# ENCYCLOPAEDIA OF
# INDIA, PAKISTAN AND BANGLADESH

# ENCYCLOPAEDIA OF INDIA PAKISTAN AND BANGLADESH

(In 9 Volumes)

(Volume 1)

OM GUPTA

ISHA

ISHA BOOKS

Delhi-110033

Encyclopaedia of India, Pakistan and Bangladesh
ISBN : 81-8205-389-7 (Set)
ISBN : 81-8205-390-0 (Vol. 1)



Published in 2006 in India by
Isha Books
D-43, Prithviraj Road,
Adarsh Nagar, Delhi - 110033
e-mail : ishabooks@hotmail.com

Laser Typesetting at : Vinayak Printers, Delhi
Printed at : Salasar Imaging, Delhi

# CONTENTS

## PART II – PAKISTAN

# Preface

Encyclopaedia is a mouthful word. Its contents are mind boggling. Why do we need such wholesomes? In our daily life, we come across the names of people, places and events, we don't know about. We have a tendency to pass them by because we can manage without them. They are important That is why they are there in the encyclopaedias. We might have heard about them. But their absence in our vocabulary didn't affect our life hence we chose to ignore them. If we had cared to refer to the encyclopaedia, we would have felt the difference in our life. Let's stop here for a while and talk about its precursor-the dictionary.

A dictionary tells us about the approximate meaning and equivalents of a word. People fight shy in consulting even a dictionary. Again because they can manage without the exact meaning or the etymology of the word. But those who dare, know what difference it makes to the reader. It is a matter of habit. Both dictionary and encyclopaedia widen the horizon of the knowledge seeker.

According to Britannica, an encyclopaedia is a reference work that contains information on all branches of knowledge or that treats a particular branch of knowledge comprehensively. It is self-contained and explains subjects in greater detail than a dictionary. It differs from an alamanc in that its information is not dated and from pedagogical texts in its attempt to be easy to consult and to be readily understood by the layperson. Though generally written in the form of many separate articles, encyclopaedias vary greatly in format and content. The prototype of modern encyclopaedias is usually acknowledged to be Ephraim Chamber's Cyclopaedia (1728), and the first modern encyclopaedia was the French Encylopedie (1751-65). The largest general encylopaedia in English is Encyclopaedia Britannica.

French encylopaedua created in the 18th century by the philosophies; one of the principal works of the Enlightenment. Under the full title

Encyclopedie ou dictionnaire raisonne des Sciences, des arts et des metiers Arts and Trades"), it was inspired by the success of E.Chambers's British Cyclopaedia; or An Universal Dictionary of Arts and Sciences (1728). Under the direction of Denis Diderot and initially aided by Jean Le Rond D'Alembert, 17, Volumes were published between 1751 and 1765; other volumes were added later for a total of 35. Though opposed by conservatives ecclesiastics and government officials and subjected to censorship, the Encyclopaedie attracted articles from many thinkers of the time, including J.J.

Rousseau, Voltaire and Diderot, who were called Encyclopedists. In its skepticism, its emphasis on scientific determinism, and its criticism of the abuses perpetrated by contemporary legal, judicial and clerical institutions, the work had widespread influence as an expression of progressive thought prior to the French Revolution.

There are various versions of encyclopaedia catering to different needs. There are encyclopaedias even for children. They are neither written by one person nor they are original texts. They are culled, collected and edited by different people. Their main purpose to put things in right perspective and to make course corrections in the quest of knowledge.

**Editor**

# Part I. India

# 1

# HISTORY

The history of India can be traced in fragments to as far back as 9,500 years ago. The Indus Valley Civilization, one of the oldest in the world, dates back over 4,000 years. This was followed by the Vedic Civilization of the Indo-Aryans. The origins of the Indo-Aryans is under some dispute. Most scholars today believe in some form of the Indo-Aryan migration hypothesis, which proposes that the Aryans, a semi-nomadic people, possibly from Central Asia or northern Iran, migrated into the north-west regions of the Indian subcontinent between 2000 and 1500 BCE. The nature of this migration, the place of origin of the Aryans, and sometimes even the very existence of the Aryans as a separate people are hotly debated. The merger of the Vedic culture with the earlier Dravidian cultures apparently resulted in classical Indian culture, though the exact details of this process are controversial.

The births of Mahavira and Buddha in the 6th century BCE mark the beginning of well-recorded Indian history. For the next 1500 years, India produced its classical civilisation, and is estimated to have had the largest economy of the ancient world between the 1st and 15th centuries CE, controlling between one third and one quarter of the world's wealth up to the time of the Mughals, from whence it rapidly declined during British rule.

Incursions by Arab and Central Asian armies in the 8th and 12th centuries were followed by inroads by traders from Europe, beginning in the late 15th century. From 1757, the British East India Company had begun colonising parts of India and by 1858, the British Crown had assumed political control over virtually all of India. Indian armed forces in the British army played a vital role in both the World Wars. Nonviolent resistance to British colonialism led, by Mohandas Gandhi, Vallabhbhai Patel and Jawaharlal Nehru brought independence in 1947.

The subcontinent was partitioned into the Secular Democratic Republic of India and the smaller Islamic Republic of Pakistan. A war between the two countries in 1971 resulted in East Pakistan becoming the separate nation of Bangladesh. In the 21st century, India has made impressive gains in economic investment and output, and stands as the world's largest democracy with a population exceeding 1 billion, is self sufficient in terms of food, and is a fast-growing, economically strong country, with the fourth largest economy (PPP) in the world.

Human civilisations in India are some of the earliest recorded, and were contemporaries of civilisations in ancient Mesopotamia and Egypt. India's history essentially includes all of the Indian subcontinent, including the more recent nations of Pakistan and Bangladesh. India is also inalienably linked with the history and heritage of the other South Asian nations like Sri Lanka, Nepal and Bhutan. India's culture, economy and politics has had an influence on the history and culture of the nations in South East Asia, East Asia and Central Asia, such as Indonesia, Cambodia, Thailand, China, Tibet, Persia and Afghanistan over thousands of years, and in turn, India has been influenced by Persia, and to an extent, China and Afghanistan.

After Arab incursions into India during the early part of the second millennium CE, similar quests for access to India's fabled wealth strongly influenced the history of medieval Europe, after the landing of Vasco Da Gama. Christopher Columbus discovered America whilst searching for a new route to India, and the British Empire gained much of its resources after the incorporation of India as the 'Jewel in the Crown', from the late 18th century to 1947.

## Paleolithic Era

Isolated remains of Homo Erectus in Hathnora in the Narmada Valley in Central India indicate that India might have been inhabited since at least the Middle Pleistocene era. The precise date of these remains is unclear, and archaeologists put it anywhere between 200,000 to 500,000 years. The fossils are the earliest human remains found in South Asia. Recent finds include a quarry along the Malaprabha and Ghataprabha rivers in the Kaladgi Basin in Karnataka. Modern humans seem to have settled the subcontinent towards the end of the last Ice Age about 12,000 years ago. The first confirmed permanent settlements appeared 9,000 years ago in Bhimbetka in modern Madhya Pradesh.

## Neolithic era

By 5100 BC, people in the Indus Valley were farming and harvesting einkorn, a primitive form of wheat. Early Neolithic culture in South Asia is represented by the Mehrgarh findings (7000 BCE onwards), in Balochistan, Pakistan. The Mehrgarh community was mostly pastoral, lived in mud houses, wove baskets and tended to goats and their farms. By 5500 BCE, pottery began to appear and later chalcolithic implements began to appear. By 2000 BCE, the settlement was abandoned.

Traces of a Neolithic culture have been found submerged in the Gulf of Khambat in 2002. Many of the finds recovered from the area have been radiocarbon dated to 7500 BCE. Late Neolithic cultures sprang up in the Indus

Valley region between 6000 and 2000 BCE, and in southern India between 2800 and 1200 BCE.

## Bronze Age

Bronze age civilisations in the Indian subcontinent laid the foundations for modern Indian civilization, including urban settlements and the development of Vedic beliefs, which form the core of Hinduism. Many historians claim that the rise, and eventual decline of the Indus Valley Civilization, and the migration of nomadic peoples from Central Asia into the Indian subcontinent shaped its history during this period.

## Indus Valley Civilisation

The irrigation of the Indus Valley, which provided enough resources to support major urban centers such as Harappa and Mohenjo-daro around 2500 BC, marked the beginning of the Harappan civilization. This period marked the beginning of the earliest urban society in India, known as the Indus Valley Civilization (or, the Harappan Civilisation), which thrived between 2500 and 1900 BCE. It was centred on the Indus River and its tributaries, including the Ghaggar-Hakra River, and extended into the Ganges-Yamuna Doab, Gujarat, and northern Afghanistan.

The civilisation is noted for its cities built of brick, road-side drainage system and multi-storeyed houses. The earliest historic references to India may be those to the Meluhha in Sumerian records, possibly referring to the Indus Valley civilization. When compared to the contemporary civilizations of Egypt and Sumeria, the Indus civilisation possessed unique urban planning techniques, covered the largest geographical area, and may have been a single state, as suggested by the amazing uniformity of its measurement systems.

The Mohenjo-daro ruins were once the centre of this ancient society. Indus Civilization settlements spread as far south as present-day Bombay, as far east as Delhi, as far west as the Iranian border, and as far north as the Himalayas. Among the settlements were the major urban centres of Harappa and Mohenjo-daro, as well as Dholavira, Ganweriwala, Lothal, Kalibanga and Rakhigarhi.

At its peak, some archaeologists are of the opinion that the Indus civilisation may have had a population of well over five million. To date, over 2,500 cities and settlements have been found, mainly in the general region to the east of the Indus River in Pakistan. It is thought by some that geological disturbances and climate change, leading to a gradual deforestation may ultimately have contributed to the civilization's downfall.

Archaeological resources suggest that the diverse geography of ancient India was increasing in the amount and specialization of faunal remains around 2400 to 1500 BCE. This specialization suggests that the Indus Valley Civilizations were dependent upon the alluvial soils of the rivers, which produced high yield crops.

By 2600 BCE, the presence of a state level society is evident, complete with hierarchical rule and large scale public works. These include accomplishments such as irrigation, warehouses for grain, public streets, and brick-lined drainage systems for sanitation. Around the middle of the second millennium BCE, the region of the Indus River basin, in which approximately two-thirds of currently known sites were located dried up, and the sites were abandoned.

## Vedic Civilisation

The Vedic civilization is the Indo-Aryan culture associated with the Vedas, which are some of the oldest extant texts, orally composed in Vedic Sanskrit. The exact connection between the genesis of this civilization and the Indus Valley civilization on one hand, and a possible Indo-Aryan migration on the other hand, is the subject of dispute. Early Vedic society was largely pastoral. After the Rigveda, Aryan society became increasingly agricultural, and was organized around the four Varnas, or classes. Several small kingdoms and tribes merged to form a few large ones, such as the Kuru and Pançala, some of which were often at war with each other. In addition to the principal texts of Hinduism (the Vedas), the great Indian epics (the Ramayana and Mahabharata) including the famous stories of Rama and Krishna are said to have their ultimate origins during this period, from an oral tradition of unwritten bardic recitation. The Bhagavad Gita, another primary text of Hinduism well-known for its philosophical nature, is contained in the Mahabharata.

Early Indo-Aryan presence probably corresponds, in part, to the presence of Ochre Coloured Pottery in archaeological findings. The kingdom of the Kurus corresponds to the Black and Red Ware culture and the beginning of the Iron Age in Northwestern India, around 1000 BCE (This date is most likely, contemporaneous with the composition of the Atharvaveda). Painted Grey Ware cultures spanning much of Northern India marks the Middle Vedic period, followed by a wave of urbanization that occurred across the Indian sub-continent, from Afghanistan to Bengal, in the 6th century BCE. A number of kingdoms and oligarchies, often called republics, emerged across the Indo-Gangetic plain and the northern part of the Deccan during this period. 16 of these Republics, called Mahajanapadas (great lands), are referred to in the ancient literature of the period.

### The Mahajanapadas

By 500 BCE, sixteen monarchies and 'republics' known as the Mahajanapadas stretched across the Indo-Gangetic plains from modern-day Afghanistan to Bangladesh. The largest of these nations were Magadha, Kosala, Kuru and Gandhara. The right of a king to his throne, no matter how it was gained, was usually legitimized through religious right and genealogies concocted by priests who ascribed divine origins to the rulers. There is some controversy about how closely the political entities of this period can be represented by those mentioned in the Vedas, and ancient epics of India. The educated speech at that time was Sanskrit, while the dialects of the general population of northern India were referred to as Prakrits.

Hindu rituals at that time were complicated and conducted by the priestly class. It is thought that the Upanishads, late Vedic texts dealing mainly with incipient philosophy, were first composed early in this period. They had a huge effect on Indian philosophy, and were contemporary to the development of Buddhism and Jainism, indicating a golden age of thought in this period, similar to that in ancient Greece. It was in 537 BCE, that Gautama Buddha gained enlightenment and founded Buddhism, which was initially intended as a supplement to the existing Vedic dharma. Around the same time period, in mid-6th century BCE, Mahavira founded Jainism. Both religions had a simple doctrine, and were preached in Prakrit, which helped it gain acceptance amongst the masses. While the geographic impact of Jainism was limited, Buddhist nuns and monks eventually spread the teachings of Buddha to Central Asia, East Asia, Tibet, Sri Lanka and South East Asia.

Recorded history from this period of fragmented states is sparse, up until the advent of Buddhism and Jainism but the Mahajanapadas were roughly equivalent to the ancient Greek city-states of the same period in the Mediterranean, producing philosophy which would eventually form the basis of much of the eastern world's beliefs, just as ancient Greece would produce philosophy that much of the western world's subsequent beliefs were based on. The period effectively ended with the onset of Persian and Greek invasion, and the subsequent rise of a single Indian empire from the kingdom of Magadha.

## Persian and Greek Invasion

Around the 5th century BCE, the northern Indian subcontinent was invaded by the Achaemenid Empire and the Greeks of Alexander the Great's army. This had important repercussions for Indian civilisation, as the political systems of the Persians would have an influence on later Indian political philosophy, including the administration of the Mauryan dynasty, and a melting pot of Indian, Persian, Central Asian and Greek culture was created in the modern region of Afghanistan, producing a unique hybrid culture.

## Achaemenid Empire

Much of the northwestern Indian Subcontinent (present day Eastern Afghanistan and most of Pakistan) was ruled by the Persian Achaemenid Empire from c. 520 BCE during the reign of Darius the Great, up until its conquest by Alexander the Great. Lands in present-day Punjab, the Indus river from the borders of Gandhara down to the Arabian Sea, and some other parts of the Indus plain, became a satrapy of Alexander's empire. According to Herodotus of Halicarnassus, it was the most populous and richest of all the twenty satrapies of the empire. Achaemenid rule lasted about 186 years. The Achaemenids used the Aramaic script for the Persian language. After the end of Achaemenid rule, the use of Aramaic in the Indus plain diminished, although we know from inscriptions from the time of Emperor Asoka that it was still in use two centuries later. Other scripts, such as Kharosthi (a script derived from Aramaic) and Greek became more common after the arrival of Alexander the Great.

## Alexander in India

The interaction between Hellenistic Greece and Buddhism began when Alexander the Great conquered Asia Minor and the Achaemenid Empire, reaching the north west frontiers of the Indian subcontinent in 334 BCE. There, he defeated King Puru in the Battle of the Hydaspes (near modern-day Jhelum, Pakistan) and conquered much of the Punjab. However, Alexander's troops refused to go beyond the Beas river, and he was forced to march his army southwest.

Alexander created garrisons for his troops in his new territories, and founded several cities in the areas of the Oxus, Arachosia, and Bactria, and Macedonian/Greek settlements in Gandhara and the Punjab. The regions included the Khyber Pass — a geographical passageway south of the Himalayas and the Hindu Kush mountains — and the Bolan Pass, on a trade route connecting Drangiana, Arachosia and other Persian and Central Asian kingdoms to the lower Indus plain. It is through these regions that most of the interaction between South Asia and Central Asia took place, generating intense cultural exchange and trade.

## Greco-Buddhist Period

Greco-Buddhism, sometimes spelled Græco-Buddhism, is the cultural syncretism between the culture of Classical Greece and Buddhism, which developed over a period of close to 800 years in the area corresponding to modern-day Afghanistan and Pakistan, between the 4th century BCE and the 5th century CE. Greco-Buddhism especially influenced the artistic development of Mahayana Buddhism, before it was adopted by Central and Northeastern Asia from the 1st century CE, ultimately spreading to China, Korea, and Japan. It was mainly centered around the area of Gandhara, or modern Afghanistan, the area of the subcontinent that had most been influenced by Persian and Greek contact. Gandhara was roughly contemporary to the other Mahajanapada kingdoms elsewhere in India.

## The Magadha Empire

Amongst the sixteen Mahajanapadas, the kingdom of Magadha rose to prominence under a number of dynasties that peaked in power under the reign of Asoka Maurya, one of India's most legendary and famous emperors. The kingdom of Magadha had emerged as a major power following the subjugation of two neighbouring kingdoms, and possessed an unparalleled military.

## Shishunaga Dynasty

According to tradition, the Shishunaga dynasty founded the Magadha Empire in 684 BCE, whose capital was Rajagriha, later Pataliputra, near the present day Patna. This dynasty lasted till 424 BCE, when it was overthrown by the Nanda dynasty. This period saw the development of two of India's major religions. Gautama Buddha in the 6th or 5th century BCE was the founder of Buddhism, which later spread to East Asia and South-East Asia, while Mahavira founded Jainism.

## Nanda Dynasty

The Nanda dynasty was established by an illegitimate son of the king Mahanandin of the previous Shishunaga dynasty. Mahapadma Nanda died at the age of 88, ruling the bulk of this 100-year dynasty. The Nandas were followed by the Maurya dynasty.

## Maurya Dynasty

In 321 BCE, exiled general Chandragupta Maurya founded the Maurya dynasty after overthrowing the reigning king Dhana Nanda to establish the Maurya Empire. During this time, most of the subcontinent was united under a single government for the first time. Capitalising on the destabilization of northern India by the Persian and Greek incursions, the Mauryan empire under Chandragupta would not only conquer most of the Indian subcontinent, but also push its boundaries into Persia and Central Asia, conquering the Gandhara region. Chandragupta was succeeded by his son Bindusara, who expanded the kingdom over most of present day India, barring the extreme south and east, which may have held tributary status.

The kingdom was inherited by his son Ashoka The Great who initially sought to expand his kingdom. In the aftermath of the carnage caused in the invasion of Kalinga, he renounced bloodshed and pursued a policy of non-violence or ahimsa after converting to Buddhism. The Edicts of Ashoka are the oldest preserved historical documents of India, and from Ashoka's time, approximate dating of dynasties becomes possible. The Mauryan dynasty under Ashoka was responsible for the proliferation of Buddhist ideals across the whole of East Asia and South-East Asia, fundamentally altering the history and development of Asia as a whole. Ashoka the Great has been described as one of the greatest rulers the world has seen.

## Shunga Dynasty

The Sunga dynasty was established in 185 BCE, about fifty years after Ashoka's death, when the king Brihadratha, the last of the Mauryan rulers, was brutally murdered by the then commander-in-chief of the Mauryan armed forces, Pusyamitra Sunga, while he was taking the Guard of Honour of his forces. Pusyamitra Sunga then ascended the throne.

## Early Middle Kingdoms

The middle period, especially that associated with the Gupta dynasty, is known as India's Golden Age, a time of unparalleled cultural development. The Kushanas invaded northwestern India about the middle of the 1st century CE, from Central Asia, and founded an empire that eventually stretched from Peshawar to the middle Ganges and, perhaps, as far as the Bay of Bengal. It also included ancient Bactria (in the north of modern Afghanistan) and southern Tajikistan. Their power also extended into Turkestan and helped spread Buddhism to China. In South India, several kingdoms emerged. The earliest of these is the Pandya kingdom in southern Tamil Nadu, with its capital at Madurai. The Indo-Greek Kingdoms following the conquests of Alexander the Great ruled much of Gandhara from 180 BCE to 10 CE. Around the same time in southern India, the Dravidian Pandyan kingdom began to take shape. An important source for the geography and history of that period is the Greek historian Arrian.

### *Satavahana Empire*

The Satavahanas, also known as the Andhras, were a dynasty which ruled in Southern and Central India starting from around 230 BCE. Although there is some controversy about when the dynasty came to an end, the most liberal estimates are of about 450 years. Long before that their kingdom had disintegrated into successor states. Conflict with the Sakas and the rising ambitions of their feudatories, led to their decline. Several dynasties divided the lands of the kingdom among themselves.

### *Indo-Greek Kingdom*

The Indo-Greek Kingdom (or sometimes Greco-Indian Kingdom) covered various parts of northwest and northern India from 180 BCE to around 10 CE, and was ruled by a succession of more than thirty Greek kings, often in conflict with each other. The kingdom was founded when the Greco-Bactrian king Demetrius invaded India in 180 BCE, ultimately creating an entity which seceded from the powerful Greco-Bactrian Kingdom centred in Bactria (today's northern Afghanistan).

### *Indo-Scythians*

The Indo-Scythians are a branch of the Indo-European Sakas (Scythians), who migrated from southern Siberia into Bactria, Sogdiana, Kashmir and finally into Arachosia and then India from the middle of the 2nd century BCE to the 1st century BCE. They displaced the Indo-Greeks and ruled in northern India from Gandhara to Mathura.

### *Indo-Parthians*

The Indo-Parthian Kingdom was established during the 1st century CE, by a Parthian leader named Gondophares, in an area covering today's Afghanistan, Pakistan and Northern India. The Parthians ended up controlling all of Bactria and extensive territories in Northern India, after fighting many local rulers such as the Kushan Empire ruler Kujula Kadphises,in the Gandhara region.

### *Kushan Empire*

The Kushan Empire (c. 1st–3rd centuries) was a state that at its height, about 105–250, stretched from Tajikistan to the Caspian Sea to Afghanistan and down into the Ganges river valley. The empire was created by Tocharians from modern East Turkestan, China, but was culturally dominated by north India. They had diplomatic contacts with Rome, Sassanian Persia and China, and for several centuries were at the centre of exchange between the East and the West, spreading Buddhism through trade with China.

### *Gupta Dynasty*

In the 4th and 5th centuries, the Gupta Dynasty unified northern India. During this period, known as India's Golden Age, Hindu culture, science and political administration reached new heights. After the collapse of the Gupta empire in the 6th century, India was again ruled by numerous regional kingdoms. The Gupta 'golden age' marked a period of significant cultural development.

Their origins are largely unknown, however the Chinese traveller I-tsing provides the first evidence of the Gupta kingdom in Magadha. The Vedic Puranas are also thought to have been written around this period. The empire came to an end with the attack of the Huns from central Asia. A minor line of the Gupta clan continued to rule Magadha after the disintegration of the empire. These Guptas were ultimately ousted by the Vardhana king Harsha, who established an empire in the first half of the seventh century that, for a brief time, rivalled that of the Guptas in extent.

### *Hun Invasion*

The Huns, (sometimes known as Alchon, and inaccurately potrayed as the Indo-Hephthalites), seem to have been part of the Hephthalite group, who established themselves in Afghanistan by the first half of the fifth century, with their capital at Bamiyan. They were responsible for the downfall of the Gupta dynasty, and thus brought an end to what historians consider a golden age in northern India. However, much of the Deccan and southern India were largely unaffected by this state of flux in the north.

The Gupta Emperor Skandagupta repelled a Hun invasion in 455 CE, but they continued to pressure India's northwest frontier (now Pakistan), and broke through into northern India by the end of the fifth century, thereby hastening the disintegration of the Gupta Empire. After the end of the sixth century, little is recorded in India about the Huns, and their ultimate fate is unclear; some historians surmise that the remaining Huns were assimilated into northern India's population. Certain historians, such as Romila Thapar, have suggested that the Huns are the ancestors of the Rajputs. Many Rajputs themselves however have hotly rejected this suggestion.

### *Indo-Sassanians*

The Sassanian empire of Persia, who were close contemporaries of the Guptas, began to expand into the northwestern part of ancient India (now Pakistan), where they established their rule. The mingling of Indian and Persian cultures in this region gave birth to the Indo-Sassanian culture, which flourished in the western part of the Punjab and the areas now known in Pakistan as the North West Frontier Province and Balochistan. The last Hindu kingdom in this region, the Shahis, also may have arisen from this culture.

## Late Middle Kingdoms

Later, the Chola kingdom emerged in northern Tamil Nadu, and the Chera kingdom in Kerala. The ports of southern India were involved in the Indian Ocean trade, chiefly involving spices, with the Roman Empire to the west and Southeast Asia to the east. In the north, the first of the Rajputs, a series of kingdoms which managed to survive in some form for almost a millennium until Indian independence from the British.

### *Harsha's Empire*

King Harsha of Kannauj succeeded in reuniting northern India during his reign in the 7th century, after the collapse of the Gupta dynasty. His kingdom collapsed after his death. From the 7th to the 9th century, three dynasties contested for control of northern India: the Pratiharas of Malwa and later Kannauj; the Palas of Bengal, and the Rashtrakutas of the Deccan.

### *Chalukyas and Pallavas*

The Chalukya Empire ruled parts of southern and central India from 550 to 750 (from Badami, Karnataka) and again from 970 to 1190 (from Kalyani, Karnataka). The Pallavas of

Kanchi were their contemporaries to the south. Over a period of roughly a century, the two kingdoms fought a series of low-intensity wars, each conquering the other's capitals at various points. The kings of Sri Lanka and the Keralan Cheras rendered support to the Pallavas, while the Pandyas rendered support to the Chalukyas. Whilst the northern concept of a pan-Indian empire had collapsed at the end of Harsha's empire, the ideal instead shifted to the south. The two dynasties were responsible for some of the greatest examples of both rock-cut and free-standing temples.

### *Chola Empire*

The Cholas emerged as the most powerful empire in the south in the 9th century and retained their pre-eminent position until the 12th century when the Hoysala empire was founded in Karnataka. The Cholas, like the Chalukyas and Pallavas before them, and the Hoysala and Vijayanagar after them, were responsible for some of India's finest monuments, and being located on the south tip of the peninsula, ruled Sri Lanka, and culturally dominated most of South East Asia, where the Hindu Srivijaya and Khmer empires of Indonesia and Cambodia used south Indian temple design. The Chola Navy was the most powerful for its time having conquered the neighbouring island of Lanka and other areas across the Bay of Bengal.

### *The Pratiharas, Palas, and Rashtrakutas*

The Pratiharas, also called the Gurjara-Pratiharas were an Indian dynasty who ruled kingdoms in Rajasthan and northern India from the sixth to the eleventh centuries. The Pala Empire controlled Bihar and Bengal, from the 8th to the 12th century. The Rashtrakutas of Malakheda (Karnataka) were a dynasty which ruled the Deccan during the 8th-10th centuries after the end of Chalukya rule. Each three kingdoms vied for north Indian domination around the same time that the Cholas were flourishing in the south.

### *The Rajputs*

The first recorded Rajput kingdoms emerged in Rajasthan in the 6th century, and Rajput dynasties later ruled much of northern India, including Mewar (Sisodias), Gujarat (Solankis), Malwa (Paramaras), Bundelkhand (Chandelas), and Haryana (Tomaras). The Pallava dynasty of Kanchipuram ruled southeastern India from the 4th century to the 9th century. The Pratihara ruled northern India before the Rajputs. Various other dynasties such as the Yadav, Chera, Hoysala of Halebidu, Sena and Pala controlled various empires of their own.

### *Vijayanagar Empire*

The brothers Harihara and Bukka founded the Karnataka Empire, also known as the Vijayanagara Empire, in 1336. The Vijayanagara empire prospered during the reign of Krishnadevaraya. It suffered a major defeat in 1565 but continued for another century or so in an attenuated form. Southern Indian kingdoms of the time expanded their influence as far as Indonesia, controlling vast overseas empires in south east Asia.

The Hindu dynasty came into conflict with Islamic rule (the Bahmani Kingdom) and the clashing of the two systems, the prevailing indigenous Hindu/Muslim religion, which caused a mingling of the indigenous and foreign culture that left lasting cultural influences on each other. The later Mughal rule also saw such influences of Gujarati and Rajasthani culture contributing towards this.

## The Islamic Sultanates

After the Arab-Turkic invasion of India's ancient northern neighbour Persia, various short lived Islamic empires invaded and spread across the subcontinent over a period of 1000 years. Prior to Turkic invasions, Muslim trading communities flourished throughout coastal South India, particularly in Kerala, where they arrived in small numbers through trade links via the Indian Ocean with the Arabian peninsula.

### *Delhi Sultanate*

In the 10th and 11th centuries, Turks and Afghans invaded parts of northern India and established the Delhi Sultanate at the beginning of the 13th century. The Slave dynasty managed to conquer large areas of northern India, approximate to the ancient extent of the Guptas, while the Khilji Empire was also able to conquer most of central India, but were ultimately unsuccessful in conquering most of the subcontinent, until the onset of the Mughals.

### *Mughal Empire*

In 1526, Babur, a Timurid descendant of Timur, swept across the Khyber Pass and established the Mughal Empire, which lasted for over 200 years. The Mughal Dynasty ruled most of the Indian subcontinent by 1600; it went into a slow decline after 1707 and was finally defeated during the Indian rebellion of 1857.

This period marked vast social change in the subcontinent as the Hindu majority were ruled over by the Mughal emperors, some of whom showed religious tolerance, while others liberally patronized Hindu culture, and some of whom destroyed historical temples and imposed taxes on non-Muslims. During the decline of the Mughal Empire, which at its peak occupied an area slightly larger than the ancient Mauryan Empire, several smaller empires rose to fill the power vacuum or themselves were contributing factors to the decline.

## Maratha Empire

The Maratha Kingdom was founded by Shivaji in 1674, when he annexed a portion of the Bijapur Sultanate. After consolidating his hold over his territories in the Deccan, Shivaji declared war on the Mughal Emperor, Aurangzeb. By the 18th century, it had transformed itself into the Maratha Confederacy under the rule of the Peshwas. By 1760, the Empire had stretched across practically the entire subcontinent. This expansion was brought to an end by the defeat of the Marathas by an Afghan army led by Ahmad Shah Abdali at the Third Battle of Panipat (1761). The last Peshwa, Baji Rao II, was defeated by the British in the Third Anglo-Maratha War.

## The Kingdom of Mysore

The Kingdom of Mysore was a kingdom of southern India, which was founded around 1400 CE by the Wodeyar dynasty. The rule of the Wodeyars was interrupted by Hyder Ali and his son Tippu Sultan. Under their rule Mysore fought a series of wars sometimes against the combined forces of the British and Marathas, but mostly against the British with some aid or promise of aid from the French. After the death of Tippu Sultan in the Fourth War of Mysore in 1799, the Wodeyar dynasty regained limited power as a Princely State under the British. The Kingdom of Mysore became part of the modern day, Indian state of Karnataka.

## Sikh Empire

The Punjabi kingdom, ruled by members of the Sikh religious movement was a political entity that ruled the region of modern day Punjab. Founded by the ten Gurus of the Sikh faith, it expanded its borders during the reign of Maharaja Ranjit Singh at the height of the Sikh Empire to include surrounding areas like Kashmir and Peshawar, and was among the last areas of the subcontinent that was conquered by the British. The Anglo-Sikh wars marked the downfall of the Sikh Empire.

## Durrani Empire

In 1748, the Afghan leader Ahmed Shah Durrani crossed the Indus River on the pretext of waging a jihad against the "Hindus". He attacked Lahore (in present day Pakistan) in 1750, his first Indian target. Subsequentley, he raided the rest of the Punjab (including Amritsar), Kashmir and finally Delhi. He also fought against the Marathas frequently. He left India with numerous treasures, including the Kohinoor diamond.

## Colonial Era

During the colonial era, India, along with several ancient nations in Asia, Africa and South America, was targeted by expansionist European powers, and was eventually incorporated into the British Empire. The subsequent freedom struggle, beginning with the First War of Independence, and later led by figures such as Mohandas Gandhi, would prove to be one of the biggest turning points in the development of modern world history.

### *Company Rule*

Vasco da Gama's discovery of a new sea route to India in 1498 paved the way for European colonization of India. The Portuguese set up bases in Goa, Daman, Diu and Bombay. They remained the longest colonial rulers for 500 years till 1962. The British established their first outpost in South Asia in 1619 at Surat on the northwestern coast of India, arriving in the wake of Portuguese and Dutch visitors. Later in the century, the British East India Company opened permanent trading stations at Madras, Bombay, and Calcutta, each under the protection of native rulers.

*French India*

The French set up base along with the British in the 17th century. They occupied large parts of southern India. However subsequent wars with the British, led to the loss of almost all their territory. They however retained the colonies of Pondicherry - (Pondicherry, Karaikal, Yanam, and Mahe.) and Chandernagore. Pondicherry was ceded to India in 1950.

The Dutch did not have a major presence in India. The towns of Travancore were ruled by the Dutch. However they were more interested in Ceylon (now Sri Lanka) and their prize of the Dutch East Indies (now Indonesia). They were responsible for training the military of the princely state of Kerala. In 1845, the Danish colony of Tranquebar was sold to the United Kingdom.

## The British Raj

The British established a foothold in Bengal when the British soldiers, funded by the East India Company, and led by Robert Clive, defeated Nawab Siraj Ud Daulah in the Battle of Plassey in 1757 and plundered the Bengali treasure. Bengal became a protectorate, and then directly went under the rule of East India Company. The British East India Company monopolized the trade of Bengal.

The Bengali craftsmen were inevitably fixed at foreign posts of the Company, where they were obliged to render their labour at minimal compensation while their collective tax burden increased harshly. The result was the famine of 1769 to 1773 in which 10 million Bengalis died, followed almost a century later by the catastrophic Great Calamity period, resulting in part from an extension of similar policies, in which up to 40 million Indians perished from famine amidst the collapse of India's native industries and skilled workforce.

By the 1850s Britain controlled most of the Indian subcontinent, which included present-day Pakistan and Bangladesh. From 1830, the defeat of the Thugs played a part in securing establishing greater control of diverse Indian provinces for the British.

The Indian rebellion of 1857 in the north, led by mutinous Indian soldiers, was crushed by the British. In the aftermath all political power was transferred from the East India Company to the Crown, which began administering most of India directly. It controlled the rest through local rulers.

## The Freedom Movement

In the late 19th century "British India" took its first steps toward self-government with the appointment of Indian councillors to advise the British viceroy, and the establishment of provincial Councils with Indian members; the British subsequently widened participation in legislative councils. Beginning in 1920, Indian leaders such as Mohandas K. Gandhi (also known as Mahatma Gandhi) and Subhas Chandra Bose transformed the Indian National Congress into a mass movement to campaign against British colonial rule.

The movement eventually succeeded in bringing independence to the people of the Indian subcontinent, by means of parliamentary action and non-violent resistance and non-cooperation. Following the division of India into the secular Republic of India and the Islamic Republic of Pakistan in August 1947, rioting broke out between Sikhs, Hindus and Muslims in several parts of India, including Punjab, Bengal and Delhi, leaving some 200,000 dead. Also, this period saw the largest mass migration ever recorded in modern history, with a total of 12 million Hindus and Muslims moved between the newly created dominions of India and Pakistan.

## Republic of India

Since independence, India has fought a number of wars against its neighbours, most notably four wars against Pakistan, and one against China. It also detonated a nuclear device in 1974 and became a declared nuclear state in 1998 following a series of tests.

From a socialist-inspired economy to the early 1990s , India continued to make slow progress away from the state the British had left the country in, however, it was only after extensive economic reforms in the early 90s that India's economy began to grow at a high rate. Today, in the 21st century, India is considered an emerging economic superpower, and is currently the tenth largest economy in terms of gross GDP, and 4th largest when accounting for purchasing power parity.

Since independence, India has fought three major wars and one minor war with Pakistan. The Indo-Pakistani War of 1947 started over the control of Kashmir. The Indo-Pakistani War of 1965 was also fought over Kashmir. In 1971, India hosted refugees from erstwhile East Pakistan and helped the Bangladeshi freedom fighters (Mukti Bahini) with resources and training during the Bangladesh Liberation War. During the final stages of that war, India became directly involved in the Indo-Pakistani War of 1971, which ultimately resulted in Pakistan's defeat and the independence of Bangladesh. India also fought a border war with China in 1962.

As well as being a declared nuclear state, India has an advanced space program designed to benefit the country economically, rather than merely create prestige. In the 1990s, following economic reform from the socialist-inspired economy of post-independence India, the country began to experience rapid economic growth, as markets opened for international competition and investment.

In the 21st century, India is an emerging economic power and labelled as a modern great power. with vast human and natural resources, and a huge knowledge base. Economists predict that by 2050, India will be among the top three economies of the world.

# 2

# GEOGRAPHY

India comprises most of the Indian subcontinent situated on the Indian Plate, the northerly portion of the Indo-Australian Plate. Having a coastline of over 7,000 km (4,300 miles), most of India lies on a peninsula in southern Asia that protrudes into the Indian Ocean. India is bounded on the southwest by the Arabian Sea and on the southeast by the Bay of Bengal. On the north, northeast, and northwest are the Himalayas. Kanyakumari constitutes the southern tip of the Indian peninsula, which narrows before ending in the Indian Ocean.

India lies to the north of the equator between 8 degree 4 minutes and 37 degree 6 minutes north latitude and 68 degrees 7 minutes and 97 degrees 25 minutes east longitude. It is the seventh-largest country in the world, with a total land area of 3,287,263 km$^2$ (1,269,219 square miles). India measures 3,214 km (1,997 miles) from north to south and 2,933 km (1,822 miles) from east to west. It has a land frontier of 15,200 km (9,445 miles) and a coastline of 7,516.5 km (4,670.5 miles). The Andaman and Nicobar Islands in the Bay of Bengal and Lakshadweep in the Arabian Sea are parts of India.

The geography of India is extremely diverse, with landscape ranging from snow-capped mountain ranges to deserts, plains, hills and plateaus. Indeed, the term Indian subcontinent aptly describes the enormous extent of the earth's surface that India occupies, and any attempt to generalize about its physiography is inaccurate. Diversity is also evident in the geographical distribution of India's ethnic and linguistic groups.

In ancient times, the major river valleys of the Indo-Gangetic Plain of South Asia were among the great cradles of civilization in Asia, as were the valleys of the Tigris and Euphrates rivers in West Asia and the Huang He (Yellow River) in East Asia. As a result of thousands of years of cultural and political expansion and amalgamation, contemporary India has come to include many different natural and cultural regions.

The Himalayas (and the nations of Nepal and Bhutan) form India's northern frontier with China. Pakistan borders India to the west and Bangladesh (formerly East Pakistan) to the east. Although both were formerly part of the British Indian Empire, India and Pakistan became separate countries in 1947 and East Pakistan became independent Bangladesh in 1971. The boundaries of the Indian polity are not fully demarcated because of regional ethnic and political disputes and are the source of occasional tensions.

India's total land mass is 2,973,190 square kilometers and is divided into three main geological regions: the Indo-Gangetic Plain, the Himalayas, and the Peninsula region. The Indo-Gangetic Plain and those portions of the Himalayas within India are collectively known as North India. South India consists of the peninsular region, often termed simply the Peninsula.

## Geographical Regions

On the basis of its physiography, India is divided into seven geographic regions. They are:

1. The northern mountains including the Himalayas and the northeast mountain ranges.

2. Indo-Gangetic plains
3. Thar Desert
4. Central Highlands and Deccan Plateau
5. East Coast
6. West Coast
7. Bordering seas and islands.

***Mountains***

A great arc of mountains, composed of the Himalaya, Hindu Kush, and Patkai ranges, define the Indian subcontinent. These mountains were formed by the ongoing tectonic collision of the Indian Plate with the Eurasian Plate which started some 50 million years ago. These mountain ranges are home to some of the tallest mountains in the world and provide a natural barrier against the cold polar winds. They also facilitate the monsoons that drive climate in India. The protection and climatic control they have provided has been a geographical quality that has assisted India's position as a Great power. The numerous rivers that originate in these mountains provide water to the fertile Indo-Gangetic plains. These mountains are recognised by biogeographers as the boundary between two of the earth's great ecozones; the temperate Palearctic that covers most of Eurasia, and the tropical and subtropical Indomalaya ecozone that includes the Indian subcontinent and extend into Southeast Asia and Indonesia. Historically, these ranges have served as barriers to invaders.

India has seven major mountain ranges having peaks of over 1,000 m (3,300 feet). The Himalayas are the only mountain ranges to have snow-capped peaks. These ranges are:

1. Aravalli
2. Eastern Ghats

3. Himalayas
4. Patkai
5. Vindhyas
6. Sahyadri or Western Ghats
7. Satpuras

The Himalaya mountain range is the world's highest mountain range. They form India's north-eastern border, separating it from the rest of Asia. The Himalayas are one of the world's youngest mountain ranges, and extend almost uninterrupted for a distance of 2,500 km (1,550 miles), covering an area of 500,000 km$^2$ (193,000 square miles).

The Himalayas extend from the state of Jammu and Kashmir in the west to the state of Arunachal Pradesh in the east. These states along with Himachal Pradesh, Uttaranchal, and Sikkim lie mostly in the Himalayan region. Some of the Himalayan peaks range over 7,000 m (23,000 feet) and the snow line ranges between 6,000 m (19,600 feet) in Sikkim to around 3,000 m (9,850 feet) in Kashmir. Kanchenjunga, which lies in Sikkim, is the highest point in the country's territory (undisputed). Most peaks in the Himalayas remain snowbound throughout the year.

The Shiwalik, or lower Himalaya, consists of smaller hills towards the Indian side. Most of the rock formations are young and highly unstable, with landslides being a regular phenomenon during the rainy season. Many of India's hill stations are located on this range. The climate varies from sub tropical in the foothills to tundra at the higher elevations of these mountain ranges.

The mountains on India's eastern border with Myanmar are called as the Patkai or the Purvanchal. They were created by the same tectonic processes that resulted in the formation of the Himalaya. The features of the Patkai ranges are conical peaks, steep slopes and deep valleys. The

Patkai ranges are not as rugged or tall as the Himalayas. There are three hill ranges that come under the Patkai: The Patkai-Bum, the Garo-Khasi-Jaintia, and the Lushai hills. The Garo-Khasi range is in the Indian state of Meghalaya. The climate ranges from temperate to alpine due to altitude. Cherrapunji, which lies on the windward side of these hills, has the distinction of being the wettest place in the world, receiving the highest annual rainfall.

The Vindhya range runs across most of central India, covering a distance of 1,050 km (652 miles). The average elevation of these hills is 300 m (1,000 feet). They are believed to have been formed by the wastes created due to the weathering of the ancient Aravalli mountains. It geographically separates northern India from southern India. The western end of the range lies in eastern Gujarat, near its border with the state of Madhya Pradesh, and the range runs east and north nearly to the Ganges River at Mirzapur.

The Satpura Range is a range of hills in central India. It begins in eastern Gujarat near the Arabian Sea coast, then runs east through Maharashtra, Madhya Pradesh and ends in the state of Chhattisgarh. It extends for a distance of 900 km with many of its peaks rising above 1000 m (3,300 feet). It is angular in shape, with its vertex at Ratnapuri and the two sides being parallel to the Tapti and Narmada river. It runs parallel to the Vindhya Range, which lies to the north, and these two east-west ranges divide the Indo-Gangetic plain of northern India from the Deccan Plateau lying in the south. The Narmada runs in the depression between the Satpura and Vindhya ranges, and drains the northern slope of the Satpura range, running west towards the Arabian Sea.

The Aravalli Range is the oldest mountain range in India, running from northeast to southwest across Rajasthan in western India, extending approximately 500 km (310 miles). The northern end of the range continues as isolated hills and rocky ridges into Haryana, ending near Delhi. The highest peak is Mount Abu, rising to 1,722 m (5,653 feet), lying near the southwestern extremity of the range, close to the border with Gujarat. The city of Ajmer with its lake lies on the southern slope of the range in Rajasthan. The Aravalli Range is the eroded stub of an ancient folded mountain system that was once snow-capped. The range rose in a Precambrian event called the Aravalli-Delhi orogen. The range joins two of the ancient segments that make up the Indian craton, the Marwar segment to the northwest of the range, and the Bundelkhand segment to the southeast.

The Western Ghats or Sahyadri mountains run along the western edge of India's Deccan Plateau, and separate the Deccan plateau from a narrow coastal plain along the Arabian Sea. The range starts south of the Tapti River near the border of Gujarat and Maharashtra, and runs approximately 1,600 km (1,000 miles) through the states of Maharashtra, Goa, Karnataka, Kerala, and Tamil Nadu, almost to the southern tip of the Indian peninsula and ends near Swamithope in Marunthuvazh Malai. The average elevation is around 1,000 m with the higher peaks occurring in the northern section of the range in Maharashtra. Two of the notable peaks lying in the western ghats are Kalsubai 1,646 m (5,427 feet) and Mahabaleshwar 1,438 m (4,710 feet).

The Eastern Ghats are a discontinuous range of mountains, which have been eroded and cut through by the four major rivers of southern India, the Godavari, Mahanadi, Krishna, and Kaveri. These mountain ranges extend from West Bengal in the north, through Orissa and Andhra Pradesh to Tamil Nadu in the south. They run parallel to the Bay of Bengal and are not as tall as the Western Ghats, though some of its peaks are over 1000 m in height.

The Eastern and Western Ghats meet at the Nilgiri knot in Tamil Nadu. The Anai Mudi in the Cardamom Hills at 2,695 m (8,841 feet) in Kerala is the highest peak in the Western Ghats. The Nilgiris are considered to be a part of the Western Ghats.

***Indo-Gangetic Plain***

In social and economic terms, the Indo-Gangetic Plain is the most important region of India. The plain is a great alluvial crescent stretching from the Indus River system in Pakistan to the Punjab Plain (in both Pakistan and India) and the Haryana Plain to the delta of the Ganga (or Ganges) in Bangladesh (where it is called the Padma). Topographically the plain is homogeneous, with only floodplain bluffs and other related features of river erosion and changes in river channels forming important natural features.

Two narrow terrain belts, collectively known as the Terai, constitute the northern boundary of the Indo-Gangetic Plain. Where the foothills of the Himalayas encounter the plain, small hills known locally as ghar (meaning house in Hindi) have been formed by coarse sands and pebbles deposited by mountain streams. Groundwater from these areas flows on the surface where the plains begin and converts large areas along the rivers into swamps. The southern boundary of the plain begins along the edge of the Great Indian Desert in the state of Rajasthan and continues east along the base of the hills of the Central Highlands to the Bay of Bengal.

The hills, varying in elevation from 300 to 1,200 meters, lie on a general east-west axis. The Central Highlands are divided into northern and southern parts. The northern part is centered on the Aravalli Range of eastern Rajasthan. In the northern part of the state of Madhya Pradesh, the Malwa Plateau comprises the southern part of the Central Highlands and merges with the Vindhya Range to the south. The main rivers that flow through the southern part of the plain—the Narmada, the

Tapti, and the Mahanadi—delineate North India from South India.

Some geographers subdivide the Indo-Gangetic Plain into three parts: the Indus Valley (mostly in Pakistan), the Punjab (divided between India and Pakistan) and Haryana plains, and the middle and lower Ganga. These regional distinctions are based primarily on the availability of water. By another definition, the Indo-Gangetic Plain is divided into two drainage basins by the Delhi Ridge; the western part consists of the Punjab Plain and the Haryana Plain, and the eastern part consists of the Ganga-Brahmaputra drainage systems. This divide is only 300 meters above sea level, contributing to the perception that the Indo-Gangetic Plain appears to be continuous between the two drainage basins. The Punjab Plain is centered in the land between five rivers: the Jhelum, the Chenab, the Ravi, the Beas, and the Sutlej. The name Punjab comes from the Sanskrit *pancha ab* , meaning five waters or rivers.

Both the Punjab and Haryana plains are irrigated with water from the Ravi, Beas, and Sutlej rivers. The irrigation projects emanating from these rivers have led to a decrease in the flow of water reaching the lower drainage areas in the state of Punjab in India and the Indus Valley in Pakistan. The benefits that increased irrigation has brought to farmers in the state of Haryana are controversial in light of the effects that irrigation has had on agricultural life in the Punjab areas of both India and Pakistan.

The middle Ganga extends from the Yamuna River in the west to the state of West Bengal in the east. The lower Ganga and the Assam Valley are more lush and verdant than the middle Ganga. The lower Ganga is centered in West Bengal from which it flows into Bangladesh and, after joining the Jamuna (as the lower reaches of the Brahmaputra are known in Bangladesh), forms the delta of the Ganga. The Brahmaputra (meaning son of Brahma) rises in Tibet (China's Xizang Autonomous Region) as the

Yarlung Zangbo River, flows through Arunachal Pradesh and Assam, and then crosses into Bangladesh. Average annual rainfall increases moving west to east from approximately 600 millimeters in the Punjab Plain to 1,500 millimeters around the lower Ganga and Brahmaputra.

### *Thar Desert*

The Thar Desert (also known as the Great Indian Desert) is a hot desert that forms a significant portion of western India. Spread over four states in India - Punjab, Haryana, Rajasthan, and Gujarat it covers an area of 208,110 $km^2$ (80,350 $mile^2$). The desert continues into Pakistan as the Cholistan Desert. Most of the Thar Desert is situated in Rajasthan, covering 61% of its geographic area. Most of the desert is rocky, with a small part of the extreme west of the desert being sandy.

The origin of the Thar Desert is uncertain. Some geologists consider it to be 4,000 to 10,000 years old, whereas others state that aridity began in this region much earlier. The area is characterised by extreme temperatures of above 45 °C (113 °F) in summer to below freezing in winters. Rainfall is precarious and erratic, ranging from below 120 mm (4.72 in) in the extreme west to 375 mm (14.75 in) eastward. The lack of rainfall is mainly due to the unique position of the desert with respect to the Aravalli range. The desert lies in the rain shadow area of the Bay of Bengal arm of the southwest monsoon. The parallel nature of the range to the Arabian Sea arm also means that the desert does not receive much rainfall.

The desert can be divided into two regions, the great Desert and the little desert. The great Desert extends northwards from the edge of the Rann of Kutch region of Gujarat. The little desert extends from the River Luni between the towns of Jodhpur and Jaisalmer, up to the northern areas. The soils of the arid region are generally sandy to sandy-loam in texture. The consistency and depth vary according to the topographical features. The low-lying loams are heavier and may have a hard pan of clay, calcium carbonate or gypsum. Due to the low population density, the effect of the population on the environment is relatively less compared to the rest of India.

### *Central Highlands and Deccan plateau*

The Central Highlands are composed of three main plateaus - the Malwa Plateau in the west, the Deccan Plateau in the south, (covering most of the Indian peninsula); and the Chota Nagpur Plateau in Jharkhand towards the east.

The Deccan plateau is a large triangular plateau, bounded by the Vindhyas to the north and flanked by the Eastern and Western Ghats. The Deccan covers a total area of 1.9 million km$^2$ (735,000 mile$^2$). It is mostly flat, with elevations ranging from 300 to 600 m (1,000 to 2,000 feet).The name Deccan comes from the Sanskrit word dakshina, which means "the south". The plateau slopes gently from west to east and gives rise to several peninsular rivers such as the Godavari, the Krishna, the Kaveri and the Narmada. This region is mostly semi-arid as it lies on the leeward side of both Ghats. Much of the Deccan is covered by thorn scrub forest scattered with small regions of deciduous broadleaf forest. Climate ranges from hot summers to mild winters.

The Chota Nagpur Plateau is a plateau in eastern India, which covers much of Jharkhand state as well as adjacent parts of Orissa, Bihar, and Chhattisgarh. The total area of Chota Nagpur Plateau is approximately 65,000 km$^2$ (25,000 mile$^2$). The Chota Nagpur Plateau is made up of three smaller plateaus, the Ranchi, Hazaribagh, and Kodarma plateaus. The Ranchi plateau is the largest of the plateaus, with an average elevation of 700 m (2,300 feet). Much of the plateau is forested, covered by the Chota Nagpur dry deciduous forests. The plateau is famous for its vast reserves of ores and coal. Besides the Great Indian peninsula, the Kathiawar Peninsula in Gujarat is another large peninsula of India.

### *East Coast*

The Eastern Coastal Plain is a wide stretch of land lying between the Eastern Ghats and the Bay of Bengal. It stretches from Tamil Nadu in the south to West Bengal in the north. Deltas of many of India's rivers form a major portion of these plains. The Mahanadi, Godavari, Kaveri and Krishna rivers drain these plains. The region receives both the Northeast and Southwest monsoon rains with its annual rainfall averaging between 1,000 mm (40 in) and 3,000 mm (120 in). The width of the plains varies between 100 to 130 km (62 to 80 miles). The plains are divided into seven regions: The Mahanadi delta; the southern Andhra Pradesh plain; the Krishna Godavari deltas; the Kanyakumari coast; Coromandel Coast and sandy littoral.

### *West Coast*

The Western Coastal Plain is a narrow strip of land sandwiched between the Western Ghats and the Arabian Sea. The strip begins in Gujarat in the north and extends across the states of Maharashtra, Goa, Karnataka and Kerala. The plains are narrow, and range from 50 to 100 km (30 to 60 miles) in width. Small rivers and numerous backwaters inundate the region. The rivers, which originate in the Western Ghats, are fast flowing and are mostly perennial. The fast flowing nature of the rivers results in the formation of estuaries rather than deltas. Major rivers flowing into the sea are the Tapi, Narmada, Mandovi and Zuari.

The coast is divided into three regions. The northern region of Maharashtra and Goa is known as the Konkan Coast, the central region of Karnataka is known as the Kanara Coast and the southern coastline of Kerala is known as the Malabar Coast. Vegetation in this region is mostly deciduous. The Malabar Coast has its own unique ecoregion known as the Malabar Coast moist forests.

### *Islands*

India has two major offshore island possessions: the Lakshadweep islands and the Andaman and Nicobar Islands. Both these island groups are administered by the Union government of India as Union Territories.

The Lakshadweep islands lie 200 to 300 km (124 to 186 miles) off the coast of Kerala in the Arabian Sea. It consists of twelve coral atolls, three coral reefs, and five banks. Ten of these islands are inhabited.

The Andaman and Nicobar island chain lies in the Bay of Bengal near the Myanmar coast. It is located 950 km (590 miles) from Kolkata (Calcutta) and 193 km (120 miles) from Cape Negrais in Myanmar. The territory consists of two island groups, the Andaman Islands and the Nicobar Islands. The Andaman islands consist of 204 islands having a total length of 352 km (220 miles). The Nicobar Islands, which lie south of the Andamans, consists of twenty-two islands with a total area of 1,841 $km^2$ (710 $mile^2$). The highest point is Mount Thullier at 642 m (2,140 feet). Indira Point, India's southernmost land point is situated in the Nicobar islands, and lies just 189 km (117 miles) from the Indonesian island of Sumatra to the southeast.

Significant islands just off the Indian coast include Diu, a former Portuguese exclave; Majuli, Asia's largest freshwater island; Salcette Island, India's most populous island, on which Mumbai (Bombay) city is located; Elephanta in Bombay Harbour; and Sriharikota barrier island in Andhra Pradesh.

### *Rivers*

All major rivers of India originate from one of the three main watersheds. They are:

1. The Himalaya and the Karakoram ranges
2. Vindhya and Satpura range in central India
3. Sahyadri or Western Ghats in western India

The Himalayan river networks are snow-fed and have a continuous flow throughout the year. The other two networks are dependant on the monsoons and shrink into rivulets during the dry season. Twelve of India's rivers are classified as major, with the total catchment area exceeding 2,528,000 km$^2$.

Himalayan rivers or the northern rivers that flow westward into Pakistan are the Indus, Beas, Chenab, Ravi, Sutlej, and Jhelum. The Ganga-Brahmaputra-Meghana system has the largest catchment area of 1,100,000 km$^2$. The river Ganga originates at the Gangotri Glacier in Uttaranchal. It flows in a south easterly direction, draining into Bangladesh. The Yamuna and Gomti rivers also arise in the Western Himalayas and join the Ganga river in the plains. The Brahmaputra, another tributary of the Ganga originates in Tibet and enters India in the far eastern state of Arunachal Pradesh. It then proceeds westwards, unifying with the Ganga in Bangladesh.

The Chambal, another tributary of the Ganga originates from the Vindhya-Satpura watershed. The river flows eastward. Westward flowing rivers from this watershed are the Narmada (also called Nerbudda) and Tapti (also spelt Tapi) rivers which drain into the Arabian Sea in Gujarat. The river network that flows from east to west constitutes 10% of the total outflow.

The Western Ghats are the source of all Deccan rivers. Major rivers in the Deccan include the Mahanadi, Godavari, Krishna, and Kaveri River (also spelt Cauvery), all draining into the Bay of Bengal. These rivers constitute 20% of India's total outflow.

The Mahanadi, rising in the state of Madhya Pradesh, is an important river in the state of Orissa. In the upper drainage basin of the Mahanadi, which is centered on the Chhattisgarh Plain, periodic droughts contrast with the situation in the delta region where floods may damage the crops in what is known as the rice bowl of Orissa. Hirakud Dam, constructed in the middle reaches of the Mahanadi, has helped in alleviating these adverse effects by creating a reservoir.

The source of the Godavari is northeast of Bombay (Mumbai in the local Marathi language) in the state of Maharashtra, and the river follows a southeasterly course for 1,400 kilometers to its mouth on the Andhra Pradesh coast. The Godavari River basin area is second in size only to the Ganga; its delta on the east coast is also one of the country's main rice-growing areas. It is known as the "Ganga of the South," but its discharge, despite the large catchment area, is moderate because of the medium levels of annual rainfall, for example, about 700 millimeters at Nasik and 1,000 millimeters at Nizamabad.

The Krishna rises in the Western Ghats and flows east into the Bay of Bengal. It has a poor flow because of low levels of rainfall in its catchment area—660 millimeters annually at Pune. Despite its low discharge, the Krishna is the third longest river in India.

The source of the Kaveri is in the state of Karnataka, and the river flows southeastward. The waters of the river have been a source of irrigation since antiquity; in the early 1990s, an estimated 95 percent of the Kaveri was diverted for agricultural use before emptying into the Bay of Bengal. The delta of the Kaveri is so mature that the main river has almost lost its link with the sea, as the Kollidam, the distributary of the Kaveri, bears most of the flow.

The Narmada and the Tapti are the only major rivers that flow into the Arabian Sea. The Narmada rises in Madhya Pradesh and crosses the state, passing swiftly through a narrow valley between the Vindhya Range and spurs of the Satpura Range. It flows into the Gulf of

Khambhat (or Cambay). The shorter Tapti follows a generally parallel course, between eighty kilometers and 160 kilometers to the south of the Narmada, flowing through the states of Maharashtra and Gujarat on its way into the Gulf of Khambhat.

Harnessing the waters of the major rivers that flow from the Himalayas is an issue of great concern in Nepal, India, and Bangladesh. Issues of flood control, drought prevention, hydroelectric power generation, job creation, and environmental quality—but also traditional lifestyles and cultural continuities—are at stake as these countries grapple with the political realities, both domestic and international, of altering the flow of the Ganga and Brahmaputra. Although India, Nepal, and Bangladesh seek to alleviate problems through cooperation over Himalayan rivers, irrigation projects altering the flow of Punjab-area rivers are likely to continue to be an irritant between India and Pakistan—countries between which cooperation is less likely to occur—in the second half of the 1990s. Internally, large dam projects, such as one on the Narmada River, are also controversial.

### *Bodies of Water*

Major gulfs include the Gulf of Cambay, Gulf of Kutch and the Gulf of Mannar. Straits include the Palk Strait which separates India from Sri Lanka and the Ten Degree Channel, separating the Andamans from the Nicobar Islands and the Eight Degree Channel separating the Laccadive and Amindivi Islands from Minicoy Island towards the south. Important capes include the Cape Comorin, the southern tip of mainland India, Indira Point, the southernmost location of India, Rama's Bridge and Point Calimere. Smaller seas include the Laccadive Sea and the Andaman Sea. There are four coral reefs in India and are located in; the Andaman and Nicobar Islands, Gulf of Mannar, Lakshadweep and Gulf of Kutch.

Important lakes include Chilka Lake, the country's largest salt-water lake in Orissa; Kolleru Lake in Andhra Pradesh; Loktak Lake in Manipur, Dal Lake in Kashmir, Sambhar Lake in Rajasthan, and the Sasthamkotta Lake in Kerala.

### *Wetlands*

India's wetland ecosystem is widely distributed from the cold and arid; from ones in the Ladakh region in the state of Jammu and Kashmir to the ones in the wet and humid climate of peninsula India. Most of the wetlands are directly or indirectly linked to India's river networks. The Indian government has identified a total of 22 wetlands for conservation. Among the protected wetlands are the tropical mangrove forests in peninsular India and the salt mudflats in western India.

Mangrove forests occur all along the Indian coastline, in sheltered estuaries, creeks, backwaters, salt marshes and mud flats. The mangrove area covers a total of 6,740 km$^2$ (2,600 mile$^2$) which comprises 7% of the world's total mangrove cover. The Andaman and Nicobar Islands; the Sundarbans; Gulf of Kutch; deltas of the Mahanadi, Godavari and Krishna; and parts of Maharashtra, Karnataka and Kerala have large mangrove covers. Most of the identified wetlands adjoin or are parts of sanctuaries, national parks and are thus protected.

### *The Sundarbans*

The Sundarbans delta is the largest mangrove forest in the world. It lies at the mouth of the Ganges and is spread across areas of Bangladesh and West Bengal, India. The Bangladeshi and Indian portions of the jungle are listed in the UNESCO world heritage list separately as the Sundarbans and Sundarbans National Park respectively, though they are parts of the same forest. The Sundarbans are intersected by a complex network of tidal waterways, mudflats and small islands of salt-tolerant mangrove forests, and presents an excellent example of ongoing ecological processes.

The area is known for its wide range of fauna. The most famous among these is the Bengal Tiger, but numerous species of birds, spotted deer, crocodiles and snakes also inhabit it. It is estimated that there are now 400 Bengal tigers and about 30,000 spotted deer in the area.

### *Rann of Kutch*

The Rann of Kutch is a marshy region located in the Gujarat state of India, which borders the Sindh region of Pakistan. The name Rann comes from the Hindi word ran meaning salt marsh. It occupies a total area of 27,900 km$^2$ (10,800 mile$^2$). The region was originally a part of the Arabian Sea. Geologic forces, most likely by earthquakes, resulted in the damming up of the region, turning it into a large salt-water lagoon. This area gradually filled with silt thus turning it into a seasonal salt marsh. During the monsoons, the area turns into a shallow marsh, often flooding to knee-depth height. After the monsoons, the region turns dry and becomes parched.

## Climate

The Himalayas isolate South Asia from the rest of Asia. South of these mountains, the climate, like the terrain, is highly diverse, but some geographers give it an overall, one-word characterization—violent. What geographers have in mind is the abruptness of change and the intensity of effect when change occurs—the onset of the monsoon rains, sudden flooding, rapid erosion, extremes of temperature, tropical storms, and unpredictable fluctuations in rainfall. Broadly speaking, agriculture in India is constantly challenged by weather uncertainty.

It is possible to identify seasons, although these do not occur uniformly throughout South Asia. The Indian Meteorological Service divides the year into four seasons: the relatively dry, cool winter from December through February; the dry, hot summer from March through May; the southwest monsoon from June through September when the predominating southwest maritime winds bring rains to most of the country; and the northeast, or retreating, monsoon of October and November.

The southwest monsoon blows in from sea to land. The southwest monsoon usually breaks on the west coast early in June and reaches most of South Asia by the first week in July. Because of the critical importance of monsoon rainfall to agricultural production, predictions of the monsoon's arrival date are eagerly watched by government planners and agronomists who need to determine the optimal dates for plantings.

Theories about why monsoons occur vary. Conventionally, scientists have attributed monsoons to thermal changes in the Asian landmass. Contemporary theory cites other factors—the barrier of the Himalayas and the sun's northward tilt (which shifts the jet stream north). The hot air that rises over South Asia during April and May creates low-pressure areas into which the cooler, moisture-bearing winds from the Indian Ocean flow.These circumstances set off a rush of moisture-rich air from the southern seas over South Asia.

The southwest monsoon occurs in two branches. After breaking on the southern part of the Peninsula in early June, the branch known as the Arabian Sea monsoon reaches Bombay around June 10, and it has settled over most of South Asia by late June, bringing cooler but more humid weather. The other branch, known as the Bay of Bengal monsoon, moves northward in the Bay of Bengal and spreads over most of Assam by the first week of June. On encountering the barrier of the Great Himalayan Range, it is deflected westward along the Indo-Gangetic Plain toward New Delhi. Thereafter the two branches merge as a single current bringing rains to the remaining parts of North India in July.

The withdrawal of the monsoon is a far more gradual process than its onset. It usually withdraws from northwest India by the beginning of October and from the remaining parts of the country by the end of November. During this period, the northeast winds contribute to the formation of the northeast monsoon over the southern half of the Peninsula in October. It is also known as the retreating monsoon because it follows in the wake of the southwest monsoon. The states of Tamil Nadu, Karnataka, and Kerala receive most of their rainfall from the northeast monsoon during November and December. However, 80 percent of the country receives most of its rainfall from the southwest monsoon from June to September.

South Asia is subject to a wide range of climates—from the subfreezing Himalayan winters to the tropical climate of the Coromandel Coast and from the damp, rainy climate in the states of Assam and West Bengal to the arid Great Indian Desert. Based on precipitation and temperature, experts define seven climatic regions: the Himalayas, Assam and West Bengal, the Indo-Gangetic Plain, the Western Ghats and coast, the Deccan (the interior of the Peninsula south of the Narmada River), and the Eastern Ghats and coast.

In the Himalayan region, climate varies with altitude. At about 2,000 meters, the average summer temperature is near 18°C; at 4,500 meters, it is rarely above 0°C. In the valleys, summer temperatures reach between 32°C and 38°C. The eastern Himalayas receive as much as 1,000 to 2,000 millimeters more precipitation than do the Western Himalayas, and floods are common.

Assam and West Bengal are extremely wet and humid. The southeastern part of the state of Meghalaya has the world's highest average annual rainfall, some 10,900 millimeters.

The Indo-Gangetic Plain has a varied climatic pattern. Rainfall and temperature ranges vary significantly between the eastern and western extremes. In the Peninsula region, the Western Ghats and the adjoining coast receive heavy rains during the southwest monsoon. Rainfall in the peninsular interior averages about 650 millimeters a year, although there is considerable variation in different localities and from year to year. The Eastern Ghats receive less rainfall than the western coast. Rainfall there ranges between 900 and 1,300 millimeters annually.

The northern Deccan region, bounded by the Western Ghats, the Vindhya Range and the Narmada River to the north, and the Eastern Ghats, receives most of its annual rainfall during the summer monsoon season. The southern Deccan area is in a "rain shadow" and receives only fifty to 1,000 millimeters of rainfall a year. Temperature ranges are wide—from some 15°C to 38°C—making this one of India's most comfortable climatic areas.

Throughout most of non-Himalayan India, the heat can be oppressive and sometimes, such as was experienced in 1994 and 1995, literally can be a killer. Hot, relatively dry weather is the norm before the southwest monsoons, which, along with heavy rains and high humidity, bring cloud cover that lowers temperatures slightly. Temperatures reach the upper 30s°C and can reach as high as 48°C during the day in the premonsoon months.

## Natural Resources

India is particularly rich in a variety of natural resources. Along with 56% arable land, it has significant sources of Coal (fourth-largest reserves in the world), Iron ore, Manganese, Mica, Bauxite, Titanium ore, Chromite, Natural gas, Diamonds, Petroleum, Limestone, Thorium (world's largest along Kerala's shores). Petroleum is found off the coast of Maharashtra, Gujarat and in Assam, but meets only 40% of India's demand. Increasing amounts of natural gas are being discovering regularly especially off the coast of Andhra Pradesh. Uranium is mined in Andhra Pradesh and gold in the Kolar Gold Fields in Karnataka.

## Natural Disasters

India is prone to several natural disasters, responsible for huge losses in life and property. Natural disasters in India include droughts; flash floods, as well as widespread and destructive flooding from monsoonal rains; severe cyclones; and earthquakes.

Floods are the most common natural disaster in India. During the monsoon season, heavy rainfall may cause rivers to distend their banks, often flooding the surrounding areas. The Brahmaputra River is prone to perennial flooding during the monsoon season. Floods are responsible for a number of deaths and property loss in many parts of India. With the exception of a few states, almost all of India is prone to flooding.

Indian agriculture is heavily dependent on the monsoon as a source of water. In some parts of India, the failure of the monsoons results in water deficiency in the region causing extensive crop losses. Drought prone regions include south Maharashtra, north Karnataka, Andhra Pradesh, Orissa, Gujarat and Rajasthan. In the past, failure of monsoons has led to famines causing great damage.

Tectonic plates beneath the earth's surface are responsible for yearly earthquakes along the Himalayan belt and in northeast India. This region is classified as a Zone V, indicating that it is a very high-risk area. Parts of western India, around the Kutch region in Gujarat and Koyna in Maharashtra, are classified as a Zone IV region (high risk). Other areas have a moderate to low risk chance of an earthquake occurring.

Cyclones are another natural disaster, affecting thousands living in the coastal regions. Cyclones are severe and bring with them heavy rains that cut off supplies and relief to the affected areas. On 2004-12-26, a tsunami caused by the 2004 Indian Ocean earthquake struck the Andaman and Nicobar Islands and India's east coast resulting in the loss of over ten thousand individuals. Until then India was thought to have negligible activity related to tsunamis, though there is historical anecdotal evidence of its occurrence in the past.

India has one active volcano: the Barren Island volcano which last erupted in May 2005. There is also a dormant volcano called the Narcondum and a Mud volcano at Baratang. All these volcanoes lie in the Andaman Islands.

Landslides are common in the Lower Himalaya owing to labile rock formations due to the young age of the hills. Parts of the Western Ghats also suffer from low intensity landslides. Avalanches occur in Kashmir, Himachal Pradesh and Sikkim.

During the summer months, dust storms cause immense property damage in northern India. These storms bring with it large amounts of dust from arid regions. Hailstones are common in parts of India, and cause severe damage to the standing crops.

# 3

# SOCIETY AND CULTURE

The culture of India is one of the oldest in the world. India has managed to preserve its culture and traditions throughout various eras of history and all the while absorbing customs, traditions and ideas from both invaders and immigrants. Many cultural practices, languages, customs and monuments are examples of this co-mingling over centuries.

It is to be noted that in modern India, there is remarkable cultural diversity throughout the country. This cultural melting pot, comprising the various regions of India, namely South, North, and North-East, have their own distinct identities and almost every state has carved out its own cultural niche. In spite of this unique yet ignoble cultural diversity, the whole country is bound as a civilization due to its common history, thereby preserving the national identity.

The Indian culture also has had a considerable impact from Persian, Arabic Turkish, and European cultures. The various religions and the multihued traditions of India have had an impact on South East Asia, China and beyond. India was the birth place of many major religious systems such as Hinduism, Sikhism, Buddhism and Jainism, which have a strong prevalence and influence not only over India, but the whole world.

Indian culture can be classified into many varied form which are existent in their totality throughout the territory of India. The culture of India has been influenced by various religions and customs of the world, which resulted in the mingling of religious values, folk idioms and art forms. While the religious influence is quite evident in the "classical" Indian culture, the urban India is now widely influenced by global culture. India is generally divided into five major cultural divisions—each with their own characterstics and styles. There are pronounced differences between the South India and the North East India, whereas the East and the West India portray a confluence of Northern and Southern influences in their typical yet exceptional forms.

## Regions

India is one of the most religiously diverse nations in the world, with one of the most deeply religious societies and cultures. Religion plays a central and definitive role in the life of the country and most of its people. The faith of more than 80.4% of the people is Hinduism, considered the world's oldest religious and philosophical system. Islam is practiced by around 13.4% of all Indians. Sikhism, Ayyavazhi, Buddhism and Jainism are Indian-born religious systems that are strong and influential not only in India but across the world. Christianity, Zoroastrianism, Judaism and the Bahá'í Faith are also influential but their numbers are smaller. Despite the strong role of religion in Indian life, atheism and agnostics are also visible influences.

### *Hinduism*

The adherents of Hinduism form the largest religious community in India, numbering approximately 900 million and comprising 80.5% of the population. About 50 million Hindus of Indian origin are living abroad (notably the USA and South Africa). Hinduism in India has a long and varied history. Indeed, India is the birth-place of Hinduism and the history of Hinduism is as old as that of India herself. Hinduism is a set of practices of the people of India. The word Hindu is derived from the word Sindhu and signifies a person coming from the land of the river Sindhu? (i.e., India). India is the home to the largest number of Hindus. Hinduism has origins of around 2500 BCE. Modern Hinduism has taken the form of a religion due to other religious influences. However, it is known as a "way of life" rather than a religion. It differs from other religions by the fact that it does not have a single founder, a specific theological system, a single system of morality, or a central religious organisation.

Despite attacks and invasions by various Arab and Afghan empires during and after the 7th century CE, Hinduism has survived. The reason is said to be the in-built tolerance and inclusiveness in Hinduism and also, in part, the tolerance of some of the invading rulers, notably Akbar.

### *Buddhism*

Buddhism, known in ancient India as Buddha Dharma, originated in northern India in what is today the state of Bihar. It rapidly gained adherents during the Buddha's lifetime. It was also the religion of the rich and the upper classes and hence Up to the 9th century, Indian followers numbered in the hundreds of thousands only compared to other religions which numbered in millions. While the exact cause of the decline of Buddhism in India is disputed, it is known that the mingling of Hindu and Buddhist societies in India and the rise of Hindu Vedanta movements began to compete against Buddhism. Many believe that Hinduism's adaptation to Buddhism resulted in Buddhism's rapid decline. Also, Muslim invaders are recorded to have caused massive devastation on monasteries, libraries, and statuary, as they did on Hindu religious life. Many Indian Buddhist populations remained intact in or migrated to places like Sri Lanka, Tibet, and other Asian countries. The loss of main centers of pilgrimage and supplanting the upper class by new islamic upper class cuased the decline of Buddhism in India.

Recently, a revival of Buddhism in India has made significant progress. In 1956, B. R. Ambedkar, a princely state official during the Indian struggle for independence from the United Kingdom, and thousands of his followers converted to Buddhism in protest against the caste system. Subsequent mass conversions on a lesser scale have occurred since then. Three-quarters of these "neo-Buddhists" live in Maharashtra. Alongside these converts are the Vajrayana Buddhists of Ladakh, Sikkim, and Arunachal Pradesh, a small number of tribal peoples in the region of Bengal, and Tibetan refugees. Today around 8 million Buddhists live in India.

### *Jainism*

Jainism, along with Hinduism, Buddhism and Sikhism, is one of the four major Dharmic religions originating in India. In general, Jains are extremely well-represented in spite of the fact that they form only 0.4% (around 4.2 million) of India's total population. Many of India's Jains are affluent, and almost all are well off. As such, it can be said that they hold power and wealth disproportionate to their small population. According to the India Census 2001, Jains have the highest literacy rate (religion-wise) of 94.1% compared to the national average of 64.8%.

### *Christianity*

Christianity, according to tradition arrived in India in the first century through the apostle Thomas. This myth has been questioned time and again by historians. It was further consolidated by the arrival of Syriac Jewish-Christians now known as Knanaya people in the second century C.E. This ancient ethnic Christian community of Kerala is known as Nasrani or Syrian Christian. The Nasrani people and especially the Knanaya people within the Nasranis have strong Jewish historical ties. Their form of Christianity is one of the most ancient: Syriac Christianity which is also known as the Eastern Orthodox Church and referred to in India as Saint Thomas Christians. It should be noted that the term "Saint Thomas Christians" is a loose term that many non-Nasranis Christians in Kerala are often labeled. The vast majority of Christians in Kerala are not the original Nasrani/Knanaya but indigenous local converts.

Roman Catholicism reached India during the period of European colonization, which began in 1498 when the Portuguese explorer Vasco da Gama arrived on the Malabar coast. Christian missionary activity increased in the early 1800s. Today Christianity is the third largest religion of India making up 2 - 2.9% of the population. Christians are most prevalent in the southern states like Kerala and Tamil Nadu, northeastern states such as Nagaland, Mizoram and in western state Goa.

### *Islam*

Islam arrived in India as early as the 8th century CE. During the following decades, Islam contributed greatly to the cultural enhancement of an already rich Indian culture, shaping not only the shape of Northern Indian classical music (Hindustani, a melding of Indian and Middle Eastern elements) but encouraging a grand tradition of Urdu (a melding of Hindi, Arabic and Persian languages) literature both religious and secular. Among other monuments, the Taj Mahal is a gift of the Mughals. As of 2001, there are about 130 million Muslims in India who are scattered throughout the country, with the highest concentrations being in the states of Jammu and Kashmir, Kerala, West Bengal, Assam and parts of the Gangetic plain. Uttar

Pradesh in the Gangetic plain has the highest population of Muslims in one state.

### *Ayyavazhi*

Ayyavazhi is a religion originated in south India in the 19th century. Officially it is considered as an offshoot section of Hinduism. But either in Philosophy or in religious practices Ayyavazhi and Hinduism varies a lot. Though it has not received official recognition, it has transformed itself into a distinctive religious phenomenon, making its presence felt in India's southern parts, mostly in southern districts of Tamil Nadu and in some parts of Kerala. But it is one of the fastest growing religions of Southern India, its rapid growth has been noted in the Christian missionary reports of the mid-19th century. It has more than 7000 worship centers throughout south India, mostly in Tamil Nadu and some in the city of Mumbai.

### *Zoroastrianism*

A form of the ancient Persian religion Zoroastrianism continues to be practiced in India, where its followers are called Parsis. Suffering persecution from Muslim rulers in what is now modern-day Iran, Zoroastrian immigrants were granted protection by a Hindu king at a place called Sanjan in the western Indian state of Gujarat many centuries ago.

### *Sikhism*

Sikhism, was founded in India's northwestern Punjab region about 400 years ago. As of 2001 there were 19.3 million Sikhs in India. Many of today's Sikhs are situated in Punjab, the largest Sikh province in the world and the ancestral home of Sikhs. The most famous Sikh temple is the Golden Temple, located in Amritsar, Punjab. Many Sikhs serve in the Indian Army. The current prime minister of India, Manmohan Singh, is a Sikh. Punjab is the spiritual home of

Sikhs and is the only state in India where Sikhs form a majority.

### *Judaism*

Trade contacts between the Mediterranean region and the west coast of India probably led to the presence of small Jewish settlements in India as long ago as the early first millennium B.C. In Kerala a community of Jews tracing its origin to the fall of Jerusalem in A.D. 70 has remained associated with the cities of Kodungallur (formerly known as Cranganore) and Kochi (formerly known as Cochin) for at least 1,000 years. The Paradesi Synagogue in Kochi, rebuilt in 1568, is in the architectural style of Kerala but preserves the ritual style of the Sephardic rite, with Babylonian and Yemenite influence as well. The Jews of Kochi, concentrated mostly in the old "Jew Town," were completely integrated into local culture, speaking Malayalam and taking local names while preserving their knowledge of Hebrew and contacts with Southwest Asia.

A separate community of Jews, called the Bene Israel, had lived along the Konkan Coast in and around Bombay, Pune, and Ahmadabad for almost 2,000 years. Unlike the Kochi Jews, they became a village-based society and maintained little contact with other Jewish communities. They always remained within the Orthodox Jewish fold, practicing the Sephardrew is coolite without rabbis, with the synagogue as the center of religious and cultural life. Following trade routes established by the expansion of the British Empire, a third group of Jews, the Baghdadi Jews immigrated to India, settling primarily in Bombay and Calcutta.

Many of the Baghdadi traders became wealthy and participated prominently in the economic leadership of these growing cities. As a result of religious pressure elsewhere, including the forced conversions of Mashhad, their numbers were increased by religious refugees. The Baghdadis came mostly from the Ottoman Empire, Persia, and Afghanistan.

The population of the Kochi Jews, always small, had decreased from 5,000 in 1951 to about fifty in the early 1990s. During the same period, the Bene Israel decreased from about 20,000 to 5,000, while the Baghdadi Jews declined from 5,000 to 250. Emigration to Australia, Israel, the United Kingdom, and North America accounts for most of this decline. According to the 1981 Indian census, there were 5,618 Jews in India, down from 5,825 in 1971. The 1991 census showed a further decline to 5,271, most of whom lived in Maharashtra and Kerala.

## Language

As well as regional diversity, languages have created diverse traditions of culture in India. There are a large number of languages in India; 216 of them are spoken by a group of 10,000 persons or more.

The languages of India primarily belong to two major linguistic families, Indo-European (whose branch Indo-Aryan is spoken by about 74% of the population) and Dravidian (spoken by about 24%). Other languages spoken in India come from the Austro-Asiatic and Tibeto-Burman linguistic families. The Andamanese languages, spoken on the Andaman Islands, are apparently not related to any other language family.

The number of mother tongues in India is as high as 1,652. There are 24 languages which are spoken by a million or more people, in addition to thousands of smaller languages. Three millennia of language contact situation have led to a lot of mutual influence among the four language families in India and South Asia. Three contact languages have played an important role in the history of India: Sanskrit, Persian and English. Two classical languages native to the land are Sanskrit and Tamil.

Article 343 of the Indian Constitution recognises Hindi in Devanagari script as the official language of the union; the Constitution also allows for the continuation of use of the English language for official purposes. Article 345 provides constitutional recognition to "regional languages" of the union to include any language adopted by a State Legislature as the official language of that state. Until the Twenty-First Amendment of the Constitution in 1967, the country recognised 14 official regional languages. The Eighth Schedule and the Seventy-First Amendment provided for the inclusion of Sindhi, Konkani, Manipuri and Nepali, thereby increasing the number of official regional languages of India to 18.

Individual states, whose borders are mostly drawn on socio-linguistic lines, are free to decide their own language for internal administration and education. The Constitution of India recognises 22 "national languages", spoken throughout the country, namely Assamese, Bengali, Bodo, Dogri, Gujarati, Hindi, Kannada, Kashmiri, Konkani, Maithili, Malayalam, Manipuri, Marathi, Nepali, Oriya, Punjabi, Sanskrit, Santhali, Sindhi, Tamil, Telugu and Urdu. Hindi, apart from being an official language of the Union of India, is the official language of the states Uttar Pradesh, Bihar, Jharkhand, Uttaranchal, Madhya Pradesh, Rajasthan, Chattisgarh, Himachal Pradesh, Haryana and the National Capital Territory of Delhi. English is the co-official language of the Indian Union, and that each of the several states mentioned above may also have another co-official language.

The two classical languages Sanskrit and Tamil have large collections of literature, with the earliest Sanskrit texts dating from 5000 years ago and the earliest Tamil literature from 2500 years ago. An official language, and the main language of Hindu liturgy, Sanskrit is used in rituals and ceremonies or as part of daily prayers in Hinduism. Though not prevalent in every-day use, it is interestingly being revived as a spoken tongue in the village of Mattur, in the Shimoga district of Karnataka. Telugu, a mellifluous language is another language with a notably ancient history and body of literature, and is widely used in Carnatic music.

The northern Indian languages from the Indo-European family evolved from Old Indo-Aryan such as Sanskrit, by way of the Middle Indo-Aryan Prakrit languages and Apabhramsha of the Middle Ages. There is no consensus for a specific time where the modern north Indian languages such as Hindi, Marathi, Panjabi, and Bengali emerged, but c. 1,000 AD is commonly accepted. Each language had different influences, with Hindi/Urdu and closely related languages being strongly influenced by Persian and Arabic.

Indian languages have corresponding distinct alphabets. The two major families are those of the Dravidian languages and those of the Indo-Aryan languages, the former largely confined to the south and the latter to the north. Urdu and sometimes Kashmiri, Sindhi and Panjabi are written in modified versions of the Arabic script. Except for these languages, the alphabets of Indian languages are native to India. There are those scholars who believe the scripts of the Northern languages to be distant derivations of the Aramaic alphabet, though this is a disputed theory primarily because the number and grouping of sounds and letters are so radically different.

## Literature

The earliest literary traditions were mostly oral and passed through descendants by the citizens. They were later transcribed. Most of these spring from Hindu tradition and are represented by sacred works like the Vedas, the epics of the Mahabharata and Ramayana. Tamil Sangam literature represents some of India's oldest secular traditions. Many

Buddhist and Jain works are in Prakrit languages like Pali. The classical works of playwright Kalidasa even today exert an important influence on Indian literrateurs. Upon the arrival of Mughal dynasty, Islamic culture dominated most of medieval Indian literature.This was due to the spreading influence of Persian and the rise of famous poets such as Amir Khusro. Colonial rule prepared the stage for modern literature exemplified by the works of Rabindranath Tagore, Bankim Chandra Chattopadhyay, Michael Madhusudan Dutt, Munshi Premchand, Devaki Nandan Khatri, among many others. Indian writers in modern times, like R. K. Narayan, Vaikom Muhammad Basheer, Arundhati Roy, Vikram Seth, Khushwant Singh, Salman Rushdie have been the cynosure of wide acclaim, both in Indian languages and English.

India has strong tradtions of poetry, as well as prose writing. This is often closely related to musical traditions, and most poetry can be attributed to religious movements. Writers and philosophers were often also skilled poets. In modern times, poetry served as an important non-violent tool of nationalism during the Indian freedom movement. A famous modern example of this tradtion can be found in such figures as Rabindranath Tagore in modern times, and poets such as Kabir in medieval times, as well as the epics of ancient times. Two examples of poetry from Tagore's Gitanjali serve as the national anthems of both India and Bangladesh.

The Ramayana and Mahabharata are not only considered epics of India and Hinduism, but serve as the folk epics of other Asian countries like Thailand, Malaysia and Indonesia. In this respect, they are considered by many to be the 'eastern' equivalents of the classical epics of Europe, namely Iliad and Odyssey. Other regional variations of these stories, and unrelated epics include such as the Tamil Silappadhikaram, Kamba Ramayana , Manimegalai and Jeevaga-chintamani, Hindi Ramacharita-manasa, Malayalam Adhyath-maramayanam.

Indian literature is generally acknowledged as the oldest in the world. India has 22 officially recognized languages, and a huge variety of literature has been produced in these languages over the years. In Indian literature, oral and written forms are both important. Hindu literary traditions dominate a large part of Indian culture. Apart from the Vedas which are a sacred form of knowledge, there are other works such as the Hindu epics Ramayana and Mahabharata, treatises such as Vaastu Shastra in architecture and town planning, and Arthashastra in political science. Islamic culture dominates most of medieval Indian literature, with the spreading influenc of Persian and the rise of famous poets such as Amir Khusro.

Devotional Hindu drama, poetry and songs span the subcontinent. Among the best known are the works of Kalidas (writer of the famed Sanskrit play Shakuntala) and Tulsidas (who wrote an epic Hindi poem based on the Ramayana, called Raamcharitmaanas). Tamil poetry of the Sangam poetry which dates back to 500 BC is well renowned.

### *Sanskrit Literature*

The most famous works in Sanskrit are the Hindu holy texts like the Vedas, Upanishads, and Manusmriti. The great epics are Ramayana and Mahabharata. Panini's Ashtadhyayi standardized Sanskrit grammar and phonetics. Kalidas is considered the greatest in Sanskrit literature. His Shakuntala and Meghaduuta are the most famous Sanskrit plays. Some other famous plays were Mricchakatika by Shudraka, Svapna Vasavadattam by Bhaasa, and Ratnavali by Sri Harsha. Later poetic works include Geeta Govinda by Jayadeva. Some other famous works are Chanakya's Arthashastra and Vatsyayana's Kamasutra.

### *Tamil Literature*

Tamil literature has existed for more than 2000 years.

Tolkaappiyam is said to be the world's oldest surviving grammar for any language has been credited as its oldest work available today, whereas the exact origins of Thirukkural is unknown. The golden age of Tamil literature was during the Third Sangam period, roughly 1800 years ago. The classic works of this period are Cilappatikaram, Manimekalai, and Sivakasinthamani. Tamil literature is known for its secular traditions, although its authors had strong religious beliefs. Thirukkural is considered to be the greatest of Tamil works.

### *Kannada Literature*

Kannada literature is the third oldest in Indian literature next to Sanskrit literature and Tamil literature. The earliest reported work in Kannada literature dates back to 5th century. The first available literary in Kannada is Kavirajamarga written in 8th century by Amoghavarsha Nrpatunga. Kannada literature can broadly studied in three phases: Hale Kannada (Old Kannada), Nadu Kannada (Middle Kannada) and Adhunika Kannada (Modern Kannada). As of today Kannada authors have distinction of winning jnanpeeth award, the highest literary award in India, most times, seven.

### *Hindi Literature*

Hindi literature started as religious and philosophical poetry in medieval periods in dialects like Avadhi and Brij. The most famous figures from this period are Kabir and Tulsidas. In modern times, the Khadi dialect became more prominent and a variety of literature was produced in Sanskrit.

Chandrakanta, written by Devaki Nandan Khatri, is considered to be the first work of prose in Hindi. Munshi Premchand was the most famous Hindi novelist. The chhayavadi poets include Surya kant tripathi "Nirala", Jaishankar Prasad, Sumitranandan Pant,and Mahadevi

Varma other renowned poets are Maithili Sharan Gupt,Agyey,Harivansh rai bachan, Dharmveer bharti etc. The progressive poets of Hindi were : Kedarnath Agrawal,Shamsher,Gajanan madhav "Muqtibodh", Ramdhari Singh "Dinkar", Nagarjun, Raghuveer sahai, and Kedar nath singh. The young generation good poets are : Kumar Vikal, Dinesh Shukla, Uday Prakash, Mohan Daheria, Shailendra Chauhan, Vinod Padraj and so on — This young generation is very much extrovert in expressions and much aware of global changes.

Now a days in Hindi poetry "Shailendra Chauhan" is known for the sensible and touchy poems. His poetry collections viz; 'Swetpatra' and 'Eashwar kee chaukhat par' were read and discussed on many forums in length. Recently in Hindi India Today there is very short but beautiful review on later collection. He has been widely published and accepted by most of Hindi literary magazines such as Pahal, Vasudha, Ashay, Aksharparva, Abhivyakti, Kriti Oar, Prerana, Swadhinta, sahmat Muktanad, Sahi samajh etc. All the important Hindi newspapers also presesented him on various ocassions eg; Jansatta, Rashtriy Sahara. Amar Ujala, Dainik Bhaskar etc. Many poems have been placed on internet also whom one can get by searching on any popular search engine particularly 'google'.

### *Prakrit Literature*

The most notable Prakrit language was Pali. Pali literature includes Buddhist philosophical works, poetry and some grammatical works. Major works in Pali are Jataka tales, Dhammapada, Addhakatha, and Mahavansha. Some of the major Pali grammarians were Kachvaayan, Moggalaan and Varruchi. Many of Ashvaghosha's plays were written in Shaurseni Prakrit. Another major work in Shaurseni was Karpoormanjari. Kalidasa, Harsha and Haal used Maharashtrian Prakrit in some of their plays and poetry. Many

Shwetambar Jain works are also written in the Maharashtri Prakrit. Many plays and Jain works were written in the Ardha Magadhi Prakrit.

### *Indian writing in Persian*

During the early Muslim period, Persian became the lingua franca of the subcontinent, used by most of the educated and the government. Although Persian literature from Persia itself was popular, several Indians became major Persian poets, the most notable being Amir Khusro and in more modern times Allama Iqbal. Much of the older Sanskrit literature was also translated into Persian. For a time, it remained the court language of the Mughals, soon to be replaced by Urdu.

Persian still held its status, despite the spread of Urdu, well into the early years of the British rule in India. Most British officials had to learn Persian on coming to India and concluded their conversations in Persian. In the early 19th century, however, the British, in an effort to expand their influence, made a government ruling to discontinue the use of Persian and commence the use of English instead. Thus started the decline of Persian as the subcontinent's lingua franca, a position to be taken up by the new language of the British Raj, English. Many modern Indian languages still show signs of heavy Persian influence, most notably Urdu and Hindi.

### *Urdu Literature*

Among other traditions, Urdu poetry is a fine example of linguistic and cultural synthesis. Arab and Persian vocabulary based on the Hindi language resulted in a vast and extremely beloved class of ghazal literature, usually written by Muslims in contexts ranging from romance and society to philosophy and devotion to Allah. Urdu soon became the court language of the Mughals and in its higher forms was once called the "Kohinoor" of Indian languages.

### *Bengali Literature*

The most internationally famous Bengali writer is Nobel laureate Rabindranath Tagore, who received the Nobel Prize for Literature; but another poet, one generation younger is equally popular, valuable, and influential in his country, though virtually unknown in foreign countries: Kazi Nazrul Islam. Other famous Indian Bengali writers were Sharat Chandra Chattopadhyay and Bankim Chandra Chattopadhyay. Bengali is the second most commonly spoken language in India (after Hindi). As a result of the Bengali renaissance in the 19th and 20th centuries, quite a bit of India's most famous, and relatively recent, literature, poetry, and songs are in Bengali.

### *Marathi Literature*

Marathi literature began with saint-poets like Dnyaneshwar, Tukaram, Ramdas, and Eknath. Modern Marathi literature was marked by a theme of social reform. Well-known figures from this phase include Mahatma Jyotiba Phule, Lokhitwadi, and others. Prominent modern literary figures include Vishnu Sakharam Khandekar, P.L. Deshpande, Vijay Tendulkar, and Vishnu Vaman Shirvadakar (Kavi Kusumagraj).

### *Indian writing in English*

In the last century, several Indian writers have distinguished themselves not only in traditional Indian languages but also in English. India's only Nobel laureate in literature was the Bengali writer Rabindranath Tagore. Other major writers who are either Indian or of Indian origin and derive much inspiration from Indian themes are R. K. Narayan, Vikram Seth, Salman Rushdie, Arundhati Roy, Raja Rao, Amitav Ghosh, Vikram Chandra, Mukul Kesavan, Shashi Tharoor, Nayantara Sehgal, Anita Desai, Ashok Banker, Shashi Deshpande, Jhumpa Lahiri, Kamala Markandaya and Bharati Mukherjee.

In recent years, English-language writers of Indian origin are being published in the West at an increasing rate. In June 1997, a special fiction issue of The New Yorker magazine devoted much space to essays by Amitav Ghosh and Abraham Verghese, a short story by Vikram Chandra, and poems by Jayanta Mahapatra and A. K. Ramanujan. John Updike profiled R.K. Narayan and Arundhati Roy's "A God of Small Things."

### *Telugu Literature*

Telugu, the second largest language spoken in India, is rich in literary traditions. The earliest written literature dates back to seventh century AD. The epic literary tradition started with Nannayya who is acclaimed as 'AADIKAVI' which means the first poet. He belongs to tenth-eleventh century AD. Kalapurnodayam by Pingali Suranna a poet of sixteenth century- is the worlds first literary work in stream of concoiuness technique. The world had to wait for four centuries to have a major work in this tradition in the form of James Joyce's magnum opus.

The father of Telugu modern poetry Gurajada created a literary marvel with his play Kanyasulkam. Kanyasulkam stands one of the best plays that have ever been written in the world literature. Sri Sri who is thse only poet deserved the title 'Mahakavi' (the greatest of the poets) in the modern era produced Mahaprasthanm. Mahaprasthanam did to telugu people, what the literature from milton to eliot/frost had done to the english. The Digambara poets shook the stragnat literary world between 1960 - 1970 and their verses were translated not only in to many other indian languages but also into many european laguages. It is Telugu lierature that led whole indian literary world in revolutionary literary movement. The tradition goes on: thus between Nannayya and 'Nandanodaya' of today, there stood literary gaints who enriched world literature.

## Performing Arts

### *Music*

The music of India includes multiple varieties of folk, popular, pop, and classical music. India's classical music tradition, including Carnatic and Hindustani music, has a history spanning millennia and, developed over several eras, remains fundamental to the lives of Indians today as sources of religious inspiration, cultural expression and pure entertainment. India is made up of several dozen ethnic groups, speaking their own languages and dialects. Alongside distinctly subcontinental forms there are major influences from Persian, Arab and British music. Indian genres like filmi and bhangra have become popular throughout the United Kingdom, South and East Asia, and around the world.

Indian pop stars now sell records in many countries, while world music fans listen to the roots music of India's diverse nations. American soul, rock and hip hop have also made a large impact, primarily on Indian pop and filmi music. Other highly popular forms are ghazal, qawwali, thumri, dhrupad, dadra, bhajan, kirtan, shabad, and gurbani. The earliest texts of Indian music are the Natya shastra, Dattilam, Brihaddeshi, and the Sangita-Ratnakara.

### *Classical music*

The two main traditions of classical music have been Carnatic music, found predominantly in the peninsular regions and Hindustani music, found in the northern and central parts. While both traditions claim Vedic origin, history indicates that the two traditions diverged from a common musical root since 13th century.

The origins of Indian classical music, the classical music of India, can be found from the oldest of scriptures, part of the Hindu tradition, the Vedas. Samaveda, one of the four Vedas, describes music at length. The two main streams of Indian classical music are Hindustani music, from North India, and Carnatic music (Karnataka Sangeeth), from South India.

Indian classical music is monophonic and based around a single melody line. The performance of a composition, based melodically on one particular raga and rhythmically on one tala, begins with the performers coming out in a ritualized order: drone instruments, then the soloist, then accompanists and percussionists. The musicians begin by tuning their instruments; this process often blends imperceptibly into the beginning of the music.

Indian musical instruments used in classical music include veena, mridangam, tabla, kanjira, tambura, flute, sitar, gottuvadyam, violin, and sarangi.

Players of the tabla, a type of drum, begin by tapping the edges with a hammer to make sure it is in tune with the soloist. Another common instrument is the stringed tambura (sometimes also called tanpura), which is played at a steady tone (a drone) throughout the raga. This task traditionally falls to a student of the soloist, a task which might seem monotonous but is, in fact, an honour and a rare opportunity for the student who gets it.

The raga begins with the melody being developed gradually, and proper rendering of any raga will take more than half an hour. The beginning of the raga is called an alap in Hindustani music and an alapana in Carnatic music. Many aficionados consider the alap their favourite part, but the alap is often inaccessible to others.

In Hindustani music, once the raga is established, the ornamentation around the mode begins to become rhythmical, gradually speeding up. This section is called the jor. After the jor climaxes, everything stops and the audiences applaud. Finally, the percussionist begins to play, interacting with the soloist, eventually reaching the spontaneous and competitive jhala section.

Carnatic raga elaborations are generally much faster in tempo and shorter. The opening piece is called a varnam, and is a warm-up for the musicians. A devotion and a request for a blessing follows, then a series of interchanges between ragams (unmetered melody) and thaalams (the ornamentation, equivalent to the jor). This is intermixed with hymns called krithis. This is followed by the pallavi or theme from the raga.

*Folk music*

Indian folk music is diverse because of India's vast cultural diversity. It has many forms including bhangra, lavani, dandiya and Rajasthani. The arrival of movies and pop music weakened folk music's popularity, but cheaply recordable music has made it easier to find and helped revive the traditions. Folk music (desi) has been influential on classical music, which is viewed as a higher art form. Instruments and styles have impacted classical ragas. It is also not uncommon for major writers, saints and poets to have large musical libraries and traditions to their name, often sung in thumri (semi-classical) style. Most of the folk music of India is dance-oriented.

***Rabindra sangeet***

A towering figure of Indian music was Rabindranath Tagore. Writing in Bengali, he created a library of over 2,000 songs now known by Bengalis as rabindra sangeet whose form is primarily influenced by Hindustani classical thumri style. Many singers in West Bengal proudly base their entire careers on the singing of Tagore musical masterpieces.

***Qawwali***

Qawwali is a Sufi form of devotional music based on the principles of Hindustani classical. It is performed with one or two lead singers, several chorus singers, harmonium, tabla, and dholak.

*Pop music*

The biggest form of Indian pop music is filmi, or songs from Indian musical films. Independent pop acts such as Alisha Chinoy, Shaan, and rock bands like Indus Creed, Indian Ocean, and Euphoria exist and have gained mass appeal with the advent of cable music television.

*Filmi music*

Many languages are spoken in India, and there are film industries for each of the major languages. Film music is mostly used in commercial Indian cinema, which is mainly produced in the centres of Mumbai, Chennai, and Hyderabad. Indian films are best-known for their music and composers (music directors). Today's most popular music director, A. R. Rahman, got his start in Tamil films and then moved to Bollywood. Well-known music directors of the past include Naushad, R.D. Burman, Bappi Lahiri, and Ilayaraaja.

**Dance**

*Classical dance*

India offers a number of Classical Indian dance forms, each of which can be traced to different parts of the country. Each form represents the culture and ethos of a particular region or a group of people. The eight main styles are Bharatanatyam, Kathak, Odissi, Kuchipudi, Mohiniattam, Bhangra, Manipuri and Kathakali. Indian classical dance, at its best, has the most powerful means to lead its worshippers – the artist – to the Divine. It is a sincere depiction of the Divine. It is a sincere depiction of the realities in life, an embodiment of the imagination and gracefulness, the very soul which thereby creates as it were the "Idol of the Beautiful".

*Folk dances*

Besides, there are several forms of Indian folk dances, and special dances observed in regional festivals. Indian folk and tribal dances are simple dances, and are performed to express joy. Folk dances are performed for every possible occasion, to celebrate the arrival of seasons, birth of a child, a wedding and festivals. The dances are extremely simple with minimum of steps or movement. The dances burst with verve and vitality. Men and women perform some dances exclusively, while in some perfomances men and women dance together. On most occasions, the dancers sing themselves, while being accompanied by artists on the instruments. Each form of dance has a specific costume. Most costumes are flamboyant with extensive jewels. While there are numerous folk and tribal dances, they are constantly improved. The skill and the imagination of the dances influence the performance.

***Drama and theatre***

Indian drama and theatre is perhaps as old as its music and dance. Kalidas' plays like Shakuntala and Meghadoot are some of the oldest plays from literary traditions. The tradition of folk theatre is alive in nearly all the linguistic regions of the country. In addition, there is a rich tradition of puppet theatre in rural India. Group Theatre is also thriving in the cities, initiated by the likes of Utpal Dutt, Khwaja Ahmad Abbas and still maintained by groups like Nandikar and Prithvi Theatre.

## Visual Arts

***Painting***

The earliest Indian paintings were the rock paintings of pre-historic times, the petroglyphs as found in places like Bhimbetka, and some of them are older than 5500 BC.

Ancient texts outlining theories of darragh and anecdotal accounts suggesting that it was common for households to paint their doorways or indoor rooms where guests resided.

Cave paintings from Ajanta, Bagh, Ellora and Sittanavasal and temple paintings testify to a love of naturalism and God. Most rock art in India is Hindu or Buddhist. A freshly made coloured flour design (Rangoli) everyday is still a common sight outside the doorstep of many (mostly South Indian) Indian homes.

Madhubani painting, Rajput painting, Tanjore painting, Mughal painting are some notable Genres of Indian Art; while Raja Ravi Varma, Nandalal Bose, Jamini Roy are some modern painters. Jehangir Art Gallery, Mumbai, has on display several good Indian paintings.

### *Sculpture*

The first sculptures in India date back to the Indus Valley civilization, where stone and bronze carvings have been discoverd. This is one of the earliest instances of sculpture in the world. Later, as Hinduism, Buddhism and Jainism developed further, India produced some of the most intricate bronzes in the world, as well as unrivaled temple carvings. Some huge shrines, such as the one at Ellora were not actually constructed using blocks, but instead carved out of solid rock, making them perhaps the largest and most intricate sculptures in the world.

The pink sandstone sculptures of Mathura evolved during the Gupta period (4th to 6th century) to reach a very high fineness of execution and delicacy in the modeling. Newer sculptures in northwest, in stucco, schist or clay, display very strong blending of Indian post-Gupta mannerism and Classical influence, Hellenistic or possibly even Greco-Roman. Meanwhile, elsewhere in India, less anatomically accurate styles of human representation evolved, leading to the classical art that the world is now familiar with, and contributing to Buddhist and Hindu sculpture throughout Asia.

*Architecture*

Indian architecture is that vast tapestry of production of the Indian Subcontinent that encompasses a multitude of expressions over space and time, transformed by the forces of history considered unique to the sub-continent, sometimes destroying, but most of the time absorbing new ideas. The result is an evolving range of architectural production that none the less retains a certain amount of continuity across history.

The earliest production in the Indus Valley Civilization was characterised by well planned cities and houses where religion did not seem to play an active role, but which demonstrated world-famous city planning. During the reign Gupta and Maurya empires, several Buddhist architecture like caves of Ajanta and Ellora and the monumental Sanchi Stupa were built. South India contains several Hindu temples like Brihadeeswara Temple, Thanjavur, the Sun Temple, Konark, Sri Ranganathaswamy Temple at Srirangam. Angkor Wat and other Buddhist and Hindu temples carry the evidence of Indian influence on South East Asian architecture, as they are built in styles almost indentical to traditional Indian temple building.

With the advent of Islamic influence from the west, the erstwhile Indian architecture was slightly adapted to allow the traditions of the new religion. Fatehpur Sikri, Taj Mahal, Gol Gumbaz, Qutub Minar, Red Fort of Delhi are the creations of this era, and are often used as the steriotypical symbols of India, despite the greater antiquity and originality of traditional architecture. The colonoal rule of the British Indian Empire saw the development of Indo-Saracenic style, and mixing of several other styles, such as European gothic. Victoria Memorial, Victoria Terminus are notable examples. Recent creations such as Lotus Temple, and the various modern urban developments of India, are also notable.

The traditional system of Vaastu Shastra serves as India's version of Feng Shui, influencing town planning, architecture, and ergonomics. It is unclear which system is older, but they contain many similarities. Though Vastu is conceptually similar to Feng Shui in that it also tries to harmonize the flow of energy, through the house, it differs in the details, such as the exact directions in which various objects, rooms, materials etc are to be placed. The idea of Prana likely formed the basis of the idea of Chi in China and other countries that were exposed to Indian philosophy, indicating there may be some connection between the two systems.

Indian archutecture has influence the world, especially eastern asia, due to the spread of ideas with Buddhism. A number of Indian archutectual features such as the temple mound or stupa, temple spire or sikhara, temple tower or pagoda and temple gate or torana, have become famous symbols of asian culture, used extensively in East Asia and South East Asia. The central spire is also sometimes called a vimanam. The varient southern temple gate, or gopuram is noted for its intricacy and majesty. The arch, a cornerstone of world archutecture, was first developed by the Indus Valley civilization, and would later be a staple of Indian archutecture.

## Recreation and Sports

In the area of recreation and sports India had evolved a number of games. The modern eastern martial arts originated as ancient games and martial arts in India and it was from here that these games were transmitted to foreign countries, where they were further modernized. Additionally, a few games introduced during the British Raj have grown quite popular in India, field hockey, football (soccer) and especially cricket.

Although field hockey is India's official national sport, cricket is by far the most popular sport not only in India, but the entire subcontinent, thriving recreationally and professionally. Cricket has even been used recently as a forum for diplomatic relations between India and long-standing rival, Pakistan. The two nations' cricket teams face off annually and such contests are quite impassioned on both sides. Traditional indigenous sports include kabaddi and gilli-danda, which are played in most parts of the country. Indoor and outdoor games like Chess, Snakes and Ladders, Playing cards, Polo, Carrom, Badminton are popular.

## Cuisine

The earliest Indians, the Harappans, probably ate mainly wheat, rice and lentils, and occasionally meats such as pork, lamb, beef, goat and chicken. It is not known exactly when beef was made forbidden in Hinduism. Some believe that vegetarianism became popular with the arrival of Buddhism and Jainism, that emphasised ahimsa (non-violence).

The cuisine of Modern India has great variety and each region has its own distinctive flavours. The staple cereals are rice and wheat. North Indian staple meals consist of chapatis or rotis, wheat based and rice as staples, eaten with a wide variety of side dishes like dals, curries, yogurt, chutney and achars. South India staple dishes dishes consist of rice, sambhar, rasam, yoghurt and curries being important side dishes. Another important ingredient in south Indian food is cocunut & most popular snacks like idli dosa are also rice-based. Fish is popular in coastal states, especially West Bengal, Orissa and Kerala. Several kind of street foods like Panipuri, Vada pav, Bhelpuri, samosa, vada are popular, though they are known by different names in different regions. Indian Chinese cuisine, a spicier and indianized version of the Chinese cuisine is also popular. This cuisine is supposed to have originated from east of India generally and Darjeeling specfically. Tea enjoys heavy popularity, while coffee is mostly popular in South India. Nimbu pani (lemonade), lassi, and coconut milk are also popular, while India also has many indigenous alcoholic beverages like Fenny and Indian beer.

## Popular Media

### *Cinema*

Bollywood is the informal name given to the popular Mumbai-based film industry in India. Bollywood and the other major cinematic hubs (Bengali, Kannada, Malayalam, Tamil, Telugu) constitute the broader Indian film industry, whose output is considered to be the largest in the world in terms of number of films produced and, possibly, number of tickets sold.

Bollywood films are usually musicals. Few movies are made without at least one song-and-dance number. Indian audiences expect full value for their money; they want songs and dances, love interest, comedy and dare-devil thrills, all mixed up in a three hour long extravaganza with intermission. Such movies are called masala movies, after the Indian spice mixture masala. Like masala, these movies are a mixture of many things. Plots tend to be melodramatic. They frequently employ formulaic ingredients such as star-crossed lovers and angry parents, corrupt politicians, kidnappers, conniving villains, courtesans with hearts of gold, long-lost relatives and siblings separated by fate, dramatic reversals of fortune, and convenient coincidences, and even movies with tri polar changes that can turn a movie and its plot upside down.

Besides the regular masala films, India has also produced many critically acclaimed cinema-makers like Satyajit Ray, Ritwik Ghatak, Adoor Gopalakrishnan, Mani Ratnam, G. Aravindan etc. In fact, with the opening up of the economy in the recent years & consequent exposure to world cinema, audience tastes have been changing. Indian commercial movies have also started following authentic, real world themes with a lower amount of melodrama & some do not even contain songs. In addition, multiplexes have mushroomed in most cities, changing the revenue patterns & allowing film makers greater liberty & scope for executing bold & innovative ideas which would not have been possible even a decade ago.

### *Television*

Indian television started off in 1959 in New Delhi with tests for educational telecasts. Indian small screen programming started off in the early 1980s. At that time there was only one national channel Doordarshan, which was government owned. The Ramayana and Mahabharat were some among the popular television series produced. By the late 1980s more and more people started to own television sets. Though there was a single channel, television programming had reached saturation. Hence the government opened up another channel which had part national programming and part regional. This channel was known as DD 2 later DD Metro. Both channels were broadcasted terrestrially.

In 1994, the government liberated its markets, opening them up to cable television. Since then, a spurt in the number of channels available. Today, Indian silver screen is a huge industry by itself, and has thousands of programmes in all the states of India. The small screen has produced numerous celebrities of their own kind some even attaining national fame. TV soaps are extremely popular with housewives as well as working women. Some small time actors have made it big in Bollywood.

### *Radio*

Radio broadcasting began in India in 1927, with two privately-owned transmitters at Mumbai and Calcutta.

These were nationalised in 1930 and operated under the name "Indian Broadcasting Service" until 1936, when it was renamed All India Radio (AIR). Although officially renamed again to Akashwani in 1957, it is still popularly known as All India Radio. All India Radio is a division of Prasar Bharati (Broadcasting Corporation of India), an autonomous corporation of the Ministry of Information and Broadcasting, Government of India. It is the sister service of Prasar Bharati's Doordarshan, the national television broadcaster.

## Festivals

A vast number of local Hindu festivals revolve around the worship of gods at the neighborhood, village, or caste level. All over India, at least once a year the images of the gods are taken from their shrines to travel in processions around their domains. The images are carried on palanquins that require human bearers or on human-drawn, large-wheeled carts. The images may be intricately made up in order for the stone or wooden statues to appear lifelike. They may wear costly vestments, and flower garlands may surround their necks or entire shrines. The gods move down village or city streets in parades that may include multiple palanquins and, at sites of major temples, even elephants decked out in traditional vestments. As the parade passes, throngs of worshipers pray and make vows to the gods while the community as a whole looks on and participates in the spectacle.

In many locations, these public parades go on for a number of days and include special events where the gods engage in "play" (lila ) that may include mock battles and the defeat of demons. The ceremonial bathing of the images and displays of the gods in all their finery in public halls also occur. In the south, where temples stand at the geographic and psychological heart of village and town, some "chariots" of the gods stand many stories tall and require the concerted effort of dozens of men to pull them through the streets.

There are a number of Hindu religious festivals that are officially recognized by the government as "closed holidays," on which work stops throughout the country. The biggest of these occur within two blocks of time after the end of the southwest monsoon. The first comes at the end of the ten-day festival of Dussehra, late in the month of Asvina (September-October) according to the Shaka calendar, India's official calendar. This festival commemorates Ram's victory over Ravana and the rescue of his wife Sita. On the ninth day of Dusshera, people bless with sandalwood paste the "weapons" of their business life, including everything from plows to computers.

On the final day of Dussehra, in North India celebrating crowds set fire to huge paper effigies of Ravana. Several weeks later comes Dipavali (Diwali), or the Festival of Lights, in the month of Kartika (October-November). This is officially a one-day holiday, but in reality it becomes a week-long event when many people take vacations. One tradition links this festival to the victory of Krishna over the demon Naraka, but for most devotees the holiday is a recreation of Ram's triumphant return with Sita, his wife, from his adventures. People light rows of lamps and place them on sills around their houses, set off gigantic amounts of fireworks, pray for wealth and good fortune, distribute sweets, and send greeting cards to friends and business associates.

The other closed holidays associated with Hindu festivals include Mahashivaratri, or the great night of Shiva, during the month of Magha (January-February). This festival celebrates Shiva's emanation of the universe through his cosmic dance, and is a day of fasting, visiting temples, and in many places staying up all night to sing devotional songs. On the fourth day in the month of Bhadra (August-September) comes the festival of Ganesh Chaturthi.

Families and businesses prepare for this festival by purchasing brightly painted images of Ganesh and worshiping them for a number of days. On the festival itself, with great celebration, participants bathe the images (and in most cases permanently dump them) in nearby rivers, lakes, or seas. Janmashtami, the birthday of Krishna, also occurs in the month of Bhadra.

There are a large number of "restricted holidays" celebrated by the vast majority of the population and resulting in closures of business establishments. Major Hindu events include Ramanavami, the birthday of Ram in the month of Chaitra (March-April), and Holi, celebrated at the end of the month of Phalguna (February-March), when people engage in cross-dressing, play tricks on each other, and squirt colored water or powder on each other. These primarily northern festivals receive varying amounts of attention in other parts of the country. A separate series of restricted holidays allow regional cultures to celebrate their own feasts, such as the harvest festival of Pongal in Tamil Nadu in mid-January, which celebrates the harvest and the sun's entrance into Capricorn.

## Indian Philosophy

Indian philosophy throughout the ages has had a tremendous impact on world thought, especially in the east. Various theistic schools of philosophy, such as the many schools of Buddhism and Hinduism, have has huge influences, but also, India produced some of the longest and most influential secular traditions of logic, rationalism, science, mathematics, materialism, atheism, agnosticism, etc, which are often overlooked due to popular conception that India is a 'mystical' country. Many of the complex scientific and mathematical concepts such as the idea of zero, found their way to Europe via Arab intermediaries. The most famous school of Indian atheism, is Carvaka, considered by some to be the oldest materialistic school of thought in the world, composed around the same time as the Hindu Upanishads, as well as the philosophy of Buddhism and Jainism. This period around 600-400 BCE marked a huge leap in both Indian philosophy and world philosophy in general, with contemporary Greek schools emerging simultaneously. Some philosophical concepts from India were introduced to the Greeks, especially during the campaigns of Alexander the Great, and vis a vis, leading some schools of classical Greek philosophy to be almost identical to prior Indian schools.

In addition to the unbroken high emphasis placed on philosophy in India, which has existed since ancient times, modern India has produced some of the world's most influential philosophers of modern times, who have written both in their native languages, and often English. During the British occupation of India, various thinkers, both secular and religious, achieved a new level of recognition across the world as both ancient Indian texts, and the work of contemporary Indian philosophers was translated into English, German and other languages. Swami Vivekananda traveled to America and participated in the 1893 World Parliament of Religions, impressing delegates with a groundbreaking speech that for the first time gave access to eastern, Indian, Hindu and dharmic philosophy to western intellectuals. As well as various religious thinkers Mahatma Gandhi, Rabindranath Tagore and other members of the Indian freedom movement, generated political philosophy, and formed the basis of modern Indian democracy, secularism and liberalism. Today, economists such as Amartya Sen, who won Asia's first nobel prize in economics, continue to give India a reputation as an important contributor to world thought.

# 4

# ECONOMY

The economy of India is the fourth largest in the world as measured by purchasing power parity (PPP), with a gross domestic product (GDP) of US $3.63 trillion. When measured in USD exchange-rate terms, it is the twelfth largest in the world, with a GDP of US $775 billion (2005). India was the second fastest growing major economy in the world, with a GDP growth rate of 8.1% at the end of the first quarter of 2005–2006. This recent economic growth has been a catalyst for India's growth as a Great power and emerging superpower. However, India's huge population results in a relatively low per capita income of $3,100 at PPP.

The country's economy is diverse and encompasses agriculture, handicrafts, industries and a multitude of services. Services are the major source of economic growth in India today, though two-thirds of the Indian workforce earn their livelihood directly or indirectly through agriculture. In recent times, India has also capitalised on its large number of highly educated people who are fluent in the English language to become an important location for global companies outsourcing customer service and technical support call centers. It is also a major exporter of skilled workers in software services, financial services, and software engineering.

India adhered to a socialist-inspired approach for most of its independent history, with strict government control over private sector participation, foreign trade, and foreign direct investment. However, since the early 1990s, India has gradually opened up its markets through economic reforms by reducing government controls on foreign trade and investment. Privatisation of public-owned industries and opening up of certain sectors to private and foreign players has proceeded slowly amid political debate.

India faces are a burgeoning population and lack of infrastructure, as well as growing inequality and unemployment. Poverty also remains a problem although it has declined significantly since independence due the green revolution and economic reforms.

## Structure of the Economy

At independence the economy was predominantly agrarian. Most of the population was employed in agriculture, and most of those people were very poor, existing by cropping their own small plots or supplying labor to other farms. Landownership, land rental, and sharecropping rights were complex, involving layers of intermediaries. Moreover, the structural economic problems inherited at independence were exacerbated by the costs associated with the partition of British India, which had resulted in about 12 million to 14 million refugees fleeing past each other across the new borders between India and Pakistan. The settlement of refugees was a considerable financial strain. Partition also divided complementary economic zones. Under the British, jute and cotton were grown in the eastern part of Bengal, the area that became East Pakistan (after 1971, Bangladesh), but processing took place mostly in the western part of Bengal, which became the Indian state of West Bengal in 1947. As a result, after independence India had to employ land previously used for food production to cultivate cotton and jute for its mills.

India's leaders—especially the first prime minister, Jawaharlal Nehru, who introduced the five-year plans—agreed that strong economic growth and measures to increase incomes and consumption among the poorest groups were necessary goals for the new nation. Government was assigned an important role in this process, and since 1951 a series of plans have guided the country's economic development. Although there was considerable growth in the 1950s, the long-term rates of growth were less positive than India's politicians desired and less than those of many other Asian countries.

From FY 1951 to FY 1979, the economy grew at an average rate of about 3.1 percent a year in constant prices, or at an annual rate of 1.0 percent per capita. During this period, industry grew at an average rate of 4.5 percent a year, compared with an annual average of 3.0 percent for agriculture. Many factors contributed to the slowdown of the economy after the mid-1960s, but economists differ over the relative importance of those factors. Structural deficiencies, such as the need for institutional changes in agriculture and the inefficiency of much of the industrial sector, also contributed to economic stagnation. Wars with China in 1962 and with Pakistan in 1965 and 1971; a flood of refugees from East Pakistan in 1971; droughts in 1965, 1966, 1971, and 1972; currency devaluation in 1966; and the first world oil crisis, in 1973-74, all jolted the economy.

## Five-Year Plans

After independence, India opted to have a centrally planned economy to ensure an effective and equitable allocation of national resources for the purpose of balanced economic development. After liberalisation, the emergence of a market economy with a fast growing private sector, planning has become indicative, rather than prescriptive in nature. The process of formulation and direction of the Five-Year Plans is carried out by the Planning Commission, headed by the Prime Minister of India as its chairperson.

## Mixed Economy

India is a mixed economy combining features of both capitalist market economies and socialist command economies. Thus, there is a regulated private sector (the regulations have decreased since liberalisation) and a public sector controlled almost entirely by the government. The public sector generally covers areas which are deemed too important or not profitable enough to leave to the instability of capitalistic markets. Thus such services as railways and postal system are carried out by the government.

Since independence, various phases have seen nationalisation of such areas as banking, thus bringing them into the public sector, on one hand, and privatisation of some of the Public Sector Undertakings during the liberalisation period on the other.

## Public Expenditure

India's public expenditure is classified as development expenditure, comprising of central plan expenditure and central assistance and non-development expenditures, comprising of capital expenditure and revenue expenditure. Central plan expenditure is money spent on development schemes outlined in the plans of the central government and public sector undertakings, while central assistance refers to financial assistance and developmental loans given for plans of the state governments and union territories. Non-development capital expenditure comprises of capital defence expenditure, loans to public enterprises, states and union territories and foreign governments, while non-development revenue expenditure comprises revenue defence expenditure, administrative expenditure, subsidies, debt relief to farmers, postal deficit, pensions, social and economic services (education, health, agriculture, science and technology), grants to states and union territories and foreign governments.

India's non-development revenue expenditure have increased nearly five-fold in 2003-04 since 1990-91 and more than ten-fold since 1985-1986. Interest payments are the single largest item of expenditure and accounted for more than 40% of the total non development expenditure in the 2003-04 budget. Defence expenditure increased four-fold during the same period and has been increasing due to growing tensions in the region, the expensive dispute with Pakistan over Jammu and Kashmir and an effort to modernise the military. Administrative expenses are compounded by a large salary and pension bill, which rises periodically due to revisions in wages, dearness allowance etc. subsidies on food, fertilizers, education and petroleum and other merit and non-merit subsidies account are not only continuously rising, especially because of rising crude oil and food prices, but are also harder to rein in, because of political compulsions.

## Public Receipts

India has a three-tier tax structure, wherein the constitution empowers the union government to levy Income tax, tax on capital transactions (wealth tax, inheritance tax, gift tax), sales tax, service tax, customs and excise duties and the state governments to levy sales tax on intra-state sale of goods, tax on entertainment and professions, excise duties on manufacture of alcohol, stamp duties on transfer of property and collect land revenue (levy on land owned). The local governments are empowered by the state government to levy property tax, Octroi and charge users for public utilities like water supply, sewage etc. More than half of the revenues of the union and state governments come from taxes, of which half come from Indirect taxes. More than a quarter of the union government's tax revenues is shared with the state governments.

The tax reforms, initiated in 1991, have sought to rationalise the tax structure and increase compliance by taking steps in the following directions:

— Reducing the rates of individual and corporate income taxes, excises, customs and making it more progressive

— Reducing exemptions and concessions

— Simplification of laws and procedures

— Introduction of Permanent account number to track monetary transactions

— Despite protests from traders, 21 of the 29 states introduced · Value added tax (VAT) on April 1, 2005 to replace the complex and multiple sales tax system

The non-tax revenues of the central government come from fiscal services, interest receipts, public sector dividends, etc., while the non-tax revenues of the States are grants from the central government, interest receipts, dividends and income from general, economic and social services.

Inter-State share in the federal tax pool is decided by the recommendations of the Finance Commission to the President.

## General Budget

The Finance minister of India presents the annual union budget in the Parliament on the last working day of February. The budget has to be passed by the Lok Sabha before it can come into effect on April 1, the start of India's fiscal year. The Union budget is preceded by an economic survey which outlines the broad direction of the budget and the economic performance of the country for the outgoing financial year.

India's union budget for 2005-06, had an estimated outlay of Rs.5,14,344 crores ($118 billion). Earnings from taxes amount to Rs. 2,73,466 crore ($63b). India's fiscal deficit amounts to 4.5% or 1,39,231 crore ($32b).

## Currency System

The Rupee is the only legal tender accepted in India. It is also accepted as legal tender in the neighbouring Nepal and Bhutan, the latter's currency value being pegged to the rupee. The rupee is divided into 100 paise. The highest currency note printed is the 1000 rupee note, and the lowest denomination in circulation is the 10 p coin.

For higher numeric figures, India uses its own numbering system of counting in lakhs and crores. A lakh is equal to a hundred thousand, and a crore equal to ten million. The exchange rate as of April 21, 2006 is about 45.05 to a US dollar, 55.59 to a Euro, and 80.30 to a UK pound, making a crore (rupees crore) approximately equal to $222,000, €179,800, or £124,500.

## Exchange Rates

Under the fixed exchange rate system, the value of the rupee was linked to the British pound sterling till 1946 and after independence, 30% of India's foreign trade was determined in pound sterling. In 1975, as per the floating exchange rate system, the value of the rupee was pegged to a basket of currencies and was tightly controlled by the Reserve Bank of India. In recent years its value has depreciated with respect to most currencies with the exception of the U.S. dollar.

Since liberalisation, the rupee is fully convertible on trade and current account. The former has enabled Indian businessmen and workers to convert their earnings abroad into rupee at market rates, while the latter has removed all restrictions on foreign exchange for current business transactions as well as travel, education, medical expenses, etc., India has committed to gradually move towards full convertibility, albeit with some restrictions on capital accounts, in order to encourage two-way flow of capital and investment.

## Determinants of Economy

### *Demographics*

India, with a population of 1.027 billion people, is the second most populous country in the world, accounting for nearly 17% of the world's population. Growth rate of population has shown signs of decrease, coming down from a compound annual growth rate of 2.15 (1951–1981) to 1.93 (1991–2001); despite the decrease in the death rates owing to improvements in healthcare.

The large population puts further pressure on infrastructure, social services like education and has magnified socio-economic problems like unemployment, illiteracy, etc. A positive factor has been the large working age population, which forms 58.2% of the total population, which is expected to substantially increase, because of the decrease in dependency ratio. Increased literacy, better healthcare and self-sufficiency in food production since independence, have ensured that a large population has not caused any serious problems.

The national labour market has been tightly regulated by successive governments ever since the Workmen's Compensation Act was passed in 1923.

### *Geography and Natural Resources*

India's geography ranges from mountain ranges to deserts, plains, hills and plateaus, while its climate varies from tropical in the south to a more temperate climate in the north. India's total cultivable area is 1,269,219 km² (56.78% of total land area), which is decreasing due to constant pressure from an ever growing population and increased urbanisation.

India has a total water surface area of 314,400 km² and receives an average annual rainfall of 1,100 mm. Irrigation accounts for 92% of the water utilisation, and comprised 380 km$^2$ in 1974, and is expected to rise to 1,050 km$^2$ by 2025, with the balance accounted for by industrial and domestic consumers. India's inland water resources comprising rivers, canals, ponds and lakes and marine resources comprising the east and west coasts of the Indian ocean and other gulfs and bays provide employment to nearly 6 million people in the fisheries sector. India is the sixth largest producer of fish in the world and second largest in inland fish production.

India's major mineral resources include Coal (fourth-largest reserves in the world), Iron ore, Manganese, Mica, Bauxite, Titanium ore, Chromite, Natural gas, Diamonds, Petroleum, Limestone and Thorium (world's largest along Kerala's shores). India's oil reserves, found in Bombay High off the coast of Maharashtra, Gujarat, and in eastern Assam meet 25% of the country's demand.

### *Physical Infrastructure*

Since independence, India has allocated nearly half of the total outlay of the five-year plans for infrastructural development. Much of the total outlay was spent on large projects in the area of irrigation, energy, transport, communications and social overheads. Development of infrastructure was completely in the hands of the public sector and was plagued by corruption, inefficiencies, urban-bias and an inability to scale investment.

India's low spending on power, construction, transportation, telecommunications and real estate, at $31 billion or 6% of GDP, compared to China's spending of $260 billion or 20% of its GDP in 2002 has prevented India from sustaining a growth rate of around 8%. This has prompted the government to open up infrastructure to the private sector and allowing foreign investment.

### Politics

India, a federal republic, has had stable democratic governments since independence. Politics is dominated by the centre-left Indian National Congress (INC), the right-wing Bharatiya Janata Party (BJP), the left-wing Communist Party of India (CPI) and CPI (Marxist) and various regional parties, which are either centre-right or centre-left. Despite the varied political spectrums they occupy, the necessity of forming coalitions for government formation, the growing middle class that generally favours liberalisation and tightening fiscal deficits, especially at the state levels, has meant that all political parties adopt a moderate view towards economic reforms.

#### *Financial Institutions*

At the time of Independence, India inherited several institutions like the civil services, central bank, railways, etc., from her British rulers. Mumbai serves as the nation's commercial capital, with the Reserve Bank of India (RBI), Bombay Stock Exchange (BSE) and the National Stock Exchange (NSE) located here. The headquarters of many financial institutions are also located within the city.

The RBI, the country's central bank was established on 1935-04-01. It serves as the nation's monetary authority, regulator and supervisor of the financial system, manager of exchange control and as an issuer of currency. The RBI is governed by a central board, headed by a governor who is appointed by the Central government of India.

The BSE Sensex or the BSE Sensitive Index is a value-weighted index composed of 30 companies with April 1979 as the base year (100). These companies have the largest and most actively traded stocks and are representative of various sectors, on the Exchange. They account for around one-fifth of the market capitalisation of the BSE. The Sensex is generally regarded as the most popular and precise barometer of the Indian stock markets. Incorporated in 1992, the National Stock Exchange is one of the largest and most advanced stock markets in India. The NSE is the world's third largest stock exchange in terms of transactions. There are a total of 23 stock exchanges in India, but the BSE and NSE comprise 83% of the volumes. The Securities and Exchange Board of India (SEBI), established in 1992, regulates the stock markets and other securities markets of the country.

## Economic Sectors

### *Agriculture*

Given below is a chart of trend of output of cereals and major foodgrains as published by the Department of Food and Public Distribution with figures in tonnes.

India ranks second worldwide in farm output. Agriculture and allied sectors like forestry, logging and fishing accounted for 20% of the GDP in 2005, employed 60% of the total workforce and despite a steady decline of its share in the GDP, is still the largest economic sector and plays a significant role in the overall socio-economic development of India. Yields per unit area of all crops have grown since 1950, due to the special emphasis placed on agriculture in the five-year plans and steady improvements in irrigation, technology, application of modern agricultural practices and provision of agricultural credit and subsidies since the green revolution. However, international comparisons reveal that the average yield in India is generally 30% to 50% of the highest average yield in the world.

The low productivity in India is a result of the following factors:

— Illiteracy, general socio-economic backwardness, slow progress in implementing land reforms and inadequate or inefficient finance and marketing services for farm produce.

— The average size of land holdings is very small (less than 20,000 $m^2$) and are subject to fragmentation, due to land ceiling acts and in some cases, family disputes. Such small holdings are often over-manned, resulting in disguised unemployment and low productivity of labour.

— Adoption of modern agricultural practices and use of technology is inadequate, hampered by ignorance of such practices, high costs and impracticality in the case of small land holdings.

— Irrigation facilities are inadequate, as revealed by the fact that only 53.6% of the land was irrigated in 2000-01 , which result in farmers still being dependent on rainfall, specifically the Monsoon season. A good monsoon results in a robust growth for the economy as a whole, while a poor monsoon leads to a sluggish growth.

Farm credit is regulated by NABARD, which is the statutory apex agent for rural development in the subcontinent.

**Industry**

India ranks fourteenth worldwide in factory output. Concerted efforts at industrialisation by the government, aiming at self-sufficiency in production and protection from foreign competition, for nearly four decades since independence, have encouraged a diverse (though small) industrial base. They together account for 28.4% of the GDP and employ 17% of the total workforce. Economic reforms bought foreign competition, led to privatisation of certain public sector industries, opened up sectors hitherto reserved for the public sector and led to an expansion in the production of fast-moving consumer goods.

Post-liberalisation, the Indian private sector, which was usually run by oligopolies of old family firms and required political connections to prosper was faced with foreign competition, including the threat of cheaper Chinese imports. It has since handled the change by squeezing costs, revamping management, focusing on designing new products and relying on low labour costs and technology.

### *Services*

India ranks fifteenth worldwide in services' output. Still, this sector, providing employment to 23% of the work force, is the fastest growing sector, with a growth rate of 7.5% in 1991-2000 up from 4.5% in 1951-80. It has the largest share in the GDP, accounting for 51% in 2005 up from 15% in 1950. Business services (including information technology (IT) and information technology enabled services), communication services, financial services, hotels and restaurants, community services and trade (distribution) services are among the fastest growing sectors contributing to one third of the total output of services in 2000.

The growth in the service sector is attributed to increased specialisation, availability of a large population of highly educated and fluent English-speaking workers on the supply side and on the demand side, increased demand from domestic consumers resulting from growth in personal incomes and from foreign consumers interested in India's service exports or those looking to outsource their operations. India's IT industry, despite contributing significantly to its balance of payments, accounted for only about 1% of the total GDP or 1/50th of the total services. Low power and telecom density, particularly in the nrthern and eastern States have stunted the growth of services there.

### *Banking and Finance*

The Indian money market is classified into: the organised sector (comprising private, public and foreign owned commercial banks and cooperative banks, together known as scheduled banks); and the unorganised sector (comprising individual or family owned indigenous bankers or money lenders and non-banking financial companies (NBFCs)). The unorganised sector and microcredit are still preferred over traditional banks in rural and sub-urban areas, especially for non-productive purposes, like ceremonies and short duration loans.

Indira Gandhi nationalised 14 banks in 1969, followed by seven others in 1980 and made it mandatory for banks to provide 40% (since reduced to 10%) of their net credit to priority sectors like agriculture, small-scale industry, retail trade, small businesses, etc. to ensure that the banks fulfil their social and developmental goals. Since then, the number of bank branches have increased from 10,120 in 1969 to 98,910 in 2003 and the population covered by a branch decreased from 63,800 to 15,000 during the same period. The total deposits increased 32.6 times between 1971 to 1991 compared to 7 times between 1951 to 1971. Despite an increase of rural branches, from 1,860 or 22% of the total number of branches in 1969 to 32,270 or 48%, only 32,270 out of 5 lakh (500,000) villages are covered by a scheduled bank.

Since liberalisation, the government has approved significant banking reforms. While some of these relate to nationalised banks (like encouraging mergers, reducing government interference and increasing profitability and competitiveness), other reforms have opened up the banking and insurance sectors to private and foreign players.

## Socio-Economic Characteristics

### *Poverty*

The National sample survey organisation (NSSO) estimated that 26.1% of the population was living below the poverty line in 1999–2000, down from 51.3% in 1977–1978. The criterion used was monthly consumption of goods below

Rs. 211.30 for rural areas and Rs. 454.11 for urban areas. 75% of the poor are in rural areas (27.1% of the total rural population) with most of them comprising daily wagers, self-employed households and landless labourers. The major causes for poverty are unemployment or under-employment, low ownership of assets (especially productive assets like land and farm equipment) and illiteracy.

Since the early 1950s, successive governments have implemented various schemes, under planning, to alleviate poverty, that have met with partial success. All those programmes have improved upon the strategies of the Food for work programme and National Rural Employment Programme of the 1980s, which attempted to use the unemployed to generate productive assets and build rural infrastructure. In August 2005, the Indian parliament passed the Rural Employment Guarantee Bill, the largest programme of this type, in terms of cost and coverage, which promises 100 days of minimum wage employment to every rural household in 200 of India's 600-odd districts. The question of whether economic reforms have reduced poverty or not has fuelled debates without generating any clear cut answers and has also put political pressure on further economic reforms, especially those involving downsizing of labour and cutting down agricultural subsidies.

### *Corruption*

Corruption has been one of the pervasive problems affecting India. It takes the form of bribes, evasion of tax and exchange controls, embezzlement, etc. The economic reforms of 1991 reduced the red tape, bureaucracy and the Licence Raj that had strangled private enterprise and was blamed for the corruption and inefficiencies. Yet, a 2005 study by Transparency International (TI) India found that more than half of those surveyed had firsthand experience of paying bribe or peddling influence to get a job done in a public office.

The chief economic consequences of corruption are the loss to the exchequer, an unhealthy climate for investment and an increase in the cost of government-subsidised services. The TI India study estimates the monetary value of petty corruption in 11 basic services provided by the government, like education, healthcare, judiciary, police, etc., to be around Rs.21,068 crores. India still ranks in the bottom quartile of developing nations in terms of the ease of doing business, and compared to China, the average time taken to secure the clearances for a startup or to invoke bankruptcy is much greater.

The Right to Information Act (2005) and equivalent acts in the states, that require government officials to furnish information requested by citizens or face punitive action, computerisation of services and various central and state government acts that established vigilance commissions have considerably reduced corruption or at least have opened up avenues to redress grievances.

### *Occupations and Unemployment*

Agricultural and allied sectors accounted for about 57% of the total workforce in 1999-2000, down from 60% in 1993-94. While agriculture has faced stagnation in growth, services have seen a steady growth. Of the total workforce, 8% is in the organised sector, two-thirds of which are in the public sector. The NSSO survey estimated that in 1999-2000, 106 million, nearly 10% of the population were unemployed and the overall unemployment rate was 7.32%, with rural areas doing marginally better (7.21%) than urban areas (7.65%).

Unemployment in India is characterised by chronic underemployment or disguised unemployment. Government schemes that target eradication of both poverty and unemployment, attempt to solve the problem, by providing financial assistance for setting up businesses, skill honing, setting up public sector enterprises, reservations in governments, etc. The decreased role of the public sector after liberalisation has further underlined the need for focusing on better education and has also put political pressure on further reforms.

**External Trade and Investment**

Until the liberalisation of 1991, India was largely and intentionally isolated from the world markets in order to protect its fledging economy and achieve self-reliance. Foreign trade was subject to import tariffs, export taxes and quantitative restrictions, while foreign direct investment was restricted by upper limit equity participation, requirements on technology transfer, export obligations and government approvals, which were needed for nearly 60% of new FDI in the industrial sector. These restrictions ensured that FDI averaged only around $200 million annually between 1985-1991 and a large percentage of the capital flows consisted of foreign aid, commercial borrowing and deposits of non-resident Indians.

India's exports were stagnant for the first 15 years, due to the predominance of tea, jute and cotton manufactures, whose demand were generally inelastic. Imports in the same period consisted predominantly of machinery, equipment and raw materials due to the nascent industrialisation. Post-liberalisation, the value of India's international trade has become more broad based and gone up to Rs. 63,080,109 crores in 2003-04 from Rs.1,250 crores in 1950-51. India's major trading partners are China, United States, UAE, UK, Japan and the European Union.

India is a founder-member of General Agreement on Tariffs and Trade (GATT) since 1947 and its successor, the World Trade Organization since its inception. While participating actively in its general council meetings, India has been crucial in voicing the concerns of the developing world. For instance, India has continued its opposition to the inclusion of such matters as labour and environment issues and other non-tariff barriers into the WTO policies.

# 5

# GOVERNMENT AND POLITICS

Politics of India takes place in a framework of a federal parliamentary representative democratic republic, whereby the Prime Minister of India is the head of government, and of a pluriform multi-party system. Executive power is exercised by the government. Federal legislative power is vested in both the government and the two chambers of the Parliament of India. The Judiciary is independent of the executive and the legislature.

According to its constitution, India is a "sovereign socialist secular democratic republic." India is said to be the largest nation on Earth with a democratically-elected government. Like the United States, India has a federal form of government. However, the central government in India has greater power in relation to its states, and its central government is patterned after the British parliamentary system. Regarding the former, "the Centre", the national government, can and has dismissed state governments if no majority party or coalition is able to form a government or under specific Constitutional clauses, and can impose direct federal rule known as President's rule.

The structure of India's federal—or union—system not only creates a strong central government but also has facilitated the concentration of power in the central government in general and in particular in the Office of the Prime Minister. This centralization of power has been a source of considerable controversy and political tension. It is likely to further exacerbate political conflict because of the increasing pluralism of the country's party system and the growing diversity of interest-group representation.

Once viewed as a source of solutions for the country's economic and social problems, the Indian polity is increasingly seen by political observers as the problem. When populist political appeals stir the passions of the masses, government institutions appear less capable than ever before of accommodating conflicts in a society mobilized along competing ethnic and religious lines. In addition, law and order have become increasingly tenuous because of the growing inability of the police to curb criminal activities and quell communal disturbances. Indeed, many observers bemoan the "criminalization" of Indian politics at a time when politicians routinely hire "muscle power" to improve their electoral prospects, and criminals themselves successfully run for public office. These circumstances have led some observers to conclude that India has entered into a growing crisis of governability.

Few analysts would deny the gravity of India's problems, but some contend they have occurred amidst the maturation of civil society and the emergence of new, more democratic political practices. Backward Classes, the Dalits, and tribal peoples increasingly have refused to rest content with the patronage and populism characteristic of the "Congress system." Mobilization of these groups has provided a viable base for the political opposition and unraveled the fabric of the Congress. Since the late 1970s, there has been a proliferation of nongovernmental organizations. These groups made new demands on the political system that required a substantial redistribution of political power, economic resources, and social status.

Whether or not developments in Indian politics exacerbate the continuing problems or give birth to greater democracy broadly hinges on efforts to resolve three key issues. How will India's political system, now more than ever based on egalitarian democratic values, accommodate the changes taking place in its hierarchical social system? How will the state balance the need to recognize the interests of the country's remarkably heterogeneous society with the imperatives of national unity? And, in the face of the declining legitimacy of the Indian state and the continuing development of civil society, can the Indian state regenerate its legitimacy, and if it is to do so, how should it redefine the boundaries between state and society? India has confronted these issues throughout much of its history. These issues, with their intrinsic tensions, will continue to serve as sources of change in the continuing evolution of the Indian polity.

## The Constitution

The constitution of India draws extensively from Western legal traditions in its outline of the principles of liberal democracy. It is distinguished from many Western constitutions, however, in its elaboration of principles reflecting the aspirations to end the inequities of traditional social relations and enhance the social welfare of the population.

According to constitutional scholar Granville Austin, probably no other nation's constitution "has provided so much impetus toward changing and rebuilding society for the common good." Since its enactment, the constitution has fostered a steady concentration of power in the central government—especially the Office of the Prime Minister. This centralization has occurred in the face of the increasing assertiveness of an array of ethnic and caste groups across Indian society.

Increasingly, the government has responded to the resulting tensions by resorting to the formidable array of authoritarian powers provided by the constitution. Together with the public's perception of pervasive corruption among India's politicians, the state's centralization of authority and increasing resort to coercive power have eroded its legitimacy. However, a new assertiveness shown by the Supreme Court and the Election Commission suggests that the remaining checks and balances among the country's political institutions continue to support the resilience of Indian democracy.

Adopted after some two and one-half years of deliberation by the Constituent Assembly that also acted as India's first legislature, the constitution was put into effect on January 26, 1950. Bhimrao Ramji (B.R.) Ambedkar, a Dalit who earned a law degree from Columbia University, chaired the drafting committee of the constitution and shepherded it through Constituent Assembly debates. Supporters of independent India's founding father, Mohandas Karamchand (Mahatma) Gandhi, backed measures that would form a decentralized polity with strong local administration—known as *panchayat* (pl., *panchayats*)—in a system known as *panchayati raj* , that is rule by *panchayats*. However, the support of more modernist leaders, such as Jawaharlal Nehru, ultimately led to a parliamentary government and a federal system with a strong central government.

Following a British parliamentary pattern, the constitution embodies the Fundamental Rights, which are similar to the United States Bill of Rights, and a Supreme Court similar to that of the United States. It creates a "sovereign democratic republic" called India, or Bharat (after the legendary king of the *Mahabharata* ), which "shall be a Union of States." India is a federal system in which residual powers of legislation remain with the central government, similar to that in Canada. The constitution provides detailed lists dividing up powers between central and state governments as in Australia, and it elaborates a set of Directive Principles of State Policy as does the Irish constitution.

The 395 articles and ten appendixes, known as schedules, in the constitution make it one of the longest and most detailed in the world. Schedules can be added to the constitution by amendment. The ten schedules in force cover the designations of the states and union territories; the emoluments for high-level officials; forms of oaths; allocation of the number of seats in the Rajya Sabha (Council of States—the upper house of Parliament) per state or territory; provisions for the administration and control of Scheduled Areas and Scheduled Tribes; provisions for the administration of tribal areas in Assam; the union (meaning central government), state, and concurrent (dual) lists of responsibilities; the official languages; land and tenure reforms; and the association of Sikkim with India.

The Indian constitution is also one of the most frequently amended constitutions in the world. The first amendment came only a year after the adoption of the constitution and instituted numerous minor changes. Many more amendments followed, and through June 1995 the constitution had been amended seventy-seven times, a rate of almost two amendments per year since 1950. Most of the constitution can be amended after a quorum of more than half of the members of each house in Parliament passes an amendment with a two-thirds majority vote. Articles pertaining to the distribution of legislative authority between the central and state governments must also be approved by 50 percent of the state legislatures.

## Executive Branch

The government exercises its broad administrative powers in the name of the President, whose duties are largely ceremonial. The president and vice president are elected indirectly for 5-year terms by a special electoral college. The vice president assumes the office of president in case of the death or resignation of the incumbent president.

Real national executive power is centered in the Council of Ministers (cabinet), led by the Prime Minister of India. The President appoints the Prime Minister, who is designated by legislators of the political party or coalition commanding a parliamentary majority. The President then appoints subordinate ministers on the advice of the Prime Minister.

## Legislative Branch

India's bicameral parliament (also known as the Sansad) consists of the Rajya Sabha (Council of States) and the Lok Sabha (House of the People). The Council of Ministers is responsible to the Lok Sabha.

The legislatures of the states and union territories elect 238 members to the Rajya Sabha, and the president appoints another 12, who are experts in science or the arts. The elected members of the Rajya Sabha serve 6 year terms, with one-third up for election every 2 years. The Lok Sabha consists of 545 members; 543 are directly elected, while the other two are appointed by the President from among the Anglo-Indian community. The term of the Lok Sabha is five years.

India has 28 states and 7 union territories. States have their own elected governments, whereas Union Territories are governed by an administrator appointed by the union (federal) government. Some of the state legislatures are bicameral, patterned after the two houses of the national parliament. The states' chief ministers are responsible to the legislatures in the same way the prime minister is responsible to parliament.

Each state also has a presidentially appointed governor who may assume certain broad powers when directed by the central government. The central government exerts greater control over the union territories than over the states, although some territories have gained more power to administer their own affairs. Local governments in India have less autonomy than their counterparts in the United States. Some states are trying to revitalize the traditional village councils, or panchayat systems, which aim to promote popular democratic participation at the village level, where much of the population still lives.

## Judicial Branch

India's independent judicial system began under the British, and its concepts and procedures resemble those of Anglo-Saxon countries. The Supreme Court consists of a chief justice and 25 other justices, all appointed by the president on the advice of the Chief Justice of India. In the 1960s India moved away from using juries for most trials, finding them to be corrupt and ineffective, instead almost all trials are conducted by judges.

## Political Parties in India

Political parties in India lists political parties in India. India has a multi-party system with a predominance of small regional parties. National parties are those that are recognized in four or more states. They are accorded this status by the Election Commission of India, which periodically reviews the election results in various states. This recognition helps the political parties to claim unique ownership of certain identities, such as the party symbol, until the next review of their status. The Constitution of India stipulates that India be a federal polity with a central government in New Delhi, and state governments for the various states and Union territories. Consequently, political parties in India are classified as national and state (regional) parties based on their realms of influence.

### *National Parties*

The recognised national political parties in India is give n below:

— Bahujan Samaj Party (BSP)
— Bharatiya Janata Party (BJP)
— Communist Party of India
— Communist Party of India (Marxist) (CPI(M))
— Indian National Congress (INC)
— Nationalist Congress Party (NCP)

***State Parties***

Parties that have received certain amount of votes or seats in a state might be recognized as a state party by the Election Commission. Recognition as a state party given the party the possibilty to reserve a particular election symbol in the concerned state. A party might be recognized in more than one state. A party recognized in four states is automatically recognized as a national party. Below is the list of recognized state parties ahead of the Maharashtra & Arunachal Pradesh state assembly elections in October 2004. The states where the party has gained recognition is also stated, although the party may very well be active in more states and territories than that.

**Political History of India**

The decline of the Congress (I) since the late 1980s has brought an end to the dominant single-party system that had long characterized India's politics. Under the old system, conflict within the Congress was often a more important political dynamic than was conflict between the Congress and the opposition. The Congress had set the political agenda and the opposition responded. A new party system, in which the Congress (I) is merely one of several major participants, was in place by 1989. As often as not in the mid-1990s, the Congress (I) seems to respond to the initiatives of other parties rather than set its own political agenda.

At least once every five years, India's Election Commission supervises one of the largest, most complex exercises of collective action in the world. India's elections in the 1990s involve overseeing an electorate of about 521 million voters who travel to nearly 600,000 polling stations to chose from some 8,950 candidates representing roughly 162 parties. The elections reveal much about Indian society. Candidates span a wide spectrum of backgrounds, including former royalty, cinema superstars, religious holy men, war heroes, and a growing number of farmers. Campaigns utilize communications technologies ranging from the latest video van with two-way screens to the traditional rumor traveling by word of mouth. Increasing violence also has come to characterize elections. In 1991, some 350 people, including former Prime Minister Rajiv Gandhi, four other parliamentary candidates, and twenty-one candidates running in state legislative assembly elections, were killed in election-related violence.

India's party system is in the throes of historic change. The 1989 general elections brought the era of Congress dominance to an end. Even though the Congress (I) regained power in 1991, it was no longer the pivot around which the party system revolved. Instead, it represented just one strategy for organizing a political majority, and a declining one at that. While the Congress (I) was encountering growing difficulties in maintaining its coalition of upper-caste elites, Muslims, Scheduled Castes, and Scheduled Tribes, the BJP was endeavoring to organize a new majority around the appeal of Hindu nationalism. The Janata Dal and the BSP, among others, were attempting to fashion a new majority out of the increasingly assertive Backward Classes, Dalits, Scheduled Castes, Scheduled Tribes, and religious minorities.

### *The Congress Era*

The Congress has, by any standards, remarkable political accomplishments to its credit. As the Indian National

Congress, its guidance fashioned a nation out of an extraordinarily heterogeneous ensemble of peoples. The party has played an important role in establishing the foundations of perhaps the most durable democratic political system in the developing world. As scholars Francis Robinson and Paul R. Brass point out, the Congress constituted one of the few political organizations in the annals of decolonialization to "make the transition from being sole representative of the nationalist cause to being just one element of a competitive party system."

The Congress dominated Indian politics from independence until 1967. Prior to 1967, the Congress had never won less than 73 percent of the seats in Parliament. The party won every state government election except two—most often exclusively, but also through coalitions—and until 1967 it never won less than 60 percent of all elections for seats in the state legislative assemblies.

There were four factors that accounted for this dominance. First, the party acquired a tremendous amount of good will and political capital from its leadership of the nationalist struggle. Party chiefs gained substantial popular respect for the years in jail and other deprivations that they personally endured. The shared experience of the independence struggle fostered a sense of cohesion, which was important in maintaining unity in the face of the party's internal pluralism.

The second factor was that the Congress was the only party with an organization extending across the nation and down to the village level. The party's federal structure was based on a system of internal democracy that functioned to resolve disputes among its members and maintain party cohesion. Internal party elections also served to legitimate the party leadership, train party workers in the skills of political competition, and create channels of upward mobility that rewarded its most capable members.

A third factor was that the Congress achieved its position of political dominance by creating an organization that adjusted to local circumstances rather than transformed them, often reaching the village through local "big men" (*bare admi* ) who controlled village "vote banks." These local elites, who owed their position to their traditional social status and their control over land, formed factions that competed for power within the Congress. The internal party democracy and the Congress's subsequent electoral success ultimately reinforced the local power of these traditional elites and enabled the party to adjust to changes in local balances of power. The nonideological pragmatism of local party leadership made it possible to coopt issues that contributed to opposition party success and even incorporate successful opposition leaders into the party. Intraparty competition served to channel information about local circumstances up the party hierarchy.

Fourth, patronage was the oil that lubricated the party machine. As the state expanded its development role, it accumulated more resources that could be distributed to party members. The growing pool of opportunities and resources facilitated the party's ability to accommodate conflict among its members. The Congress enjoyed the benefits of a "virtuous cycle," in which its electoral success gave it access to economic and political resources that enabled the party to attract new supporters.

The halcyon days of what Indian political scientist Rajni Kothari has called "the Congress system" ended with the general elections in 1967. The party lost seventy-eight seats in the Lok Sabha, retaining a majority of only twenty-three seats. Even more indicative of the Congress setback was its loss of control over six of the sixteen state legislatures that held elections. The proximate causes of the reversal included the failure of the monsoons in 1965 and 1966 and the subsequent hardship throughout northern and eastern India, and the unpopular currency devaluation in

1966. However, profound changes in India's polity also contributed to the decline of the Congress.

The rapid growth of the electorate, which increased by 45 percent from 1952 to 1967, brought an influx of new voters less appreciative of the Congress's role in the independence movement. Moreover, the simultaneous spread of democratic values produced a political awakening that mobilized new groups and created a more pluralistic constellation of political interests. The development of new and more-differentiated identities and patterns of political cleavage made it virtually impossible for the Congress to contain the competition of its members within its organization. Dissidence and ultimately defection greatly weakened the Congress's electoral performance.

It was in this context that Indira Gandhi asserted her independence from the leaders of the party organization by attempting to take the party in a more populist direction. She ordered the nationalization of India's fourteen largest banks in 1969, and then she supported former labor leader and Acting President Varahagiri Venkata Giri's candidacy for president despite the fact that the party organization had already nominated the more conservative Neelam Sanjiva Reddy. After Giri's election, the party organization expelled Indira Gandhi from the Congress and ordered the parliamentary party to choose a new prime minister. Instead, 226 of the 291 Congress members of Parliament continued to support Indira Gandhi. The Congress split into two in 1969, the new factions being the Congress (O)—for Organisation—and Mrs. Gandhi's Congress (R)—for Requisition. The Congress (R) continued in power with the support of non-Congress groups, principally the Communist Party of India (CPI) and the Dravida Munnetra Kazhagam (DMK—Dravidian Progressive Federation).

With the Congress (O) controlling most of the party organization, Indira Gandhi adopted a new strategy to mobilize popular support. For the first time ever, she ordered parliamentary elections to be held separately from elections for the state government. This delinking was designed to reduce the power of the Congress (O)'s state-level political machines in national elections. Mrs. Gandhi traveled throughout the country, energetically campaigning on the slogan *"garibi hatao "* (eliminate poverty), thereby bypassing the traditional Congress networks of political support. The strategy proved successful, and the Congress (R) won a dramatic victory. In the 1971 elections for the Lok Sabha, the Congress (R) garnered 44 percent of the vote, earning it 352 seats. The Congress (O) won only sixteen seats and 10 percent of the vote. The next year, after leading India to victory over Pakistan in the war for Bangladesh's independence, Indira Gandhi and the Congress (R) further consolidated their control over the country by winning fourteen of sixteen state assembly elections and victories in 70 percent of all seats contested.

The public expected Indira Gandhi to deliver on her mandate to remove poverty. However, the country experienced a severe drought in 1971 and 1972, leading to food shortages, and the price of food rose 20 percent in the spring of 1973. The decision by the Organization of the Petroleum Exporting Countries (OPEC) to quadruple oil prices in 1973-74 also led to inflation and increased unemployment. Jayaprakash (J.P) Narayan, a socialist leader in the preindependence Indian National Congress who, after 1947, left to conduct social work in the Sarvodaya movement (*sarvodaya* means uplift of all), came out of retirement to lead what eventually became widely known as the "J.P. movement." Under Narayan's leadership, the movement toppled the government of Gujarat and almost brought down the government in Bihar; Narayan advocated a radical regeneration of public morality that he labelled "total revolution."

After the Allahabad High Court ruled that Mrs. Gandhi had committed electoral law violations and

Narayan addressed a massive demonstration in New Delhi, at Indira Gandhi's behest, the president proclaimed an Emergency on June 25, 1975. That night, Indira Gandhi ordered the arrest of almost all the leaders of the opposition, including dissidents within the Congress. In all, more than 110,000 persons were detained without trial during the Emergency.

Indira Gandhi's rule during the Emergency alienated her popular support. After postponing elections for a year following the expiration of the five-year term of the Lok Sabha, she called for new elections in March 1977. The major opposition party leaders, many of whom had developed a rapport while they were imprisoned together under the Emergency regime, united under the banner of the Janata Party. By framing the key issue of the election as "democracy versus dictatorship," the Janata Party—the largest opposition party—appealed to the public's democratic values to rout the Congress (R). The vote share of the Congress (R) dropped to 34.5 percent, and the number of its seats in Parliament plunged from 352 to 154. Indira Gandhi lost her seat.

The inability of Janata Party factions to agree proved the party's undoing. Indira Gandhi returned to win the January 1980 elections after forming a new party, the Congress (I—for Indira), in 1978.

The Congress (I) largely succeeded in reconstructing the traditional Congress electoral support base of Brahmans, Muslims, Scheduled Castes, and Scheduled Tribes that had kept Congress in power in New Delhi during the three decades prior to 1977. The Congress (I)'s share of the vote increased by 8.2 percent to 42.7 percent of the total vote, and its number of seats in the Lok Sabha grew to 353, a majority of about two-thirds. This success approximated the levels of support of the Congress dominance from 1947 to 1967. Yet, as political scientist Myron Weiner observed, "The Congress party that won in 1980 was not the Congress party that had governed India in the 1950s and 1960s, or even the early 1970s. The party was organizationally weak and the electoral victory was primarily Mrs. Gandhi's rather than the party's." As a consequence, the Congress's appeal to its supporters was much more tenuous than it had been in previous decades.

Indira Gandhi's dependence on her flamboyant son Sanjay and, after his accidental death in 1980, on her more reserved son Rajiv gives testimony to the personalization and centralization of power within the Congress (I). Having developed a means to mobilize support without a party organization, she paid little attention to maintaining that support. Rather than allowing intraparty elections to resolve conflicts and select party leaders, Indira Gandhi preferred to fill party posts herself with those loyal to her. As a result, party leaders at the state level lost their legitimacy among the rank and file because their positions depended on the whims of Indira Gandhi rather than on the extent of their popular support. In addition, centralization and the demise of democracy within the party disrupted the flow of information about local circumstances to party leaders and curtailed the ability of the Congress (I) to adjust to social change and incorporate new leaders.

When Rajiv Gandhi took control after his mother's assassination in November 1984, he attempted to breathe new life into the Congress (I) organization. However, the massive electoral victory that the Congress (I) scored under Rajiv's leadership just two months after his mother's assassination gave him neither the skill nor the authority to succeed in this endeavor. Rajiv did, however, attempt to remove the more unsavory elements within the party organization. He denied nominations to one-third of the incumbent members of Parliament during the 1984 Lok Sabha campaign, and he refused to nominate two of every five incumbents in the state legislative assembly elections held in March 1985.

Another of Rajiv's early successes was the passage of the Anti-Defection Bill in January 1985 in an effort to end the bribery that lured legislators to cross partisan lines. Speaking at the Indian National Congress centenary celebrations in Bombay (officially called Mumbai as of 1995), Rajiv launched a vitriolic attack on the "culture of corruption" that had become so pervasive in the Congress (I). However, the old guard showed little enthusiasm for reform. As time passed, Rajiv's position was weakened by the losses that the party suffered in a series of state assembly elections and by his government's involvement in corruption scandals. Ultimately, Rajiv was unable to overcome the resistance within the party to internal elections and reforms. Ironically, as Rajiv's position within the party weakened, he turned for advice to many of the wheelers and dealers of his mother's regime whom he had previously banished.

The frustration of Rajiv Gandhi's promising early initiatives meant that the Congress (I) had no issues on which to campaign as the end of his five-year term approached. On May 15, 1989, just months before its term was to expire, the Congress (I) introduced amendments that proposed to decentralize government authority to *panchayat* and municipal government institutions. Opposition parties, many of whom were on record as favoring decentralization of government power, vehemently resisted the Congress (I) initiative. They charged that the initiative did not truly decentralize power but instead enabled the central government to circumvent state governments (many of which were controlled by the opposition) by transferring authority from state to local government and strengthening the links between central and local governments. After the Congress (I) failed to win the two-thirds vote required to pass the legislation in the Rajya Sabha on October 13, 1989, it called for new parliamentary elections and made *"jana shakti"* (power to the people) its main campaign slogan.

The Congress (I) retained formidable campaign advantages over the opposition. The October 17, 1989, announcement of elections took the opposition parties by surprise and gave them little time to form electoral alliances. The Congress (I) also blatantly used the government-controlled television and radio to promote Rajiv Gandhi. In addition, the Congress (I) campaign once again enjoyed vastly superior financing. It distributed some 100,000 posters and 15,000 banners to each of its 510 candidates. It provided every candidate with six or seven vehicles, and it commissioned advertising agencies to make a total of ten video films to promote its campaign.

The results of the 1989 elections were more of a rebuff to the Congress (I) than a mandate for the opposition. Although the Congress (I) remained the largest party in Parliament with 197 seats, it was unable to form a government. Instead, the Ja-nata Dal, which had 143 seats, united with its National Front allies to form a minority government precariously dependent on the support of the BJP (eighty-five seats) and the communist parties (forty-five seats). Although the Congress (I) lost more than 50 percent of its seats in Parliament, its share of the vote dropped only from 48.1 percent to 39.5 percent of the vote. The Congress (I) share of the vote was still more than double that of the next largest party, the Janata Dal, which received support from 17.8 percent of the electorate. More grave for the long-term future of the Congress (I) was the erosion of vital elements of the traditional coalition of support for the Congress (I) in North India. Alienated by the Congress (I)'s cultivation of Hindu activists, Muslims defected to the Janata Dal in large numbers. The Congress (I) simultaneously lost a substantial share of Scheduled Caste voters to the BSP in Haryana, Madhya Pradesh, and Uttar Pradesh and to the Indian People's Front in Bihar.

To offset these losses, the Congress (I) attempted to play a "Hindu card." On August 14, 1989, the Supreme Court ruled that no parties or groups could disturb the status quo of the Babri Masjid, a sixteenth-century mosque in Ayodhya, Uttar Pradesh. The mosque was controversial because Hindu nationalists claim it was on the site of the birthplace of the Hindu god Ram and that, as such, the use by Muslims was sacrilegious.

Despite the court ruling, in September the Congress (I) entered into an agreement with the Vishwa Hindu Parishad (VHP—World Hindu Council), a conservative religious organization with close ties to Hindu nationalists, to allow the VHP to proceed with a ceremony to lay the foundation for the Ramjanmabhumi (birthplace of Ram) Temple. (The VHP had been working toward this goal since 1984.) In return, the Congress (I) secured the VHP's agreement to perform the ceremony on property adjacent to the Babri Masjid that was not in dispute. By reaching this agreement, the Congress (I) attempted to appeal to Hindu activists while retaining Muslim support. Rajiv Gandhi's decision to kick off his campaign less than six kilometers from the Babri Masjid and his appeal to voters that they vote for the Congress (I) if they wished to bring about "Ram Rajya" (the rule of Ram) were other elements of the Congress (I)'s strategy to attract the Hindu vote.

The 1991 elections returned the Congress (I) to power but did not reverse important trends in the party's decline. The Congress (I) won 227 seats, up from 197 in 1989, but its share of the vote dropped from 39.5 percent in 1989 to 37.6 percent. Greater division within the opposition rather than growing popularity of the Congress (I) was the key element in the party's securing an increased number of seats. Also troubling was the further decline of the Congress (I) in heavily populated Bihar and Uttar Pradesh, which together account for more than 25 percent of all seats in Parliament. In Uttar Pradesh, the number of seats that the Congress (I) was able to win went down from fifteen to two, and its share of the vote dropped from 32 percent to 20 percent. In Bihar the seats won by the Congress (I) fell from four to one, and the Congress (I) share of the vote was reduced from 28 percent to 22 percent. The Congress (I) problems in these states, which until 1989 had been bastions of its strength, were reinforced by the party's poor showing in the November 1993 state elections. These elections were characterized by the further disintegration of the traditional Congress coalition, with Brahmans and other upper castes defecting to the BJP and Scheduled Castes and Muslims defecting to the Janata Dal, the Samajwadi Party (Socialist Party), and the BSP.

Strong evidence indicates that the Congress (I) would have fared significantly worse had it not been for the assassination of Rajiv Gandhi in the middle of the elections. A wave of sympathy similar to that which helped elect Rajiv after the assassination of his mother increased the Congress (I) support. In the round of voting that took place before Rajiv's death, the Congress (I) won only 26 percent of the seats and 33 percent of the vote. In the votes that occurred after Rajiv's death, the Congress (I) won 58 percent of the seats and 40 percent of the popular vote. It may also be that Rajiv's demise ended the "anti-Congressism" that had pervaded the political system as a result of his family's dynastic domination of Indian politics through its control over the Congress.

Rajiv Gandhi was assassinated by a Tamil suicide bomber affiliated with the Sri Lankan Liberation Tigers of Tamil Eelam (LTTE) during a political campaign in May 1991. Only after his assassination did hope for reforming the Congress (I) reappear. The end of three generations of Nehru-Gandhi family leadership left Rajiv's coterie of political manipulators in search of a new kingpin. The bankruptcy of the Congress (I) leadership was highlighted by the fact that they initially turned to Sonia Gandhi, Rajiv's Italian-born wife, to lead the party. Sonia's primary qualification was that she was Rajiv's widow. She had never held elected office and, during her early years in India, she had expressed great disdain for political life. However, although she did not assume a leadership role, she continued to be seen as a "kingmaker" in the Congress (I). Her advice was sought after, and she was called on to lead the party in the mid-1990s. An unusual public speech by Sonia Gandhi criticizing the government of P.V. Narasimha Rao in August 1995 further fueled speculation that she was a candidate for political leadership.

Sonia Gandhi's refusal in 1991 to become president of the Congress (I) led the mantle of party leadership to fall on Rao. Rao was a septuagenarian former professor who had retired from politics before the 1991 elections after undergoing heart-bypass surgery. Rao had a conciliatory demeanor and was acceptable to the party's contending factions. Paradoxically, the precariously positioned Rao was able to take more substantial steps in the direction of party reform than his predecessors. First, Rao had to demonstrate that he could mobilize popular support for himself and the party, a vital currency of power for any Congress (I) leader. He did so in the November 15, 1991, by-elections by winning his own seat in Andhra Pradesh unopposed and leading the party to victory in a total of eight of the fifteen parliamentary by-elections. By the end of 1991, Rao had succeeded in initiating the first intraparty elections in the Congress in almost twenty years. Although there was widespread manipulation by local party bosses, the elections enhanced the legitimacy of party leaders and held forth the prospect of a rejuvenated party organization. The process culminated in April 1992 at the All-India Congress (I) Committee at Tirupati, Andhra Pradesh, where elections were held for the ten vacant seats in the Congress Working Committee.

In the wake of the Tirupati session, Rao became less interested in promoting party democracy and more concerned with consolidating his own position. The change was especially apparent in the 1993 All-India Congress (I) Committee session at Surajkund (in Haryana), where Rao's supporters lavishly praised the prime minister and coercively silenced his opponents. However, Rao's image was damaged in July 1993 after Harshad Mehta, a stockbroker under indictment for allegedly playing a leading role in a US$2 billion stock scam in 1992, accused Rao of personally accepting a bribe that he had delivered on November 4, 1991. The extent of the press coverage of the charges and their apparent credibility among the public was evidence of the pervasive public cynicism toward politicians. Rao's stock in the party and Congress (I)'s position within Parliament were greatly weakened. On July 28, 1993, his government barely survived a no-confidence motion in the Lok Sabha.

Rao's position was temporarily strengthened at the end of 1993 when he was able to cobble together a parliamentary majority. However, support for Rao and the Congress (I) declined again in 1994. The party was rocked by a scandal relating to the procurement of sugar stocks that cost the government an estimated Rs 6.5 billion and by losses in legislative assembly elections in Andhra Pradesh—Rao's home state, where he personally took control over the campaign—and Karnataka. The Congress (I) again lost in three of four major states in elections held in the spring of 1995. The political fallout in New Delhi was an increase in dissident activity within the Congress (I) led by former cabinet members Narain Dutt Tiwari and Arjun Singh and other Rao rivals who sought to split the Congress and form a new party.

The 1990s was a period of prolonged crisis for the Congress. After gradually losing political influence the party asked the widow of Rajiv Gandhi, the Italian-born Sonia Gandhi, to accept the position as Congress President. Refusing in 1991, the Congress stuck with Narasimha Rao and after him, Sitaram Kesri. Although Rao was Prime Minister of a coalition Congress administration from 1991-1996, Kesri led the Congress to a historic low in the 1998 elections. It appeared that the Congress was politically impotent, with no real future. In 1998, Sonia Gandhi is considered by some to have finally saved the Congress from extinction by accepting the presidency of the party.

After the election of Sonia Gandhi as party leader, a section broke away and formed Nationalist Congress Party. Where breakaway factions are active, the use of "Congress (I)" to denote the party run by Indira Gandhi's successors continues. There have been repeated attempts by the Indian nationalist groups (such as the BJP) to discredit Sonia Gandhi's leadership on the basis of her foreign origin. Nonetheless she has emerged as one of the most popular political leaders of India, suggesting that the legacy of the Nehru-Gandhi dynasty is still considered to be a mark of legitimacy for broad sections of the Indian population.

In the 2004 general elections, the Congress alliance won the largest number of seats and got an assurance of support from the Left Front upsetting the Atal Behari Vajpayee-led National Democratic Alliance, which according to all forecasts was going to coast to victory. Shortly thereafter, Sonia Gandhi was nominated by the Congress-led 19-party alliance to be the next Prime Minister. But in what was described as the dropping of a political bombshell, Sonia Gandhi refused to take the position based on her "inner voice". She backed eminent economist, former Union Finance Minister and senior Congress leader Dr. Manmohan Singh for the post of Prime Minister, and he was sworn-in as Prime Minister on 22 May 2004.

### *Opposition Parties*

Opposition to the Congress has always been fragmented. Opposition parties range from Hindu nationalist parties such as the BJP on the right to communist parties on the left. The divisiveness of the opposition, combined with the "first-past-the-post" electoral system, has enabled the

Congress to dominate Indian politics without ever winning a majority of the vote from the national electorate. The extent of electoral alliances among the opposition is an important predictor of its ability to win seats in Parliament. The first two instances when the opposition succeeded in forming a government at the center occurred after it united under the Janata Party banner in 1977 and after the formation of the Janata Dal and the National Front in 1988. In each of these cases, the unity that was facilitated by anti-Congress sentiment prior to the elections collapsed in the face of rivalry and ambition once the opposition came into power.

***Rise and Decline of Janata Politics***

Prior to 1967, the opposition was divided into an array of small parties. While the Congress garnered between 45 percent and 48 percent of the vote, no opposition party gained as much as 11 percent, and during the entire period, only two parties won 10 percent. Furthermore, in each election, independent candidates won between 12 percent and 20 percent of the vote.

The opposition's first significant attempt to achieve electoral unity occurred during the 1967 elections when opposition party alliances won control of their state governments in Bihar, Kerala, Orissa, Punjab, and West Bengal. In Rajasthan an opposition coalition prevented the Congress from winning a majority in the state legislature and forced it to recruit independents to form a government. The Congress electoral debacle encouraged even more dissidence within the party, and in a matter of weeks after the elections, defections brought down Congress governments in Haryana, Madhya Pradesh, and Uttar Pradesh. By July 1967, state governments of two-thirds of the country were under opposition rule. However, opposition rule in many cases was short-lived. The aftermath of the 1967 elections initiated a climate of politics by defection in which the Congress, and to a lesser extent the opposition, attempted to overthrow governments by winning over their state legislators with promises of greater political power and outright bribes. Needless to say, this period seriously undermined the ability of most parties to discipline their members. The increase in opposition-ruled state governments after 1967 also prompted the Congress to use President's Rule to dismiss opposition-led state governments with increasing frequency.

Although the centrist and right-wing opposition formed a "grand alliance" during the 1971 parliamentary elections, it was not until the general elections of 1977 that opposition efforts culminated in electoral success at the national level. Imprisoned together under the authoritarian measures of the Emergency, India's senior opposition leaders found their personal animosity toward Indira Gandhi and the Congress to be a powerful motivation to overcome their division and rivalry. In January 1977, opposition parties reactivated a pre-Emergency multiparty front, campaigned under the banner of the Janata Party, and won a dramatic electoral victory in March 1977. The Janata Party was made up of the Congress (O), the Jana Sangh, the Bharatiya Lok Dal (Indian People Party), the Samajwadi Party (Socialist Party), a handful of imprisoned Congress dissidents, and the Congress for Democracy—a group led by Scheduled Caste leader Jagjivan Ram that had splintered off from the Congress during the election campaign.

Despite the diversity of this assemblage of parties and the different social strata that they represented, members of the Ja-nata Party achieved surprising ideological and programmatic consensus by passing a program stressing decentralization, development of rural industries, and employment opportunities. It was not ideology, but rather an inability to consolidate partisan organizations and political rivalry among the leadership that led to the demise of the Janata government in 1979. The Janata's three most senior leaders—Morarji Desai, Charan Singh, and Jagjivan Ram—each aspired to be prime minister. The rivalry continued during Desai's tenure (March 1977-July 1979). Desai, Charan Singh, and Ram continually conspired to discredit each other. Their connivances ultimately discredited the Janata Party and allowed the Congress (I) to return to power in 1980.

Just as key defections from the Congress were essential to the Janata electoral success in 1977, so too did V.P. Singh's defection from the Congress (I) in 1987 enable opposition factions from the Janata Party and Bharatiya Lok Dal to unite the Janata Dal in 1988. Regional parties, such as the Telugu Desam Party (Telugu National Party), the DMK, and the Asom Gana Pa-rishad (AGP—Assam People's Assembly), together formed the National Front, led by Janata Dal, which defeated Rajiv Gandhi's Congress (I) in the 1989 parliamentary elections. With V.P. Singh as prime minister, the National Front government earned the appellation of "the crutch government" because it depended on the support of the Communist Party of India (Marxist—CPI (M)) on its left and the BJP on the right.

On August 7, 1990, V.P. Singh suddenly announced that his government would implement the recommendations of the Mandal Commission to reserve 27 percent of central government jobs for the Backward Classes, defined to include around 52 percent of the population. Although Singh's Janata Dal had pledged to implement the Mandal Commission recommendations as part of its election manifesto, his announcement led to riots throughout North India. Some seventy-five upper-caste youths died after resorting to self-immolation to dramatize their opposition, and almost 200 others were killed in clashes with the police.

BJP president Lal Kishan (L.K.) Advani announced that he would traverse the country on a pilgrimage to Ayodhya where he would lead Hindu activists in the construction of the Ramjanmabhumi Temple on the site of the Babri Masjid. As the pilgrimage progressed, riots between Hindus and Muslims broke out throughout the country. The National Front government decided to end the agitation, and Janata Dal chief minister of Bihar, Laloo Prasad Yadav, arrested Advani on October 23, 1990. On October 30, religious militants attempted to storm the Babri Masjid despite a massive military presence, and as many as twenty-six activists were killed. The BJP's withdrawal of support for the National Front government proved fatal, and V.P. Singh lost a parliamentary vote of confidence on November 7, 1990.

Two days before the vote, Chandra Shekhar, an ambitious Janata Dal rival who had been kept out of the National Front government, joined with Devi Lal, a former deputy prime minister under V.P. Singh, to form the Samajwadi Janata Party—Samajwadi meaning socialist—with a total of sixty Lok Sabha members. The day after the collapse of the National Front government, Chandra Shekhar informed the president that by gaining the backing of the Congress (I) and its electoral allies he enjoyed the support of 280 members of the Lok Sabha, and he demanded the right to constitute a new government. Even though his rump party accounted for only one-ninth of the members of the Lok Sabha, Chandra Shekhar succeeded in forming a new minority government and becoming prime minister (with Devi Lal as deputy prime minister). However, Chandra Shekhar's government fell less than four months later, after the Congress (I) withdrew its support.

The Janata Dal and the Samajwadi Janata Party declined after the fall of the Chandra Shekhar government. In the May-June 1991 parliamentary elections, their share of the vote dropped from 17.8 percent to 15.1 percent, and the number of seats in Parliament that they won fell from 142 to sixty-one. The parties were able to win seats only in Bihar, Orissa, and Uttar Pradesh. The factional rivalry and ineffectiveness that impeded the National Front government's efforts to provide effective government tarnished the Janata Dal image.

In the absence of strong national leadership, the party was rendered a confederation of ambitious regional leaders whose rivalry prevented the establishment of a united party organization. The Janata Dal's persistent backing of the Mandal Commission recommendations made the party highly unpopular among high-caste people in the middle and upper classes, creating fund-raising difficulties. Although the Janata Dal won state elections in Karnataka in 1994 and Bihar in the spring of 1995, its poor showing in most other states gave the impression that its support was receding to a few regional bastions.

### *Bharatiya Janata Party and the Rise of Hindu Nationalism*

The BJP is unique among India's political parties in that neither it nor its political predecessors were ever associated with the Congress. Instead, it grew out of an alternative nationalist organization—the Rashtriya Swayamsevak Sangh (RSS—National Volunteer Organisation). The BJP still is affiliated with the network of organizations popularly referred to as the RSS family. The RSS was founded in 1925 by Keshav Baliram Hedgewar. Until 1928 a member of the Congress with radical nationalist political leanings, Hedgewar had grown increasingly disenchanted with the leadership of Mahatma Gandhi. Hedgewar was particularly critical of Gandhi's emphasis on nonviolence and civil disobedience, which he felt discouraged the forceful political action necessary to gain independence. He established the RSS as an organization that would provide training in martial arts and spiritual matters to rejuvenate the spiritual life of the Hindu community and build its unity.

Hedgewar and his successor, M.S. Golwalkar, scrupulously endeavored to define the RSS's identity as a cultural organization that was not directly involved in politics. However, its rapidly growing membership and the paramilitary-like uniforms and discipline of its activists made the political potential of the RSS apparent to everyone on the political scene. There was considerable sentiment within the Congress that RSS members should be permitted to join, and, in fact, on October 7, 1947, the Congress Working Committee voted to allow in RSS members. But in November 1947, the Congress passed a rule requiring RSS members to give up their affiliation before joining. The RSS was banned in 1948 after Nathuram Godse, a former RSS member, assassinated Mahatma Gandhi. The ban was lifted in 1949 only after the RSS drafted an organizational constitution that was acceptable to the government. Intensely loyal RSS members refused to give up their affiliation to join the Congress and, instead, channeled their political energies to the Jana Sangh (People's Union) after its founding in 1951.

The Jana Sangh grew slowly during the 1950s and 1960s, despite the efforts of RSS members, who quickly took control of the party's organization. Although the Jana Sangh succeeded in displacing the Hindu Mahasabha (a communal party established in 1914 as a counter to Muslim separatists) as the preeminent party of Hindu activists in the Indian political system, it failed to develop into a major rival to the Congress. According to political scientist Bruce Graham, this failure occurred because of the Jana Sangh's inability "to transcend the limitations of its origins," in particular, its identification with the Hindi-speaking, northern heartland and its Brahmanical interpretation of Hinduism rather than the more inclusive and syncretic values of popular Hinduism. However, the experience of the Jana Sangh during the 1970s, especially its increasing resort to populism and agitational tactics, provided essential ingredients for the success of the BJP in the 1980s.

In 1977 the Jana Sangh joined the Janata Party, which defeated Indira Gandhi and the Congress (I) in parliamentary elections and formed a government through the end of 1979. The rapid expansion of the RSS under Janata rule soon brought calls for all members of the RSS family to merge with Janata Party affiliates. Ultimately, intraparty tensions impelled those affiliated with the Jana Sangh to leave the Janata Party and establish a new party—the BJP.

The BJP was formed in April 1980, under the leadership of Atal Behari Vajpayee. Although the party welcomed members of the RSS, the BJP's effort to draw from the legacies of the Ja-nata Party as well as that of the Jana Sangh were suggested by its new name, its choice of a green and saffron flag similar to that of the Janata Party rather than the solid saffron flag of the old Jana Sangh, its adoption of a decentralized organizational structure along the lines of the Janata Party rather than the more centralized model of the Jana Sangh, and its inclusion in its working committee of several non-Jana Sangh individuals, including Sikandar Bakht—a Muslim. The invocation of Gandhian socialism as one of the guiding principles of the BJP rather than the doctrine of "integral humanism" associated with the Jana Sangh was another indication of the impact of the party members' experience in the Janata Party and "J.P. movement."

The new synthesis, however, failed to achieve political success. In 1984 the BJP won only two seats in the parliamentary elections. In the wake of the 1984 elections, the BJP shifted course. Advani replaced Vajpayee as party president. Under Advani's leadership, the BJP appealed to Hindu activists by criticizing measures it construed as pandering to minorities and advocating the repeal of the special status given to the Muslim majority state of Jammu and Kashmir. Simultaneously, it cooperated more closely with other RSS affiliates, particularly the VHP. During the 1980s, the BJP-VHP combine developed into a dynamic political force through its brilliant use of religious symbolism to rouse the passions of the public. The BJP and VHP attained national prominence through their campaign to convert back to Hinduism members of the Scheduled Castes who had converted to Islam. The VHP also agitated to reclaim the Babri Masjid site and encouraged villagers throughout the country to hold religious ceremonies to consecrate bricks made out of their own clay and send them to be used in the construction of the Ramjanmabhumi Temple in Ayodhya.

In the general elections of 1991, the BJP expanded its support more than did any other party. Its number of seats in the Lok Sabha increased from eighty-five to 119, and its vote share grew from 11.4 percent to 21.0 percent. The party was particularly successful in Uttar Pradesh, where it increased its share of the vote from 7.6 percent (eight seats) in 1989 to 35.3 percent (fifty seats) in 1991, and in Gujarat, where its votes and seats climbed from 30 percent (twelve seats) to 52 percent (twenty seats). In addition, BJP support appeared to be spreading into new areas. In Karnataka, its vote rose from 2.6 percent to 28.1 percent, and in West Bengal the BJP's share of the vote expanded from 1.6 to 12.0 percent. However, the elections also revealed some of the limitations of the BJP juggernaut. Exit polls showed that while the BJP received more upper-caste support than all other parties and made inroads into the constituency of Backward Classes, it did poorly among Scheduled Castes and Scheduled Tribes, constituencies that it had long attempted to cultivate. In Himachal Pradesh, Madhya Pradesh, and Rajasthan, three state governments run by the BJP since 1990, the BJP lost parliamentary seats although its share of the vote increased. In Uttar Pradesh, where the BJP also won control of the state government in 1991, veteran political analyst Paul R. Brass cogently argued that the BJP had reached the limits of its social base of support.

The limits of the BJP's Hindu nationalist strategy were further revealed by its losses in the November 1993 state elections. The party lost control over the state-level governments of Himachal Pradesh, Madhya Pradesh, and Uttar Pradesh while winning power in Gujarat and the National Capital Territory of Delhi. In the aftermath of the Hindu activists' dismantling of the Babri Masjid in December 1992, the evocative symbolism of the Ramjanmabhumi controversy had apparently lost its capacity to mobilize popular support. Nevertheless, the BJP, by giving more emphasis to anticorruption and social issues, achieved unprecedented success in South India, where it won 28 percent of the vote and came in second in elections in Karnataka in November 1994. In the spring of 1995, the BJP won state elections in Gujarat and became the junior partner of a coalition with Shiv Sena (Army of Shivaji—Shivaji Bhonsle was a seventeenth-century Maratha guerrilla leader who kept Mughal armies at bay) in Maharashtra. In view of the potential demise of the Congress (I), the BJP stands poised to emerge as India's largest party in the 1990s. However, it is likely to have to play down the more divisive aspects of Hindu nationalism and find other issues to expand its support if it is to win a majority in the Lok Sabha.

Lok Sabha elections were again held in 1998, and the BJP again won the largest number of seats. This time, the BJP formed the National Democratic Alliance (NDA) with allied political parties. NDA had a slim majority, and A.B. Vajpayee returned as Prime Minister. But the coalition ruptured in May 1999, and fresh elections were again called.

On October 13, 1999, the BJP-led NDA won as many as 303 seats. The BJP won an all-time high of 183. Vajpayee won his third-term as Prime Minister, and L.K. Advani became the Deputy Prime Minister and held the Home Ministry. This NDA Government lasted for its full 5 years.

Under Prime Minister Atal Bihari Vajpayee, the new Government sent the country bursting into the new era, with the 5 nuclear tests at Pokhran, in Rajasthan in 1998, making India a new-age nuclear power with a considerable weapons arsenal and technology. The Vajpayee administration also oversaw the country's defenses during the Kargil conflict, where thousands of soldiers supplied with artillery and aircraft performed extremely dangerous assaults and operations, recovered strategic hills from Pakistani soldiers who had incurred across and occupied ground on the Indian side of the Line of Control.

The BJP-led National Democratic Alliance passed the Prevention of Terrorist Activities Act in 2002, a stringent law increasing the powers of police authorities and intelligence agencies in an effort to destroy subversive political activities and terrorism. The POTA was promulgated chiefly in response to the December 13, 2001 terrorist attacks on the Union Parliament.

The Vajpayee administration presided over the longest-sustained economic boom in the country's history, starting in late 2002. Record increases in agricultural and industrial production were matched by hungry middle-class consumers, and increasing foreign trade and investment. In 2004, the Government signed the South Asia Free Trade Agreement with Pakistan, Nepal, Bangladesh, Bhutan, Sri Lanka and the Maldives, a decision intended to vastly benefit over 1.6 billion people.

Vajpayee was single-handedly responsible for three monumental efforts to build peaceful relations with Pakistan. In 1999, he rode on the Delhi-Lahore bus inaugural, and signed the Lahore Declaration with the Pakistani PM, committing India to peace. Despite the betrayal to come three months later in Kargil, Vajpayee in 2001 invited the military ruler, Pervez Musharaff to Delhi, though the summit failed with no result. And despite the terrorist attacks that froze relations for two and a half years, Vajpayee, in a stunning and emotive speech to Parliament in August 2004, spoke of his "absolute last attempt of my life" to foster peace with Pakistan, de-freezing relations and invoking praise from world leaders.

The BJP was severely discredited by the 2002 Gujarat riots, where the Gujarat Chief Minister Narendra Modi of the BJP was accused of protecting murderous Hindu mobs and obstructing the work of police to stop the anti-Muslim violence. Many BJP activists and party members were involved in orchestrating the violence. Over 2,000 innocent people were killed and tens of thousands displaced in the carnage. Though BJP attempted to defend and justify Modi's leadership, the moderate wing of the party was embarrassed and weakened by the effects of the fiasco on the party's image and its efforts to woo Muslim voters. International reprimands followed. In 2005, BJP Chief Minister Modi was refused a US visa following an outcry by human rights activists. The 2000 Tehelka scam severely affected the credibility of the NDA, while the charge sheeting of L.K. Advani and others in the Babri Mosque demolition case in 2003 proved a further embarrassment.

The BJP and the NDA suffered a defeat in the general elections in 2004, and failed to muster a parliamentary majority. A.B. Vajpayee passed on the premiership to Dr. Manmohan Singh of the Congress Party, and its United Progressive Alliance. The defeat was incomprehensible to many political analysts, who assumed that the BJP would win on the basis of Vajpayee's widespread popularity, the national economic boom and the revival of the peace process with Pakistan. Following the defeat, there was a perception amongst parts of the party cadre that the party had expected victory to come easy and thus volunteers of the organisation had not worked hard enough to canvass voters and recruit supporters, and that the political campaign of BJP had remained confined to television and radio. Independent analysts saw the defeat arising from a backlash by large classes of people who had not benefitted from the economic growth as well as a failure by the party to secure strong allies. The BJP slogan of "India Shining" and the "Feel Good Factor" boomeranged especially in economically isolated states such as Andhra Pradesh.

# Part II. Pakistan

# 6

# HISTORY

The nation-state of Pakistan was established in 1947 as one of the two successor states of British India, yet the land and its people possess an extensive and continuous history that can be traced back to very ancient times. The history of Pakistan for times preceding 1947 sometimes partially overlaps with that of India, Afghanistan, and Iran.

## Prehistory

The oldest evidence of human life (8,000 to 6,000 years ago) in Pakistan was found in the Soan River valley of Pothohar region of Punjab. This human activity, called Soan Culture, discovered in the form of pebble tools scattered long the river. In Peshawar Valley of ancient Gandhara, there is evidence of existence of Stone Age men found at Sanghao near Mardan. Stone tools and burnt bones dated 7,000 years were found near caves. Cave dwellers of middle Stone Age used quartz flakes tools.

The Bolan River runs through the Bolan Pass in Balochistan, Pakistan, a natural passageway connecting the Indus plain to the Iranian plateau. The Bolan region is home to Mehrgarh, the earliest known agricultural settlement in Pakistan, dating from about 7000 BCE. Mehrgarh's remains are located in Balochistan, on the Kachi plain west of the Indus River valley. Somewhere between 2600 and 2000 BCE, the site seems to have been largely abandoned, which is the time of the Indus Valley Civilisation was in its initial stages of development. It has been surmised that the inhabitants of Mehrgarh migrated to the fertile Indus valley as Balochistan became more arid due to climatic changes.

The Indus Valley Civilization (2800-1800 BCE) was one of the most ancient civilizations, on the banks of Indus River. The natives of the region were the first inhabitants of the Indus valley, although some scholars believe that they invaded from the Iranian plateau and settled in the Indus valley around 4000 BCE. The Indus culture blossomed over the centuries and gave rise to the Indus Valley Civilization around 3000 BCE.

Indus Civilization settlements spread as far south as the Arabian Sea coast of India, as far west as the Iranian border, and as far north as the Himalayas. Among the settlements were the major urban centers of Harappa and Mohenjo-daro, as well as Dholavira, Ganweriwala, Lothal, and Rakhigarhi. The Mohenjo-daro ruins were once the center of this ancient society. At its peak, some archeologists opine that the Indus Civilization may have had a population of well over five million.

The founders of this civilisation are believed to be a Dravidian people, but this remains difficult to verify as the Indus Valley script has not yet been deciphered. To date, over 1,052 cities and settlements have been found, mainly in the general region to the east of the Indus River in Pakistan and India. The Kulli culture was an approximate contemporary of the Indus Valley Civilization.

## Ancient Empires

### *Vedic Civilization*

The Indus Valley Civilization spanned much of what is today Pakistan, but suddenly went into decline just prior to the migration of Indo-Aryan tribes from Central Asia. Their introduced culture mingled with that of the natives to produce the Vedic Civilization, that existed between the Sarasvati River and Ganges River around 1500 BCE. This civilization helped shape subsequent cultures in South Asia. Some scholars claim that the Vedic Aryan migration instituted the caste system to enslave the native population and the aborigine tribes. This apartheid prohibited inter-marriage and relegated the natives into low caste untouchables while elevating the status of Vedic Aryans, although nowadays it is considered likely that a form of the caste system already existed in India prior to the migration, and that this merged with the social structure of the Indo Aryans to produce the caste system seen in later periods.

The origin of the Vedic civilization and its relation to the Indus Valley Civilization remains highly controversial and politically charged. There exist much controversy surrounding the Aryan Invasion Theory. Mainstream scholarship places the Vedic civilization into the second and first millennias BCE, with some claims dating it as early as the fifth millennium BCE based on alleged astronomical information in the texts. Historical records set in only after the end of the Vedic period, and remain scarce throughout the Middle Ages. The end of Vedic period is marked by linguistic, cultural and political changes. The grammar of Panini marks a final apex in the codification of sacred texts, and at the same time the beginning of Classical Sanskrit.

### *Achaemenid Rule*

The part of ancient Afghanistan and Pakistan was ruled by the Persian Achaemenid Empire (c.520 BCE) during the reign of Darius the Great until Alexander the Great's conquest. It became part of the empire as a satrapy that included the lands of present-day Pakistani Punjab, the Indus River, from the borders of Gandhara down to the Arabian Sea, and other parts of the Indus plain. According to Herodotus of Halicarnassus, it was the most populous and richest satrapy of the twenty satrapies of the empire. It was during the Persian rule that name India was coined. When the Indus River valley became the eastern most satrapy of Persians, they named it because of the Indus River. Vedic Aryans called the area Saptha Sindhu with the main river was called Sindhu. Persians had difficulty in pronouncing s, called it Hindu. As per the inscriptions of Darius, they called the satrapy Hindush. Greeks took this name from Persians and called the river Indus and the region India.

Achaemenid rule lasted about 186 years. The Achaemenids used Aramaic script for the Persian language. After the end of Achaemenid rule, the use of Aramaic script in the Indus plain was diminished, although we know from Asokan inscriptions that it was still in use two centuries later. Other scripts, such as Kharosthi and Greek became more common after the arrival of the Macedonians and Greeks.

### *Alexander the Great*

The interaction between Hellenistic Greece and Buddhism started when Alexander the Great conquered Asia Minor, the Achaemenid Empire and ancient Pakistan in 334 BCE, defeating Porus at the Battle of the Hydaspes (near modern-day Jhelum) and conquering much of the Punjab region. Alexander's troops refused to go beyond the Beas River — which today runs along part of the Indo-Pakistan border — and he took most of his army southwest, adding nearly all of ancient Pakistan to his empire.

Alexander created garrisons for his troops in his new territories, and founded several cities in the areas of the Oxus, Arachosia, and Bactria, and Macedonian/Greek settlements in Gandhara, such as Taxila, and Punjab. The regions included the Khyber Pass — a geographical passageway south of the Himalayas and the Hindu Kush mountains — and the Bolan Pass, on a trade route connecting Drangiana, Arachosia and other Persian and Central Asia areas to the lower Indus plain. It is through these regions that most of the interaction between South Asia and Central Asia took place, generating intense cultural exchange and trade.

### *Greco-Buddhist Period*

Greco-Buddhism, sometimes spelled Græco-Buddhism, is the cultural syncretism between the culture of Classical Greece and Buddhism, which developed over a period of close to 800 years in the area corresponding to modern-day Afghanistan and Pakistan, between the fourth century BCE and the fifth century CE. Greco-Buddhism influenced the artistic development of Buddhism, and in particular Mahayana Buddhism, before it was adopted by Central and Northeastern Asia from the 1st century AD, ultimately spreading to China, Korea and Japan.

### *Mauryan Period*

The Mauryan dynasty lasted about 180 years, nearly as long as Achaemenid rule, and began with Chandragupta Maurya, not to be confused with Chandragupta I of the much-later Gupta Dynasty. Chandragupta Maurya lived in Taxila and met Alexander and had many opportunities to observe the Macedonian army there. According to Plutarch, Alexander encouraged him to invade the Gangetic Kingdom by capitalizing on the extreme unpopularity of the reigning monarch. Chandragupta recruited warriors from among the northwestern hill tribes and trained them in Macedonian fighting techniques, With this army, and with Macedonian mercenaries, Chandragupta went east to the Gangetic plain to overthrow the Nanda dynasty in Magadha, thereby founding the Maurya dynasty.

Following Alexander's death on June 10, 323 BCE, his Diadochi (generals) founded their own kingdoms in Asia

Minor and Central Asia. General Seleucus set up the Seleucid Kingdom, which included ancient Pakistan. Chandragupta Maurya, taking advantage of the fragmentation of power that followed Alexander's death, invaded and captured the Punjab and Gandhara. Later, the Eastern part of the Seleucid Kingdom broke away to form the Greco-Bactrian Kingdom.

Chandragupta's grandson Asoka (273-232 BCE), is said to have been the greatest of the Mauryan emperors. Ashoka the Great was the ruler of the Mauryan empire from 273 BCE to 232 BCE. A convert to Buddhism, Ashoka reigned over most of South Asia and parts of Central Asia, from present-day Afghanistan to Bengal and as far south as Mysore. He converted to the Buddhist faith following remorse for his bloody conquest of the kingdom of Kalinga in Orissa. He became a great proselytiser of Buddhism and sent Buddhist emissaries to many lands.

Brhadrata, the last ruler of the Mauryan dynasty, ruled territories that had shrunk considerably from the time of emperor Ashoka, but he was still upholding the Buddhist faith. He was assassinated in 185 BCE by his Brahmin general Pusyamitra Sunga, who made himself the ruler and established the Sunga dynasty. The assassination of Brhadrata and the rise of the Sunga empire led to a wave of decline of Buddhists in eastern South Asia, but not in what is today Pakistan and Afghanistan.

### *Greco-Bactrians and Indo-Greeks*

The Sunga persecution also triggered the 180 BCE invasion of northern India by the king Demetrius (the son of theGreco-Bactrian king Euthydemus) going as far as Pataliputra and established an Indo-Greek kingdom that lasted nearly two centuries, until around 10 BCE. To the south, the Greeks captured Sindh and nearby Arabian Sea coastal areas. The invasion was completed by 175 BCE, and the Sungas were confined to the east, although the Indo-

Greeks lost some territory in the Gangetic plain. Meanwhile in Bactria, the usurper Eucratides overcame the Euthydemid dynasty, killing Demetrius in battle.

Menander I was one of the Greek kings of the Indo-Greek Kingdom in ancient Pakistan from 155 to 130 BCE. He had been a general under King Demetrius, who was killed in battle. As a general, Menader drove the Greco-Bactrians out of Gandhara and beyond the Hindu Kush, becoming king shortly after his victory.

The Indo-Greeks suffered a new attack from the descendants of Eucratides around 125 BCE, as the Greco-Bactrian king Heliocles, son of Eucratides, was fleeing from the invasion of the Yuezhi in Bactria and trying to relocate in Gandhara. The Indo-Greeks retreated to their territories east of the Jhelum River as far as Mathura, and the two houses coexisted in the northern South Asia. Various kings ruled into the beginning of the first century CE, as petty rulers and as administrators, after the conquests of the Scythian, Parthians and Yuezhi, a Central Asian people possibly of Tocharian origins who founded the Kushan dynasty.

### *Kushan Empire*

The kingdom was founded by King Heraios, and greatly expanded by his successor, Kujula Kadphises. Kadphises' son Vima Takto conquered territory now in India, but lost much of the western parts of the kingdom, including Gandhara, to the Parthian king Gondophares. The rule of Kanishka I, the fourth Kushan emperor, who flourished for at least 28 years from c. 127, was administered from a winter capital in Purushapura (now Peshawar) and a summer capital in Bagram (then known as Kapisa).

The rule of the Kushans linked the seagoing trade of the Indian Ocean with the commerce of the Silk Road through the long-civilized Indus Valley. At the height of the dynasty, the Kushans loosely oversaw a territory that extended to the Aral Sea through present-day Uzbekistan, Afghanistan, and Pakistan into northern India. The loose unity and comparative peace of such a vast expanse encouraged long-distance trade, brought Chinese silks to Rome, and created strings of flourishing urban centers. Kanishka is renowed in Buddhist tradition for having convened a great Buddhist council in Kashmir. This council is attributed with having marked the official beginning of the pantheistic Mahayana Buddhism and its scission with Nikaya Buddhism. Kanishka also had the original Gandhari vernacular, or Prakrit, Mahayana Buddhist texts translated into the high literary language of Sanskrit. Along with the Indian king Ashoka, the Indo-Greek king Menander I (Milinda), and Harsha Vardhana, Kanishka is considered by Buddhism as one of its greatest benefactors.

The art and culture of Gandhara, at the crossroads of the Kushan hegemony, are the best known expressions of Kushan influences to Westerners. The interaction of Greek and Buddhist cultures continued over several centuries until it ended in the fifth century CE with the invasions of the White Huns, and later the expansion of Islam. During the remaining centuries before the coming of Islam in 711, the White Huns, Indo-Parthians, and Kushans shared control of what is today Pakistan with the Sassanid Persian empire which dominated much of western and southern Pakistan.

### *The Gupta Empire*

The Gupta Empire arose in northern India around the second century CE and much of what is today Sindh made up the northwesternmost province of the empire. The era of the Guptas was marked by a local Hindu revival, although Buddhism continued to flourish.

### *Movements of the Pakhtuns and Balochis*

From 2nd century BC to 5th century AD Pakistan and West

India came under continuous invasions of different Turko-Iranian peoples; Bacterians, Sakas, Parthians, Kushans, and Huns. During those centuries ethnic composition of the the area now comprised Pakistan remained in flex. By 7th century it was stabilized. Rajputs, Jats, and Gujjars, never heard before became integral part of the population. With the introduction of the Iranian peoples a physical feature became predominated which resemble to Iranian or other Caucasoid races to the west. This made people of Pakistan and West India distinct from the rest of the South Asia. These Caucasoid physical features beccome more prominent with the movement of Pakhtunes and Balochis.

It is surmised that Iranian tribes existed in what is today western Pakistan very early and that Pakhtun tribes were inhabitants around the area of Peshawar prior to the period of Alexander the Great as Herodotus refers to the local peoples as the "Paktui" and as a fearsome pagan tribe similar to the Bactrians. Iranian Balochi tribes did not arrive at least until the first millennium CE and would not expand as far as Sindh until the 2nd millennium.

## Arrival of Islam

### *Arab Rule*

Prior to the 8th century what is today Pakistan was dominated by native rulers in the east and the Sassanid Persians in the west. During this period, another event occurred in the history of Pakistan which would drastically transform the region, the coming of Islam. A Syrian Muslim chieftain named Muhammad bin Qasim conquered Pakistan early in the 8th century and extended Umayyad Muslim rule to the Indus Valley. Like Alexander the Great, Qasim travelled and subdued the whole of Pakistan from Karachi to Kashmir. Muhammad Bin Qasim, himself a youth of only 20, managed this feat by leading a small force of only 6,000 Syrian tribesmen and reached the borders of Kashmir within three years.

Muhammad Bin Qasim's conquests up to Kashmir could not be sustained by the Muslim Arabs for very long. Umayyad rule stretched too far and any further conquests without consolidation would prove futile. From Lisbon in Portugal to Lahore in the Punjab were the apogee of this vast Muslim empire. Following Muhammad Bin Qasim's departure and demise, after being recalled to Baghdad, Muslim rule shrank to Sindh and southern Punjab where consolidation took place and conversion to Islam was widespread, especially amongst the Buddhist majority.

In many regions several non-Muslim groups would remain numerous north of Multan. However, from this period onward Pakistan was divided into two parts: the northern region comprising the Panjab remained under the control of Hindu Rajas while the southern area came under Muslim control and comprised Multan, Sindh and Balochistan until Mahmud Ghaznavi appeared on the scene and conquered all of what is today Pakistan. During this 300-year period (712-1000) both the northern and southern parts had their own independent governments — the latter owing nominal allegiance to the Umayyad and Abbasid Caliphs. During the Arab rule, the territories of Pakistan were known as 'Sindh' and India was known as 'Hind'.

***Ghaznavid Period***

In 1001 Sultan Mahmud Ghaznavi defeated Jeebal the king of Kabulistan and marched further into Peshawer and in 1005 made it the center for his forces. From this strategic location Mahmud was able to capture Panjab in 1007, Tanseer fell in 1014, Kashmir was captured in 1015 and Qanoch fell in 1017. By 1027 Sultan Mahmud had captured Pakistan and parts of northern India.

On 1010 Mahmud captured what is today the Ghowr Province (Ghor) and by 1011 annexed Balochistan. Sultan Mahmud had already had relationships with the leadership in Balkh through marriage and its local emir Abu Nasr

Mohammad offered his services to Sultan Mahmud and offered his daughter to Muhammad son of Sultan Mahmud. After Nasr's death Mahmud brought Balkh under his leadership. This alliance greatly helped Mahmud during his expeditions into Pakistan and northern India.

In 1030 Sultan Mahmud fell gravely ill and died at the age of 59. Sultan Mahmud was an accomplished military commander and speaker as well as a patron of poetry, astronomy, and math. Mahmud had no tolerance for other religions however and only praised Islam. Universities were formed to study various subjects such as math, religion, the humanities and medicine were taught, but only within the laws of the Sharia. Islam was the main religion of his kingdom and the Perso-Afghan dialect of Dari language was made the official language.

Ghaznavid rule in Pakistan lasted for over one hundred and seventy five years from 1010 to 1187. It was during this period that Lahore assumed considerable importance as the eastern-most bastion of Muslim power and as an outpost for further advance towards the riches of the east. Apart from being the second capital and later the only capital of the Ghaznavid kingdom, Lahore had great military and strategic significance. Whoever controlled this city could look forward to and be in a position to sweep the whole of East Punjab to Panipat and Delhi.

By the end of his reign, Mahmud's empire extended from Kurdistan in the west to Samarkand in the northeast, and from the Caspian Sea to the Yamuna. All of what is today Pakistan and Kashmir came under the Ghaznavid empire. The wealth brought back to Ghazni was enormous, and contemporary historians give detailed descriptions of the building activity and importance of Lahore, as well as of the conqueror's support of literature.

### *Invasions of Muhammad Ghori*

Muhammad Ghori was a Perso-Afghan conqueror from the

region of Ghor in Afghanistan. Before 1160, the Ghaznavid Empire covered an area running from central Afghanistan east to the Punjab, with capitals at Ghazni, a city on the banks of Ghazni river in present-day Afghanistan, and at Lahore in present-day Pakistan. In 1160, the Ghorids conquered Ghazni from the Ghaznevids, and in 1173 Muhammad was made governor of Ghazni. He raided eastwards into the remaining Ghaznevid territory, and invaded Gujarat in the 1180's, but was rebuffed by Gujarat's Solanki rulers. In 1186-7 he conquered Lahore, ending the Ghaznevid empire and bringing the last of Ghaznevid territory under his control.

In 1191, he invaded the territory of Prithviraj III, the Chauhan Rajput Emperor of Ajmer and Delhi, who ruled much of present-day Rajasthan, Haryana, and Punjab, but was defeated at Tarain, near Bhatinda, by Govinda-raja of Delhi, Prithviraj's vassal. Within a year Muhammad controlled northern Rajasthan and the northern part of the Ganges-Yamuna Doab. Muhammad returned east to Ghazni to deal with the threat to his eastern frontiers from the Turks and Mongols, but his armies, mostly under Turkish generals, continued to advance through northern India, raiding as far east as Bengal.

Muhammad returned to Lahore after 1200 to deal with a revolt of the Rajput Ghakkar tribe in the Punjab. He suppressed the revolt, but was killed during a Ghakkar raid on his camp on the Jhelum River in 1206. Upon his death, his most capable general, Qutb-ud-din Aybak took control of Muhammad Ghori's Indian conquests and declared himself the first Sultan of Delhi.

### *Delhi Sultanate*

Muhammad's successors established the first dynasty of the Delhi Sultanate, while the Mamluk Dynasty in 1211 seized the reins of empire. The territory under control of the Muslim rulers in Delhi expanded rapidly. By mid-century, Bengal and much of central India was under the Delhi Sultanate. Several

Turko-Afghan dynasties ruled from Delhi: the Mamluk (1211-90), the Khalji (1290-1320), the Tughlaq (1320-1413), the Sayyid (1414-51), and the Lodhi (1451-1526). As Muslims extended their rule into southern India, only the Hindu kingdom of Vijayanagar remained immune, until it too fell in 1565. Although some kingdoms remained independent of Delhi in the Deccan and in Gujarat, Malwa, and Bengal, almost all of the area in present-day Pakistan came under the rule of the Delhi Sultanate.

The sultans of Delhi enjoyed cordial relations with Muslim rulers in the Near East but owed them no allegiance. The sultans based their laws on the Quran and the sharia and permitted non-Muslim subjects to practice their religion only if they paid the jizya or head tax. Perhaps the greatest contribution of the sultanate was its temporary success in insulating the South Asia from the potential devastation of the Mongol invasion from Central Asia in the thirteenth century, which nonetheless led to the loss of Afghanistan and western Pakistan to the Mongols. The sultanate ushered in a period of Indian cultural renaissance resulting from the stimulation of Islam by Hinduism. The resulting "Indo-Muslim" fusion left lasting monuments in architecture, music, literature, and religion. The sultanate suffered from the sacking of Delhi in 1398 by Timur but revived briefly under the Lodhis before it was conquered by the Mughals in 1526.

## Mughal Rule

The arrival of people from the Central Asian nations such as the Turks and Mongols was a significant turning point in the history of present-day Pakistan. The Qalandars (wandering Sufi saints) from Central Asia, Persia and Middle East preached a mystical form of Islam that appealed to the Buddhist and Hindu populations of Pakistan. The concepts of equality, justice, spiritualness, and secularism of the Sufi strain of Islam greatly attracted the masses towards it. Present-day

Pakistan was a place of great cultural and religious diversity. The Muslim Sufi missionaries played a pivotal role in converting the millions of native people to Islam.

The Mughals were the descendants of Persianized Central Asian Turks and would establish a formidable empire over the breadth of South Asia and beyond. The Mughal Empire included modern Pakistan and reached as far north as eastern Afghanistan and as far south as southern India. It was one of the three major Islamic empires of its day and sometimes contested its northwestern holdings such as Qandahar against invasions from the Uzbeks and the Safavid Persians. Although the first Mughal emperor Babur favored the cool hills of Kabul, his conquests would lay the foundations for a dynasty that would hold sway over South Asia for over two centuries. Most of his successors were capable rulers and during the Mughal period the Shalimar Gardens were built in Lahore during the reign of Shah Jehan and the Badshahi Mosque was erected during the reign of Aurangzeb. One notable emperor, Akbar the Great was both a capable ruler and an early proponent of religious and ethnic tolerance and favored an early form of multiculturalism.

Pakistan still bears marvellous architectural monuments built by the Mughal emperors. During the Mughal period, the cities of Delhi and Lahore were made the capitals of the empire. The Taj Mahal and other architectural marvels were the results of the growth of Islamic culture and rule over the South Asia. The Mughals also implemented federal regulations including taxation, social welfare reforms, justice, development of the transport and agricultural system and water canals.

### *Iranian and Afghan Rule*

In 1739 Nadir Shah attacked India and after defeating the Mughal Emperor Mohammed Shah claimed Punjab (from Lahore westward), the North-West Frontier Province,

Balochistan and Sind as provinces of his Empire. Upon the death of Nadir Shah one of his generals, a Pashtun named Ahmed Shah Abdali estabished the kingdom of Afghanistan in 1747 and made Pakistan part of his newly created state. He claimed Kashmir, Peshawar, Daman, Multan, Sindh and Punjab up to the Sutlej.

When the Abdali kingdom weakened early in the 19th century due to internecine warfare, the Abdali kingdom began to decline and an independent kingdom arose in Punjab headed by the Sikh leader Ranjit Singh. The British who had established their control over Delhi in 1803 warned Ranjit Singh not to try to impose his authority on the Sikh Sardars of East Punjab i.e., beyond Sutlej. As for Sind, from as early as the last days of Aurangzeb, it had begun to assert its independence and a succession of semi-independent dynasties under the Daudpotas, Kalhoras and Talpurs continued to rule over this province till British conquest in 1843 A.D. Meanwhile, Balochistan came under the sway of the Khan of Kalat with a few coastal cities such as Gwadar coming under the control of the Sultan of Oman.

## Sikh Rule in Punjab

In the early 19th century, the Mughal empire and the Afghan Durrani empire weakened in power. Taking advantage of the situation, Sikhs conquered most of the Punjab, and parts of Kashmir and Eastern Afghanistan. Sikh warrior Ranjit Singh defeated the Afghans and took the title of Maharaja of the Punjab and eventually sovereign of the Sikh empire, stretching from within the shadows of Delhi to beyond Peshawar, with his capital at Lahore. It was also the last territory of South Asia to fall to the British Empire mainly due to the betrayal by its top Dogra Generals, during the two bloody Anglo-Sikh wars in 1845-6 and 1848-49. The outcome was a very narrow victory for the British resulting in the annexition of the Punjab and the fall of Sikh rule.

## British Conquest and Colonization

During the middle of the second millennium, several European countries, such as Great Britain, Portugal, Holland and France were initially interested in trade with South Asian rulers including the Mughals and leaders of other independent Kingdoms. The Europeans took advantage of the fractured kingdoms and the divided rule to colonize the country. Most of India came under the crown of the British Empire in 1857 after a failed insurrection, popularly known as the First War of Indian Independence, against the British East India Company by Bahadur Shah Zafar. Present-day Pakistan remained part of British South Asia until August 14, 1947.

### *Anglo-Afghan Wars*

The two Anglo-Afghan wars that involved Pakistan directly took place in 1839 and again in 1842 and 1878 and resulted in the eventual loss of Pashtun/Afghan territory to the expanding British Indian empire. Following the 2nd Anglo-Afghan war, a tenuous peace resulted between Afghanistan and the British empire based in India. Decades later, what is today western Pakistan would come to be annexed by the British.

For Afghan ruler Abdur Rahman Khan, delineating the boundary with India was far more significant, and it was during his reign that the Durand Line was drawn. Under pressure, Abdur Rahman agreed in 1893 to accept a mission headed by the British Indian foreign secretary, Sir Mortimer Durand, to define the limits of British and Afghan control in the Pashtun territories. Boundary limits were agreed on by Durand and Abdur Rahman before the end of 1893, but there is some question about the degree to which Abdur Rahman willingly ceded certain regions. There were indications that he regarded the Durand Line as a delimitation of separate areas of political responsibility, not a permanent international frontier, and that he did not explicitly cede control over certain parts that were already in British control under the Treaty of Gandamak.

The Durand Line cut through both tribes and villages and bore little relation to the realities of topography, demography, or even military strategy. The line laid the foundation, not for peace between the border regions, but for heated disagreement between the governments of Afghanistan and British India, and later, Afghanistan and Pakistan. The issue revolves around the Pashtun nationalist movement known as Pashtunistan.

During much of the 19th century, the British and Russian Empires engaged in what came to be known as the Great Game as both sides intrigued over Afghanistan and western Pakistan. Often arming local Pashtun and Tajik tribesmen, both sides sought to undermine the other, while the rulers of Afghanistan were able to maintain some measure of independence in-spite of the loss of territories to the east to British India.

### *Muslims in the Raj*

The first proponents of an independent Muslim nation began to appear in the late nineteenth and early twentieth century under the British Raj. Following the first War for Indepdence, the Indian National Congress was founded in 1885. Some Muslims felt the need to address the issue of the Muslim identity within India, leading to Sir Syed Amir Ali forming the Central National Muhammadan Association in 1877 to work towards the political advancement of the Muslims.

The organisation declined towards the end of the nineteenth century but was replaced in 1906 by the All-India Muslim League. Although the League originally demanded constitutional guarantees for Muslims, several factors including sectarian violence prompted a reconsideration of the League's aims. The All India Muslim League was founded on the sidelines of the 1905 conference of the Muslim Anglo-Oriental Conference. This party was not, right until 1940, separatist. The idea of a separate nation was mooted in humor, satire and on the fringes of the political milieu.

### *Pakistan Movement*

By 1930, Mohammad Ali Jinnah, who ultimately led the movement for a separate state, had despaired of Indian politics and particularly of getting mainstream parties like the Congress to be sensitive to minority priorities. Among the first to make the demand for a separate state was the writer/ philosopher Allama Iqbal, who, in his presidential address to the 1930 convention of the Muslim League said that he felt that a separate nation for Muslims was essential in an otherwise Hindu-dominated South Asia. The Sindh Assembly passed a resolution making it a demand in 1935. Iqbal, Jauhar and others then worked hard to draft Mohammad Ali Jinnah to lead the movement for this new nation. Jinnah later went on to become known as the Father of the Nation, with Pakistan officially giving him the title Quaid-e-Azam or "Great Leader".

### *Lahore Resolution of 1940*

In 1940, Jinnah called a general session of the All India Muslim League in Lahore to discuss the situation that had arisen due to the outbreak of the Second World War and the Government of India joining the war without taking the opinion of the Indian leaders. The meeting was also aimed at analyzing the reasons that led to the defeat of the Muslim League in the general election of 1937 in the Muslim majority provinces. Jinnah, in his speech, criticised the Congress and the nationalist Muslims, and espoused the Two-Nation Theory and the reasons for the demand for separate Muslim homelands. Sikandar Hayat Khan, the Chief Minister of the Punjab, drafted the original Lahore Resolution, which was placed before the Subject Committee of the All India Muslim League for discussion and amendments. The resolution, radically amended by the subject committee, was moved in the general session by Shere-Bangla A.K. Fazlul Huq, the Chief Minister of Bengal, on 23 March and was supported by Choudhury Khaliquzzaman and other Muslim leaders. The Resolution was adopted on 23 March 1940 with great enthusiasm.

### *Origin of Name*

The name was coined by Cambridge student and Muslim nationalist Choudhary Rahmat Ali. He devised the word and first published it on January 28, 1933 in the pamphlet Now or Never . He saw it as an acronym formed from the names of the "homelands" of Muslims in South Asia. (P for Punjab, A for the Afghan areas of the region, K for Kashmir, S for Sindh and tan for Baluchistan, thus forming 'Pakstan.' An i was later added to the English rendition of the name to ease pronunciation, producing Pakistan.) The word also captured in the Persian language the concepts of "pak", meaning "pure", and "stan", meaning "land" or "home", thus giving it the meaning "Land of the Pure".

## Partition of India

As the British granted independence to their dominions in India in mid-August 1947, the two nations joined the British Commonwealth as self-governing dominions. The partition left Punjab and Bengal, two of the biggest provinces, divided between India and Pakistan. In the early days of independence, more than two million people migrated across the new border and more than one hundred thousand died in a spate of communal violence. The partition also resulted in tensions over Kashmir leading to the Indo-Pakistani War of 1947.

## The Islamic Republic of Pakistan

Pakistan's independence was won through a democratic and constitutional struggle. Although the country's record with parliamentary democracy has been mixed, Pakistan, after lapses, has returned to this form of government. Pakistani political history is divided into alternating periods of authoritarian military government and democratic civilian/parliamentary rule. Since independence, Pakistan has also been in constant dispute with India over the territory of Kashmir. The Kashmir dispute has complicated relations between Pakistan and India. In addition, Pakistan has been at odds with Afghanistan over the Pashtunistan issue for much of its history as well.

### *Military Coup and Wars (1956-1968)*

Just two years following the formation of a Constitution and a declaration as an Islamic Republic, the military took control of the nation in 1958. Field Marshall Ayub Khan also started Basic Democracy in which the people elected electors who in turn voted to select the President. He nearly lost the national elections to Fatima Jinnah. During Ayub's rule, relations with the United States and the West grew stronger. A formal alliance including Pakistan, Iran, Iraq, and Turkey was formed during the Ayub Khan period and was called the Baghdad Pact (later known as CENTO), which was to defend the Middle East and Persian Gulf from Soviet designs. Pakistan engaged in the Indo-Pakistani War of 1965 with India over Kashmir and the Rann of Kutch.

### *The War of 1971 and Separation of Bangladesh*

After a nationwide uprising in 1969, Ayub Khan stepped down and handed over power to General Yahya Khan who promised general elections to be held at the end of 1970. On the eve of the 1970 elections, approximately 500,000 people died when a cyclone hit East Pakistan on 12 November 1970. Despite the tragedy, elections went on, and the results showed a clear division between the Eastern and the Western provinces of the country. The Awami League led by Sheikh Mujibur Rahman won a majority in the National Assembly, with 167 of the 169 East Pakistani seats, but with no seats from West Pakistan, where the Pakistan Peoples Party led by Zulfikar Ali Bhutto, won 85 seats in the National Assembly. Khan and Bhutto refused to hand over power to Sheikh Mujib. Meanwhile, Mujib initiated a civil disobedience movement, strongly supported by the general population of East Pakistan and most of its government workers.

A round-table conference between Yahya, Bhutto and Mujib was convened in Dhaka, and after it ended without a solution, the Pakistani Army started Operation Searchlight, an organized and brutal crackdown on the East Pakistani army, police, politicians, innocent civilians and students in Dhaka. Mujib and many other Awami League leaders were arrested, while others fled to India. On March 27, 1971, Major Ziaur Rahman, a decorated Bengali war-veteran of the East Bengal Regiment of Pakistan Army, declared the independence of Bangladesh on behalf of Mujib. The crackdown broadened and later escalated into a guerrilla warfare between the Pakistani Army and the Mukti Bahini-Bengali "freedom fighters".

Although the killing of Bengalis was mostly unsupported by the people of West Pakistan, it continued for 9 months. India supplied the Bengali rebels with arms and training, and also hosted more than 10 million Bengali refugees who fled the turmoil. The Indian Army officially joined the war, and launched a massive assault into East Pakistan, where, by that time, the Pakistani Army led by General A. A. K. Niazi, had been weakened and exhausted.

Being outflanked by the Indian Army and overwhelmed, it surrendered to the Indian Army-Mukti Bahini joint command on December 16, 1971, in one of the largest surrenders since WW2 - as nearly 90,000 soldiers become PoWs. The official figure of Bengali civilian death toll from the war is reported to be 3 million, although some other sources put the number as low 1.25 to 1.5 million. The result was the emergence of the new nation of Bangladesh. Discredited by the defeat, President Gen. Yahya Khan resigned.

### *Civilian Rule and the 1973 Constitution*

Civilian rule returned after the war when General Yahya Khan handed over power to Zulfikar Ali Bhutto. In 1972, Pakistani intelligence learned that India was close to developing a nuclear bomb, and in response, Bhutto formed a group of engineers and scientists, headed by nuclear scientist Abdus Salam - who later won the Nobel Prize in Physics -to develop nuclear devices. In 1973, Parliament approved the 1973 Constitution.

During Bhutto's rule, a serious rebellion also took place in Balochistan and led to harsh suppression of Baloch rebels with purported assistance from the Shah of Iran lending air support in order to avoid a spilling over the conflit into Sistan Baluchistan in Iran. Elections were held in 1977, with Bhutto winning. Bhutto's victory was challenged by the opposition, which accused him of rigging the vote. General Muhammad Zia-ul-Haq took power in a coup, Bhutto was later executed after being convicted of murdering a political opponent in a controversial 4-3 split decision by Pakistan's Supreme Court.

### *Civilian Democracy*

From 1988 to 1998, Pakistan was ruled by civilian governments, alternately headed by Benazir Bhutto and Nawaz Sharif, who were each elected twice and removed from office on charges of corruption. Economic growth declined towards the end of this period, hurt by the Asian financial crisis, and economic sanctions imposed on Pakistan after its first tests of nuclear devices in 1998. The Pakistani testing came shortly after India tested nuclear devices and increased fears of a nuclear arms race in South Asia. The next year, the Kargil Conflict in Kashmir threatened to escalate to a full-scale war. During the late 1990s, Pakistan was one of three countries which recognized the Taliban government and Mullah Mohammed Omar as the legitimate ruler of Afghanistan. Allegations have been made of Pakistan, and other countries providing economic and military aid to the group from 1994 as a part of supporting the anti-Soviet alliance. It is alleged that some post-invasion Taliban fighters were recruits, drawn from Pakistan's madrassahs.

In the election that returned Nawaz Sharif as Prime Minister in 1997, his party received a heavy majority of the vote, obtaining enough seats in parliament to change the constitution, which Sharif amended to eliminate the formal checks and balances that restrained the Prime Minister's power. Institutional challenges to his authority, led by the civilian President Farooq Leghari, military chief Jehangir Karamat and Chief Justice Sajjad Ali Shah were put down and all three were forced to resign, Shah doing so after the Supreme Court was stormed by Sharif partisans.

### *1999 Coup*

On 12 October 1999, Sharif attempted to dismiss army chief Pervez Musharraf and install ISI director Khwaja Ziauddin in his place. Musharraf, who was out of the country, boarded a commercial airliner to return to Pakistan. Senior Army generals refused to accept Musharraf's dismissal. Nawaz Sharif ordered the Karachi airport to prevent the landing of the airliner, which then circled the skies over Karachi. In a coup, the generals ousted Sharif's administration and took over the airport. The plane landed with only a few minutes of fuel to spare, and General Pervez Musharraf assumed control of the government.

General Musharraf arrested Nawaz Sharif and his cabinet ministers which took part in this conspiracy. President Clinton felt that his pressure to force Nawaz Sharif withdraw Pakistan forces from Kargil in Indian controlled Kashmir was one of the main reason for Nawaz Sharif's disagreements with Pakistan army. President Clinton and King Fahd pressured General Musharraf to exile Nawaz Sharif in Saudi Arabia and guaranteeing he would not be involved in politics for five years. General Musharraf later expelled Nawaz Sharif to Saudi Arabia. Nawaz Sharif lived in Saudi Arabia for more than six years before moving to London in 2005.

## Pakistan in the 21st Century

On May 12, 2000 the Supreme Court of Pakistan ordered Pervez Musharraf to hold general elections by October 12, 2002. In an attempt to legitimize his presidency and assure its continuance after the impending elections, he held a national referendum on April 30, 2002, which extended his presidential term to a period ending five years after the October elections. General Musharraf continues to hold post of the army chief.

General elections were held in October 2002 and the centrist, pro-Mushararraf PML-Q won a plurality of the seats in the Parliament. However, parties opposed to Musharraf's Legal Framework Order effectively paralyzed the National Assembly for over a year. The deadlock ended in December 2003, when Musharraf and some of his parliamentary opponents agreed upon a compromise, and pro-Musharraf legislators were able to muster the two-thirds supermajority required to pass the Seventeenth Amendment, which retroactively legitimized Musharraf's 1999 coup and many of his subsequent decrees. In a vote of confidence on January 1, 2004, Musharraf won 658 out of 1,170 votes in the Electoral College of Pakistan, and according to Article 41(8) of the Constitution of Pakistan, was elected to the office of President.

While economic reforms undertaken during his regime have yielded some results, social reform programmes appear to have met with resistance. Musharraf's power is threatened by extremists who have grown in strength since the September 11, 2001 attacks and who are particularly angered by Musharraf's close political and military alliance with the United States, including his support of the 2001 invasion of Afghanistan, and his liberal views on reforming Islam. Musharraf has survived assassination attempts by terrorist groups believed to be part of Al-Qaeda, including at least two instances where the terrorists had inside information from a member of his military security detail.

Pakistan continues to be involved in a dispute over Kashmir, with allegations of support of terrorist groups being leveled against Pakistan by India, while Pakistan charges that the Indian government abuses human rights in its use of military force in the region. That both India and Pakistan possess nuclear weapons makes this dispute a source of special concern for the world community. Pakistan also has been accused of contributing to nuclear proliferation; indeed, its leading nuclear scientist, Abdul Qadeer Khan, admitted to selling nuclear secrets, though he denies any governmental knowledge of his activities.

The Pakistani government sent thousands of troops into the region of Waziristan in 2002 to hunt for bin Laden and other al-Qaeda fugitives. In March 2004, heavy fighting broke out at Azam Warsak, near the South Waziristan town of Wana, between Pakistani troops and an estimated 400 militants holed up in several fortified settlements. It was speculated that bin Laden's deputy Ayman al-Zawahiri was among those trapped by the Pakistani Army.

# 7

# GEOGRAPHY

Pakistan geologically overlaps onto both South Asia and the Eurasian landplate. The provinces of Sind and Punjab are found in the northwestern corner of the Indian tectonic plate, while Balochistan and most of the North West Frontier Province exist on the Eurasian Plate tectonic plate, and on the Iranian plateau and are coextensive with the Middle East and Central Asia. The Northern Areas and Azad Kashmir also lie mainly in Central Asia along the edge of the Indian plate and as a result are prone to severe earthquakes where Eurasian and the Indian plates collide.

Pakistan western borders include the Khyber Pass and Bolan Pass, traditional invasion routes between Central Asia and the South Asia.

### Boundaries

Pakistan occupies a position of great geostrategic importance, bordered by Iran on the west, Afghanistan on the northwest, China on the northeast, India on the east, and the Arabian Sea to the south. The total land area is estimated at 803,940 square kilometers.

The boundary with Iran, some 800 kilometers in length, was first delimited by a British commission in 1893, separating Iran from what was then British Balochistan. In

1957 Pakistan signed a frontier agreement with Iran, and since then the border between the two countries has not been a subject to any border dispute.

Pakistan's boundary with Afghanistan is about 2,640 kilometers long. In the north, it runs along the ridges of the Hindu Kush mountains and the Pamirs, where a narrow strip of Afghan territory called the Wakhan Corridor extends between Pakistan and Tajikistan. The Hindu Kush was traditionally regarded as the last northwestern outpost where Hindus could venture in safety.

The boundary line with Afghanistan was drawn in 1893 by Sir Mortimer Durand, then foreign secretary in British India, and was acceded to by the amir of Afghanistan that same year. This boundary, called the Durand Line, was not in doubt when Pakistan became independent in 1947, although its legitimacy was in later years disputed periodically by the Afghan government as well as by Pashtun tribes straddling the Pakistan-Afghanistan border. On the one hand, Afghanistan claimed that the Durand Line had been imposed by a stronger power upon a weaker one, and it favored the establishment of still another state to be called Pashtunistan or Pakhtunistan. On the other hand, Pakistan, as the legatee of the British in the region, insisted on the legality and permanence of the boundary. The Durand Line remains in effect today.

In the northeastern tip of the country, Pakistan controls about 84,159 square kilometers of the former princely state of Jammu and Kashmir. This area, consisting of Azad Kashmir (11,639 square kilometers) and most of the Northern Areas (72,520 square kilometers), which includes Gilgit and Baltistan, is the most visually stunning of Pakistan. The Northern Areas has five of the world's fourteen highest mountains known as the "Eight-thousanders" (8,000+ m high). It also has such extensive glaciers that it has sometimes been called the "third pole."

The boundary line has been a matter of pivotal dispute between Pakistan and India since 1947, and the Siachen Glacier in northern Kashmir has been an important arena for fighting between the two sides since 1984, although far more soldiers have died of exposure to the cold than from any skirmishes in the conflict.

From the eastern end of the Afghanistan-Pakistan border, a boundary of about 500 kilometers runs generally southeast between China and Pakistan, ending near the Siachen Glacier Pass. This line was determined from 1961 to 1965 in a series of agreements between China and Pakistan. By mutual agreement, a new boundary treaty is to be negotiated between China and Pakistan when the dispute over Kashmir is finally resolved between India and Pakistan.

The Pakistan-India cease-fire line runs from the Siachen Glacier vicinity west-southwest to a point about 130 kilometers northeast of Lahore. This line, about 770 kilometers long, was arranged with United Nations (UN) assistance at the end of the Indo-Pakistani War of 1947-48. The cease-fire line came into effect on January 1, 1949, after eighteen months of fighting and was last adjusted and agreed upon by the two countries in the Simla Agreement of July 1972. Since then, it has been generally known as the Line of Control.

The Pakistan-India boundary continues irregularly southward for about 1,280 kilometers, following the line of the 1947 Radcliffe Award, named for Sir Cyril Radcliffe, the head of the British boundary commission on the partition of Punjab and Bengal in 1947. Although this portion of the boundary is not formally disputed, passions still run high on both sides of the border. Many Indians had expected the original boundary line to run farther to the west, thereby ceding Lahore to India; Pakistanis had expected the line to run much farther east, possibly granting them control of Delhi, the imperial capital of the Mughal Empire.

The southern borders are far less contentious than those in the north. The Thar Desert in the province of Sindh is separated in the south from the salt flats of the Rann of Kutch by a boundary that was first delineated in 1923-24. After partition, Pakistan contested the southern boundary of Sindh, and a succession of border incidents resulted. They were less dangerous and less widespread, however, than the conflict that erupted in Kashmir in the Indo-Pakistani War of August 1965. These southern hostilities were ended by British mediation, and both sides accepted the award of the Indo-Pakistan Western Boundary Case Tribunal designated by the UN secretary general. The tribunal made its award on February 19, 1968, delimiting a line of 403 kilometers that was later demarcated by joint survey teams. Of its original claim of some 9,100 square kilometers, Pakistan was awarded only about 780 square kilometers.

## Geographic Areas

Pakistan is divided into three major geographic areas: the northern highlands; the Indus River plain, with two major subdivisions corresponding roughly to the provinces of Punjab and Sindh; and the Balochistan Plateau. Some geographers designate additional major regions. For example, the mountain ranges along the western border with Afghanistan are sometimes described separately from the Balochistan Plateau, and on the eastern border with India, south of the Sutlej River, the Thar Desert may be considered separately from the Indus Plain. Nevertheless, the country may conveniently be visualized in general terms as divided in three by an imaginary line drawn eastward from the Khyber Pass and another drawn southwest from Islamabad down the middle of the country. Roughly, then, the northern highlands are north of the imaginary east-west line; the Balochistan Plateau is to the west of the imaginary southwest line; and the Indus Plain lies to the east of that line.

The northern highlands include parts of the Hindu Kush, the Karakoram Range, and the Himalayas. This area includes such famous peaks as K2 (Mount Godwin Austen, at 8,611 meters the second highest peak in the world), and Nanga Parbat (8,126 meters), the twelfth highest. More than one-half of the summits are over 4,500 meters, and more than fifty peaks reach above 6,500 meters. Travel through the area is difficult and dangerous, although the government is attempting to develop certain areas into tourist and trekking sites. Because of their rugged topography and the rigors of the climate, the northern highlands and the Himalayas to the east have been formidable barriers to movement into Pakistan throughout history.

South of the northern highlands and west of the Indus River plain are the Safed Koh Range along the Afghanistan border and the Sulaiman Range and Kirthar Range, which define the western extent of the province of Sindh and reach almost to the southern coast. The lower reaches are far more arid than those in the north, and they branch into ranges that run generally to the southwest across the province Balochistan. North-south valleys in Balochistan and Sindh have restricted the migration of peoples along the Makran Coast on the Arabian Sea east toward the plains.

Several large passes cut the ranges along the border with Afghanistan. Among them are the Khojak Pass, about eighty kilometers northwest of Quetta in Balochistan; the Khyber Pass, forty kilometers west of Peshawar and leading to Kabul; and the Baroghil Pass in the far north, providing access to the Wakhan Corridor.

Less than a one-fifth of Pakistan's land area has the potential for intensive agricultural use. Nearly all of the arable land is actively cultivated, but outputs are low by world standards. Cultivation is sparse in the northern mountains, the southern deserts, and the western plateaus, but the Indus River basin in Punjab and northern Sindh has fertile soil that enables Pakistan to feed its population under usual climatic conditions.

The name Indus comes from the Sanskrit word sindhu, meaning ocean, from which also come the words Sindh, Hindu, and India. The Indus, one of the great rivers of the world, rises in southwestern Tibet only about 160 kilometers west of the source of the Sutlej River, which joins the Indus in Punjab, and the Brahmaputra, which runs eastward before turning southwest and flowing through Bangladesh. The catchment area of the Indus is estimated at almost 1 million square kilometers, and all of Pakistan's major rivers—the Kabul, Jhelum, Chenab, Ravi, and Sutlej—flow into it. The Indus River basin is a large, fertile alluvial plain formed by silt from the Indus. This area has been inhabited by agricultural civilizations for at least 5,000 years.

The upper Indus Basin includes Punjab; the lower Indus Basin begins at the Panjnad River (the confluence of the eastern tributaries of the Indus) and extends south to the coast. In Punjab (meaning the "land of five waters") are the Indus, Jhelum, Chenab, Ravi, and Sutlej rivers. The Sutlej, however, is mostly on the Indian side of the border. In the southern part of the province of Punjab, the British attempted to harness the irrigation power of the water over 100 years ago when they established what came to be known as the Canal Colonies. The irrigation project, which facilitated the emergence of intensive cultivation despite arid conditions, resulted in important social and political transformations.

Pakistan has two great river dams: the Tarbela Dam on the Indus, near the early Buddhist site at Taxila, and the Mangla Dam on the Jhelum, where Punjab borders Azad Kashmir. The Warsak Dam on the Kabul River near Peshawar is smaller. These dams, along with a series of headworks and barrages built by the British and expanded since independence, are of vital importance to the national economy and played an important role in calming the raging floodwaters of 1992, which devastated large areas in the northern highlands and the Punjab plains.

Pakistan is subject to frequent seismic disturbances because the tectonic plate under the Indian plate hits the plate under Eurasia as it continues to move northward and to push the Himalayas ever higher. The region surrounding Quetta is highly prone to earthquakes. A severe quake in 1931 was followed by one of more destructive force in 1935. The small city of Quetta was almost completely destroyed, and the adjacent military cantonment was heavily damaged. At least 20,000 people were killed. Tremors continue in the vicinity of Quetta; the most recent major quake occurred in January 1991. Far fewer people were killed in the 1991 quake than died in 1935, although entire villages in the North-West Frontier Province were destroyed. A major earthquake centered in the North-West Frontier Province's Kohistan District in 1965 also caused heavy damage.

## Climate

Pakistan lies in the temperate zone. The climate is generally arid, characterized by hot summers and cool or cold winters, and wide variations between extremes of temperature at given locations. There is little rainfall. These generalizations should not, however, obscure the distinct differences existing among particular locations. For example, the coastal area along the Arabian Sea is usually warm, whereas the frozen snow-covered ridges of the Karakoram Range and of other mountains of the far north are so cold year round that they are only accessible by world-class climbers for a few weeks in May and June of each year.

Pakistan has four seasons: a cool, dry winter from December through February; a hot, dry spring from March through May; the summer rainy season, or southwest monsoon period, from June through September; and the retreating monsoon period of October and November. The onset and duration of these seasons vary somewhat according to location.

The climate in the capital city of Islamabad varies from an average daily low of 2° C in January to an average daily high of 40° C in June. Half of the annual rainfall occurs in July and August, averaging about 255 millimeters in each of those two months. The remainder of the year has significantly less rain, amounting to about fifty millimeters per month. Hailstorms are common in the spring.

Pakistan's largest city, Karachi, which is also the country's industrial center, is more humid than Islamabad but gets less rain. Only July and August average more than twenty-five millimeters of rain in the Karachi area; the remaining months are exceedingly dry. The temperature is also more uniform in Karachi than in Islamabad, ranging from an average daily low of 13° C during winter evenings to an average daily high of 34° C on summer days. Although the summer temperatures do not get as high as those in Punjab, the high humidity causes the residents a great deal of discomfort.

Most areas in Punjab experience fairly cool winters, often accompanied by rain. Woolen shawls are worn by women and men for warmth because few homes are heated. By mid-February the temperature begins to rise; springtime weather continues until mid-April, when the summer heat sets in. The onset of the southwest monsoon is anticipated to reach Punjab by May, but since the early 1970s the weather pattern has been irregular. The spring monsoon has either skipped over the area or has caused it to rain so hard that floods have resulted. June and July are oppressively hot. Although official estimates rarely place the temperature above 46° C, newspaper sources claim that it reaches 51° C and regularly carry reports about people who have succumbed to the heat. Heat records were broken in Multan in June 1993, when the mercury was reported to have risen to 54° C. In August the oppressive heat is punctuated by the rainy season, referred to as barsat, which brings relief in its wake. The hardest part of the summer is then over, but cooler weather does not come until late October.

## Natural Resources

Pakistan's principal natural resources are arable land, water, and extensive natural gas and Oil reserves. About 28% of Pakistan's total land area is under cultivation and is watered by one of the largest irrigation systems in the world. The most important crops are cotton, wheat, rice, sugarcane, maize, sorghum, millets, pulses, oil seeds, barley, fish, fruits and vegetables, which together account for more than 75% of the value of total crop output.

Pakistan also exports wood, cement, tiles, marbles, cotton textiles, leather goods, sports goods, surgical instruments, electrical appliances, carpets, rugs and hides & skins. The Salt Range in Punjab Province has large deposits of pure salt. Pakistan has extensive energy resources, including fairly sizable natural gas reserves, oil reserves, coal, gypsum, limestone, chromites, iron ore, rock salt, silver, gold, precious stones, gems, marbles, tiles, copper, sulphur, Fire clay, silica sand and large hydropower potential. However, the exploitation of energy resources has been slow due to a shortage of capital and domestic and international political constraints.

## Environmental Issues

Little attention was paid to pollution and environmental issues in Pakistan until the early 1990s. Related concerns, such as sanitation and potable water, received earlier scrutiny. In 1987 only about 6 percent of rural residents and 51 percent of urban residents had access to sanitary facilities; in 1990 a total of 97.6 million Pakistanis, or approximately 80 percent of the population, had no access to flush toilets. Greater success has been achieved in bringing potable water within reach of the people; nearly half the population enjoyed such access by 1990. However, researchers at the Pakistan Medical Research Council, recognizing that a large proportion of diseases in Pakistan are caused by the consumption of polluted water, have been questioning the "safe" classification in use in the 1990s. Even the 38 percent of the population that receives its water through pipelines runs the risk of consuming seriously contaminated water, although the problem varies by area. In Punjab, for example, as much as 90 percent of drinking water comes from groundwater, as compared with only 9 percent in Sindh.

The central government's Perspective Plan (1988-2003) and previous five-year plans do not mention sustainable development strategies. Further, there have been no overarching policies focused on sustainable development and conservation. The state has focused on achieving self sufficiency in food production, meeting energy demands, and containing the high rate of population growth, not on curtailing pollution or other environmental hazards.

In 1992 Pakistan's National Conservation Strategy Report attempted to redress the previous inattention to the nation's mounting environmental problem. Drawing on the expertise of more than 3,000 people from a wide array of political affiliations, the government produced a document outlining the current state of environmental health, its sustainable goals, and viable program options for the future.

Of special concern to environmentalists is the diminishing forest cover in watershed regions of the northern highlands, which has only recently come under close scrutiny. Forest areas have been thoughtlessly denuded. Deforestation, which occurred at an annual rate of 0.4 percent in 1989-90, has contributed directly to the severity of the flooding problem faced by the nation in the early 1990s.

As industry has expanded, factories have emitted more and more toxic effluents into the air and water. The number of textile and food processing mills in rural Punjab has grown greatly since the mid-1970s, resulting in pollution of its rivers and irrigation canals. Groundwater quality throughout the country has also suffered from rapidly increasing use of pesticides and fertilizers aimed at promoting more intensive cropping and facilitating self-sufficiency in food production.

The National Conservation Strategy Report has documented how solid and liquid excreta are the major source of water pollution in the country and the cause of widespread waterborne diseases. Because only just over half of urban residents have access to sanitation, the remaining urban excreta are deposited on roadsides, into waterways, or incorporated into solid waste. Additionally, only three major sewage treatment plants exist in the country; two of them operate intermittently. Much of the untreated sewage goes into irrigation systems, where the wastewater is reused, and into streams and rivers, which become sewage carriers at low-flow periods. Consequently, the vegetables grown from such wastewater have serious bacteriological contamination. Gastroenteritis, widely considered in medical circles to be the leading cause of death in Pakistan, is transmitted through waterborne pollutants.

Low-lying land is generally used for solid waste disposal, without the benefit of sanitary landfill methods. The National Conservation Strategy has raised concerns about industrial toxic wastes also being dumped in municipal disposal areas without any record of their location, quantity, or toxic composition. Another important issue is the contamination of shallow groundwater near urban industries that discharge wastes directly into the ground.

Water in Karachi is so contaminated that almost all residents boil it before consuming it. Because sewerage and water lines have been laid side by side in most parts of the city, leakage is the main cause of contamination. High levels of lead also have been found in water in Islamabad and Rawalpindi.

Air pollution has also become a major problem in most cities. There are no controls on vehicular emissions, which account for 90 percent of pollutants. The National Conservation Strategy Report claims that the average Pakistani vehicle emits twenty-five times as much carbon monoxide, twenty times as many hydrocarbons, and more than three and one-half times as much nitrous oxide in grams per kilometer as the average vehicle in the United States.

Another major source of pollution, not mentioned in the National Conservation Strategy Report, is noise. The hyperurbanization experienced by Pakistan since the 1960s has resulted in loose controls for heavy equipment operation in densely populated areas, as well as in crowded streets filled with buses, trucks, automobiles, and motorcycles, which often honk at each other and at the horse-drawn tongas (used for transporting people) and the horse-drawn rehras (used for transporting goods).

New data from millennium-long tree-ring analyses are indicating that mountains in northern Pakistan have grown significantly wetter over the past century than they have been over the last millennium — quite possibly due to human-induced global warming. In Karakorum and Himalaya mountains in northern Pakistan, the upper reaches of the Indus Valley, a group of researchers collected samples of Juniper tree rings that dated back as far as 828 CE.

# 8

# SOCIETY AND CULTURE

Pakistan, a nation-state established in 1947, has a rich and unique cultural heritage that has actively preserved its established traditions throughout history. Many cultural practices and monuments have been inherited from the rule of Mughal empire. Its culture stems from the mainstream South Asian Muslim culture, which is also found in India and, to some extent, Bangladesh.

Pakistan has a very rich cultural and traditional background going back to Indus Valley Civilization, 2800 BC–1800 BC. The region of Pakistan has in the past been invaded, occupied and settled by many different peoples, including Dravidians, Aryans, Greeks, White Huns, Persians, Arabs, Turks, Mongols and various Eurasian groups. There are differences in culture among the different ethnic groups in matters such as dress, food, and religion, especially where pre-Islamic customs differ from Islamic practices. The orgin of Pakistanis however comes from Arab lands.

The pleasures of Pakistan are ancient: Buddhist monuments, Hindu temples, Palaces and Monuments built by Emperors, tombs, pleasure grounds and Anglo-Mogul mansions - some in a state of dereliction which makes their former grandeur more emphatic. Sculpture is dominated by Graeco-Buddhist friezes, and crafts by ceramics, jewellery, silk goods and engraved woodwork and metalwork.

## Pakistani Society

Pakistani society is largely multilingual and multicultural. As a result, cultures differ so much that they may be more alien to each other than to foreign ones. However over 50 years of integration, a distinctive "Pakistani" Culture has sprung up especially in the urban areas.Religious practices of various faiths are an integral part of everyday life in society. Education is highly regarded by members of every socio-economic stratum. The traditional family values are highly respected and considered sacred, although urban families have grown into a nuclear family system, owing to the socio-economic constraints imposed by the traditional joint family system.

The past few decades have seen emergence of a middle class in cities such as Karachi, Lahore, Rawalpindi, Hyderabad, Quetta, Faisalabad, Sukkur, Peshawar, Abbottabad and Multan. The North-western part of Pakistan, bordering with Afghanistan, is highly conservative and dominated by regional tribal customs dating back hundreds of years.

One of the most familiar sights in Pakistan, is that traditionally Pakistani men wear Shalwar Qameez. They come in many different styles, fabrics, colours and patterns that make them look really stylish. Pakistani women also wear Shalwar Qameez but the designs differ.

The Sherwani or Achkan with Karakuli hat is the national dress of Pakistan for men, as it is not specifically associated with any of the provinces. Most government officials wear the formal black Sherwani on state occasions.

## Religions

Census data indicates that over 98% of the population are Muslims. The Muslims are divided into different sects which are called schools of jurisprudence i.e. 'Maktab-e-Fikr' (School of Thought) in Urdu. Nearly 80% of Pakistani

Muslims are Sunni Muslims and 20% are Shi'a Muslims. The nearly all Pakistani Sunni Muslims belong to Hanafi school with a small Hanbali school represented by Wahabis and Ahle Hadith. The Hanafi school is divided into Barelvis and Deobandis schools. While majority of Pakistani Shia Muslims belong to Ithna 'ashariyah school with significant minority of Nizari Khoja Ismailis (Aga Khanis) and a small Mustaali Dawoodi Bohra schools.

By one estimate, in Pakistan, Muslims are divided into following schools: the Barelvis 48%, Deobandis 25%, Ithna Ashari 19%, Ahle Hadith 4%, Ismailis 1%, Bohras 0.25%, and other smaller sects. The Ahle-e-Hadith are part of Hanbali school. Nearly 65% of the total seminaries (Madrassah) are run by Deobandis, 25 per cent by the Barelvis, six percent by the Ahle Hadith and three percent by various Shia organizations. Zikris are considered to be a heretical sect by mainstream Muslims.

There are small non-Muslim religious groups: Christians 1%, Hindus, Sikhs, Qadianis, Buddhists, Parsis, Bahais and others 1%. Over 98% of 166 million peoples of Pakistan are Muslims. There is a small minority of non-Muslims including: Christians, Hindus, Sikhs, Buddhists, Bahais, Ahmadis, and Parsis.

Islam arrived in the area now known as Pakistan in 713 CE, when the Umayyad dynasty sent an Muslim Arab army led by Muhammad bin Qasim against the ruler of Sindh, Raja Dahir, whose pirates attacked Arab ships. The army conquered the northwestern part of ancient India from Kashmir to the Arabian Sea. The arrival of the Arab Muslims to the provinces of Sindh and Punjab, along with subsequent Muslim dynasties, set the stage for the religious boundaries of South Asia that would lead to the development of the modern state of Pakistan as well as forming the foundation for Islamic rule which quickly spread across much of South Asia. Following the rule of various Islamic empires, including the Ghaznavid Empire, the Ghorid kingdom, and the Delhi Sultanate, the region was controlled by the Mughals from 1526 until 1739. The Muslim technocrats, bureaucrats, soldiers, traders, scientists, architects, teachers, theologians and Sufis flocked from the rest of the Muslim world to Islamic Sultanate in South Asia. The Muslim Sufi missionaries played a pivotal role in converting the millions of native people to Islam. As in other areas where it was introduced by Sufis, Islam to some extent syncretized with pre-Islamic influences, resulting in a religion traditionally more flexible than in the Arab world. Two Sufis whose shrines receive much national attention are Data Ganj Baksh (Ali Hajweri) in Lahore (ca. eleventh century) and Shahbaz Qalander in Sehwan, Sindh (ca. twelfth century).

Data Durbar in Lahore, Pakistan is the tomb of Ali Hajweri, eleventh century Sufi. People come each year to pay their respects and to say prayers. The large complex also includes Jamia Hajweri, or Hajweri Mosque.

The Muslim poet-philosopher Sir Muhammad Iqbal first proposed the idea of a Muslim state in the South Asia in his address to the Muslim League at Allahabad in 1930. His proposal referred to the four provinces of Punjab, Sindh, Balochistan, and the NorthWest Frontier—essentially what would became the post-1971 boundary of Pakistan. Iqbal's idea gave concrete form to the "Two Nations Theory" of two distinct nations in the South Asia based on religion (Islam and Hinduism) and with different historical backgrounds, social customs, cultures, and social mores.

### *Islam*

Islam was thus the basis for the creation and the unification of a separate state, but it was not expected to serve as the model of government. Mohammad Ali Jinnah made his commitment to secularism in Pakistan clear in his inaugural address when he said, "You will find that in the course of time Hindus would cease to be Hindus and Muslims would cease to be Muslims, not in the religious sense, because that is the personal faith of each individual, but in the political sense as citizens of the State." This vision of a Muslim majority state in which religious minorities would share equally in its development was questioned shortly after independence. The debate continues amid questions of the rights of Qadianis (a small group known to be outside the pale of Islam according to the teachings and tenets of all branches of Islam, both Sunni and Shia), issuance of identity cards denoting religious affiliation, and government intervention in the personal practice of Islam.

### *Christianity*

The adherents of Christianity are the largest religious minority community in the Pakistan, numbering only around 1.6 million people, or 1% of Pakistan's entire population, according to the sources cited in the Demographics of Pakistan, although other sources claim lower

Christians have made immense contributions to the Pakistani national life. Pakistan's first non-Muslim and certainly most respected Chief Justice of Pakistan Supreme Court was Justice A R Cornelius. Pakistani Christians also distinguished themselves as great fighter pilots in the Pakistan Air Force. Notable amongst them are Cecil Chaudhry, Peter O'Reilly and Mervyn L Middlecoat. Christians have also contributed as educationists, doctors, lawyers and businessmen. Apart from the Catholics, Christians of other denominations re-organized themselves, in India, into the Churches of North and South India respectively, and as the Church of Pakistan in 1948.

### *Hinduism*

Hinduism is one of the smallest religions in Pakistan, but has played a major role in its history, culture and politics.

The term Hindu is etymologically derived from the Sindhu (Indus River) of Pakistan. The Sindhu is one of the holy rivers of Hinduism. Thus, in many ways, the land which is today's heavily Muslim Pakistan has played an important part in the origin of Hinduism.

Hinduism, once the main religion in Pakistan, has endured many conquests and invasions, different rulers, and ultimately political separation from the Hindu-majority India. What is today Pakistan is where the ancient Mehrgarh and Indus Valley Civilization thrived. Various archaeological finds such as what appears to be like a "Pasupati" image that was found on the seals of the people of Mohenjo-daro, in Sindh, point to early influences that may have shaped Hinduism.

The Elamo-Dravidian arrived from Eastern Iran and settled in Indus valley. According to a widely prevalent theory, a group of people known as Aryans migrated from regions like Iran or Eastern Europe, crossed the river Sindhu, and mingled with the Dravidians and indigenous people. The religious beliefs and folklore of the Indus valley people have become a major part of the Hindu faith that evolved in this part of the South Asia.

The Sindh kingdom and its rulers play an important role in the Indian epic story of the Mahabharata. In addition, there is the legend that the Pakistani city of Lahore was first founded by Lava, the son of Rama of the Ramayana. The Gandhara kingdom of the Northwest, and the legendary Gandhara peoples are also a major part of Hindu literature such as the Ramayana and the Mahabharata.

### *Sikhism*

Sikhism is a very small minority religion in the Islamic Republic of Pakistan but has many cultural, historical and political ties to the country, and to the historical region of Punjab.

Today, Pakistan, a nation of over 150 million, is 96% Muslim, with Christians and Hindus making up the largest minority faiths, each absorbing about 1.5% of the population. Sikhs, Zoroastrians, Buddhists, members of heterodox (according to Pakistani law) Islamic faiths and some adherents to animist religions make up the remainder. Information is scarce on minority adherents.

Prior to the Partition of India in 1947, which divided British India into its successor states of Pakistan and India, Sikhs were spread all across the region of Punjab and played an important role in its economy as businessmen and traders. Lahore, the capital of (now Pakistani) Punjab was then and still is today the location of many important religious and historical sites for Sikhs, including the Samadhi of Ranjit Singh. The nearby town of Nankana Sahib has nine gurdwaras, and is the birthplace of Sikhism's founder, Guru Nanak Dev. Each of Nankana Sahib's gurdwaras are associated with different events in Guru Nanak Dev's life. The town remains an important site of pilgrimage for Sikhs worldwide.

Nationwide, there are no reliable numerical figures for Sikhs in the country. Estimates vary wildly, from 60,000 nationwide to as little as 700 families, with little methodology or scientific technique cited by sources. The largest Sikh population in Pakistan is found in Peshawar, in the Northwest Frontier Province, which was spared the scale of violence during partition that raged in Punjab.

Sikhs are also found in sizable communities in Waziristan and Swat of the Northwest Frontier Province. There are also pockets of Sikhs in Lahore, Nankana Sahib, and Hasan Abdal in Punjab, and Gwadar, Kalat, and Quetta districts of Baluchistan. The (West) Punjab and Sindh provinces of Pakistan were mostly emptied of their Sikh and Hindu population in the communal massacres of partition, with nearly all fleeing for India. Today, very large segments of the populations of East Punjab and Haryana states and Delhi in India can trace their ancestry back to towns and villages now in Pakistan, including current Prime Minister Manmohan Singh.

## Languages

Most of the languages of Pakistan are part of the family of Indo-European languages and span the Indo-Iranian range of that family with the Indo-Aryan languages predominant in the east and the Iranian languages the most significant in the west as well as Dardic languages in the north and northwest.

Urdu is the national language of Pakistan and has historical significance as a language developed during the Islamic conquests in the Indian Subcontinent during the period of the Mughal Empire and was chosen as a neutral language to unite the various groups of modern Pakistan. Urdu also refers to a standardized register of Hindustani. However, the language of the government and commerce is English. Most secondary educational institutes and almost all universities use English as the medium of instruction. Many other languages are spoken in Pakistan, including the following regional tongues from largest to smallest: Punjabi, Pashtu, Sindhi, and Balochi.

Other languages spoken include from largest to smallest: Seraiki (sometimes included within Punjabi, also called Seraiki, Sira'iki, Lahndi, Multani - from the city of Multan, Derawali, Southern Punjabi, and Western Punjabi), Hindko, Brahui, Burushaski, Balti, Shina, and Khowar. Brahui is a Dravidian language, its closest relatives being spoken primarily in southern India, far removed from Pakistan. Balti is Sino-Tibetan and Burushaski is a language isolate.

In addition, according to Ethnologue, Pakistan has a million speakers of Persian, a few of whom are refugees from Afghanistan (mainly Tajiks and Hazaras) whose dialects vary from the Hazaragi-speaking population, while others include an ethnic group called the Dehwaris. Smaller groups include the Uzbeks and there is a large Kashmiri speaking population, largely refugees as well who fled from the Vale of Kashmir.

Arabic and Persian are still taught as classical languages to a small number of students. Arabic is popular due to its religious significance, but some Pakistanis do not learn to speak Arabic beyond that required to read and recite Islamic prayers. Persian is an important literary language in Pakistan.

According to the census, Pakistanis identified the following languages as their mother tongues [figures rounded to nearest percent]: Punjabi 44%, Pashto 15%, Sindhi 14%, Seraiki 11%, Urdu 8%, Balochi 4%, others 4%.

## Pakistani Literature

Pakistani literature, that is, the literature of Pakistan, as a distinct literature came into being when Pakistan gained its nationhood as a sovereign state in 1947. The common and shared tradition of Urdu literature and English literature of the South Asia was inherited by the new state. Over a period of time, a body of literature unique to Pakistan has emerged in nearly all major Pakistani languages, including Urdu, English, Punjabi, Balochi, Pushto and Sindhi.

The nature of Pakistani literature soon after independence aroused controversy among writers due to its being centred heavily on the negative events related to the India-Pakistan partition. According to Gilani Kamran (GC University), Pakistani literature was expected to take a new direction along with the new state of Pakistan at this point, but did not immediately meet this expectation.

Saadat Hassan Manto (1912-1955), a prominent writer of short stories of the South Asia, produced great literature out of the events relating to the India-Pakistan independence. The literature, which came out of the period that followed, is considered to have been progressive in its tone and spirit. According to several critics it had not only evolved its own identity, but also had played a significant role in documenting the hardships and hopes of Pakistan in the latter part of the 20th century.

## Popular Media

### *Film and Television*

Traditionally, the government-owned Pakistan Television Corporation (PTV) has been the dominant media player in Pakistan. However past decade has seen emergence of several private TV channels (news , entertainment) such as the GEO TV, AAJ TV, ARY Digital and a dozen or so more channels. Traditionally the bulk of TV shows have been plays or soap operas some of them critically acclaimed. Various American, European, Asian and Indian TV channels and movies are available to a majority of the population via Cable TV.

### *Cinema*

An indigenous movie industry exists in Pakistan, and is known as Lollywood as it is based in Lahore, producing over forty feature-length films a year. In contrast, Indian movies are popular in Pakistan despite a ban since the Pakistan-India War in 1965.

## Performing Arts

### *Music*

The music of Pakistan can be categorized into six general groups: classical, semi-classical/ghazal, folk, qawwali/ devotional, film, pop/rock. These categories overlap considerably, and many artists are able to perform in more than one of the listed genres. It has much in common with Indian music, although it has a regional flavour of its own.

In Pakistan the main form of classical music is a performing art, classical music in Pakistan is fast disappearing, however it still forms the basis of most other musical genres (save for pop/rock). Ghazal and qawwali music make use of many musical instruments such as the (sitar, tabla, harmonium, santoor etc). Pakistani folk, film and even some pop and rock also hold some classical elements.

Many Pakistani musicians of other genre (particularly ghazal, qawwali and folk musicians) therefore are nonetheless trained in subcontinent classical, and often belong to a gharana. One of the most prominent gharanas in Pakistan is the Patiala gharana, to which the great Ustad Bade Ghulam Ali Khan, and the brothers Ustad Amanat Ali Khan and Ustad Bade Fateh Ali Khan belong.

### *Ghazal Gayaki*

Ghazal is the name of a poetic form, but musically Ghazal gayaki refers to the form of music in which the poem is sung. Ghazal gayaki is often termed semi classical music. Most Ghazal singers are trained in classical music and sing in either Khyal or Thumri. Some of the most famous Pakistani Ghazal singers are Mehdi Hassan, Ghulam Ali, Farida Khanum, Iqbal Bano, Abida Parveen, Nayyera Noor, Malika Phukhraj and Tahira Syed. Mehdi Hassan Khan Sahib is considered the greatest Ghazal singer in South Asia.

### *Folk music*

Each of Pakistan's four provinces has its own variation of popular folk music. Bhangra is a Punjabi folk dance that has become popular all over Pakistan.

*Qawwaii*

One of the most dynamic and popular music of Pakistan is qawwali, which has been internationally popularized by stars like Sabri Brothers, Aziz Mian and Nusrat Fateh Ali Khan. Qawwali, in multiple forms, is widespread throughout Pakistan and Northern India.

Qawwali refers to both the performance and the genre of music. Qawwals typically consist of a lead vocalist, two back-up vocalists and any number of percussionists. Qawwalis are traditionally led by a sheikh and are meant to help the audience realize the mystical ideals of Sufi Islam. Amir Khusrau is said to have invented qawwali in the 13th century; the legendary poet and composer is also said to have invented the tabla and sitar. The idea of music (sama) inspiring an understanding and love for the divine and communication with spiritual guides is known from at least the 9th century. Orthodox Muslims sometimes criticize qawwali for its erotic imagery and sometimes frank sensuality.

Qawwali is similar to Subcontinent's musical genres; it has three components: a rhythm (traditionally played on the dholak), the melodic line of the vocals, and the pitch of the melody which is reinforced on harmonium. Poetic verses are usually mixed with a chorus and instrumental passages. Traditional languages used include Urdu containing much Persian and Arabic, an ancient form of Sanskrit called braj bhasha, as well as Punjabi.

The ancient tradition of tarana, a rhythmic series of nonsensical syllables with meaning only to the singers, if anyone, has helped lead a fusion with qawwali and jazz, due to the parallel practice of scat singing. Qawwali fusion with filmi and Western pop music have achieved some popularity, with attendant criticism from purists for allegedly watering down the sacred sound of qawwali. Nusrat Fateh Ali Khan, Aziz Mian Sabri Brothers and

Rizwan-Muazzam Qawwali Group have become especially popular, especially after Nusrat's collaborations with Michael Brook (a Canadian producer), resulting in the unexpected hit of "Mustt Mustt", remixed by Massive Attack and popularized by its use in a Coca-Cola television commercial. Nusrat's compositions have also been used in Last Temptation of Christ, Natural Born Killer, Dead Man Walking.

*Film music*

Pakistan's film industry known as "Lollywood" is based in Lahore. One of the most famous singers of the Pakistan film industry is Malika-e-Tarranum Madame Noor Jehan. Noor Jehan had a brief and successful acting career before devoting herself completely to music. She sang extensively for Pakistani films and also sang Ghazals, folk songs and patriotic songs (milli naghmay) for Pakistan television.

Until the 1960's Pakistani film music enjoyed a robust period of creative activity with a great number of songs acquiring popularity across the sub-continent. The major music directors of this period (with the noted exception of Khawaja Khurshid Anwar) were mostly rababis. Some of the great names were, Ustad Inayat Hussain, G.A. Chishti, Rashid Attre, Ustad Tasadduq, Master Abdullah, Firoze Nizami, Tufail Farooqi and Ustad Nazar.

During the early 1960s Urdu film and music quality declined as the result of various factors. The dominance of trend-setting music directors who had experience of seasoned pre-partition artists declined and they were replaced by a new and younger generation who tapped the Punjabi film market. Music from India's film industry, Bollywood, is also very popular in Pakistan. It combines Indian classical music, with its sophisticated, melismatic vocals and traditional instruments, with catchy tunes and stylings from Western pop music.

### *Pop Music*

The privatisation of Pakistani television has resulted in an explosion in the Pakistani pop music scene. New private television stations like Indus Music and The Musik regularly feature the latest pop music videos.

Artists such as Nazia Hasan and the Vital Signs (pop band) were pioneers of Pakistani pop music in the 1980's. Pakistan Pop and Rock Music Industry has also begun to make a mark on the Global Music scene. The Pakistani band Junoon popularised a genre of music called Sufi rock. Their music blended traditional Pakistani folk and Sufi music with western rock. Bands like Strings, Jal, Fuzon , Mekaal Hassan Band, Atif Aslam and Noori have millions of fans across the border in India, and other parts of South Asia and beyond.

### *Stage Shows*

These are very similar to stage plays in theatres. They are performed by many well-known actors and actresses in the Lollywood industry. The are many types of themes that are brought across with lots of humour.

## Sports

Sport is played with great passion in in Pakistan. Even with field hockey as the national sport, cricket is far more popular. Pakistan has also many traditional games that are still played and very fascinating to watch.

Muhammad Ali Jinnah had a great love for sport and fully released the vital role it played in the development of Nations and inculcation of discipline among the masses.

In a meeting with the Organizing Committee of the First Pakistan Olympic Games held at Karachi the Quaid-i-Azam said to the first President of Pakistan Olympic Association Mr. Ahmed E.H. Jaffar: "Dedicate yourself to sports promotion, for when you and I are gone, leadership will go into the hands of Youth, and Youth is our wealth, a raw material, that must be hammered into shape, into burnished steel to strive and smite in defence - the defence of the integrity and solidarity of Pakistan - the defence of the ideology of Pakistan."

The first National Games were held at Polo Ground, Karachi from 23rd to 25th April, 1948. Sportsmen and officials from East Pakistan (now Bangladesh) and all the integrated Provincial units of West Pakistan took part in these Games. The total number of athletes was 140. No competitors were, however, invited from any foreign country. Competitions were held in track and field athletics, basketball, boxing, cycling, volleyball, weightlifting and wrestling.

The most popular sport, followed religiously in Pakistan, is cricket. Pakistan has historically produced several multi-talented players who have been among the best batsmen and bowlers in the world, including Imran Khan, Wasim Akram, Waqar Younis, Javed Miandad and Inzamam-ul-Haq. Almost every district and neighborhood in Pakistan has its cricket team and most people start playing from a young age. Pakistan has won some international cricket events, including the World Cup in 1992.

Pakistan has one of the top bowlers and batsmen ranked in the world. Pakistan's bowlers are known for developing and perfecting the art of reverse swing bowling to a high degree of proficiency.

## Festivals & Celebrations

### *Eid*

The two Eids, Eid ul-Fitr and Eid ul-Adha commemorate the passing of the month of fasting, Ramadan, and the willingness of Prophet Ibrahim to sacrifice his son Prophet Ishmael for Allah. During these days there are national holidays and many festivals and events take place to celebrate Eid.

### *Basant*

Basant is a Punjabi festival that marks the coming of spring. Basant celebrations in Pakistan are centered in Lahore and people from all over the country and abroad come to the city for the annual festivities. Kite flying competitions take place all over the city's rooftops during Basant.

### *Independence Day*

On August 14, every year all over Pakistan, the people of Pakistan celebrate the day Pakistan gained its independence from the British Raj for an independent state for Muslims. There are lots of celebrations in Lahore, the streets are full of joyful people singing and dancing. Concerts are held with many pop and classical singers.

## Cuisine

Pakistani food is similar that of northern India, with a dollop of Persian, Turkish and Middle Eastern influences thrown in for good measure. This means menus peppered with baked and deep-fried breads (roti, chapattis, puri, halwa and nan), vegetables, meat curries, lentils (dhal), spicy spinach, cabbage, peas and rice, and of course that staple of hippies, the sturdy Hunza pie. Street snacks are popular in cities - samosas and tikkas (spiced and barbecued beef, mutton or chicken) - are delicious, while a range of desserts will satisfy any sweet tooth. The most common sweet is barfi (it pays to overlook the name), which is made of dried milk solids and comes in a variety of flavours. Though Pakistan is officially 'dry' (alcohol-free), it does brew its own beer and spirits which can be bought (as well as imported alcohol) from designated bars and hotels.

## Mercantile Culture

Pakistan's service sector accounts for 53% of the country's GDP. Wholesale and retail trade is 30% of this sector. Shopping is a popular pastime for many Pakistanis, especially among the well-to-do and the thirty-million strong middle class. The cities of Lahore, Karachi, Peshawar, Islamabad, Faisalabad and Quetta are especially known for the great contrast in shopping experiences - from burgeoning bazaars to modern multi-story shopping malls. In particular, Lahore and Karachi are peppered with colourful shopping plazas.

Increasing globalization has increased the influence of "Western culture" in Pakistan. Pakistan ranks 46th in the world on the Kearney/FP Globalization index. Many Western restaurant chains have established themselves in Pakistan, and are found in the major cities.

A large Pakistani diaspora exists in the West. Whereas Pakistanis in the United States, Canada and Australia tend to be professionals, the majority of them in the United Kingdom, Germany and the Scandinavian nations come from a rural background and belong to the working class. A large number of Pakistani expatriates are also living in the Middle East. These emigrants and their children influence Pakistan culturally and economically, keeping close ties with their roots by travelling to Pakistan and especially by returning or investing there.

## Cultural Taboos

Pakistanis are highly spiritual people. The translation of Pakistan's name meaning land of the pure, implies spiritual purity. And one of the pillars of this spiritual purity is sexual purity, which over time, has become a part of the Pakistani sense of national identity.

Sexual purity does not imply not having sex rather it only implies a complete avoidance of pre or extra marital sex. The roots of this spirituality are based on the Islamic faith, which prescribes strict sexual conservatism, especially when compared to the west. Therefore, the following norms of a western society are usually strict cultural taboos in Pakistan:

— Public displays of affection, even by married couples. This however varies from place to place.

— Consumption of alcoholic beverages. (Having alcohol in public is illegal. But wine shops, especially in Karachi and the Sindh province and Islamabad operate for non-Muslims. Only non-Muslims are allowed to buy alcohal with a permit, which is issued by the government of Pakistan. However, there are not many bars. Pakistan does have a few notable companies making local alcohol beverages out of which beer made by Murree Brewery, is the most popular).

Some strict cultural taboos in the west, are the norm in Pakistan, such as:

— The staying of children in their parents' house after a certain age. In Pakistan, the girl child is supposed get married between the ages 18 to 25, and move with her husband after marriage. But the boys are there always - acting as the parents' social security, since there is no government run official 'social security' that is administered.

The boys stay with their parents all their lives (at least one of the sons does) and take care of them in their old age. This being the reason for the commonly strong desire in Pakistani parents to have sons as compared to daughters. In fact, if a young man moves out of his parents' family home and gets a place of his own, the move is usually considered highly offensive and insulting to the parents. It therefore, only rarely happens, especially if the son is an only child or an only son.

Contrary to popular belief, although the law of Islam and Pakistani law allow Muslim men to have up to four wives under certain strict conditions, monogamy is in reality the norm in the vast majority of Pakistan. It is highly unusual for a Muslim Pakistani man to have more than one wife.

# 9

# ECONOMY

Pakistan is a developing country with the world's sixth-largest population, and an economic growth rate that has been consistently positive since a 1951 recession. At purchasing power parity, Pakistan GDP in 2005 was estimated at approximately $384.9 billion, larger than that of Saudi Arabia, but slightly smaller than the GDP of the Philippines.

During much of its history, underdevelopment and poverty in parts of Pakistan—as well as fiscal mismanagement obscured the potential of a country with the resources and entrepreneurial skill to support rapid economic growth. However, the economy averaged an impressive growth rate of 6% per year during the 1980s and early 1990s.

In the twentieth century overall, its economic growth rate was better than the world average, but imprudent policies led to a slowdown in the late 1990s. Since then, the Pakistani government has instituted wide-ranging reforms, and economic growth has accelerated in the current century. Pakistan's economic outlook has brightened and it's manufacturing and financial services sectors have experienced rapid expansion. There has been a great improvement in its foreign exchange position and a rapid growth in hard currency reserves as a result of its current account surplus.

## Economic History

Economically, Pakistan was a very poor and predominantly agricultural country at the time of its independence in 1947 from British South Asia. Current GDP per capita grew 112% in the Sixties and 81% in the Seventies but this proved unsustainable and growth fell sharply to 22% in the Eighties and 18% in the Nineties.

Industrial-sector growth, including manufacturing, was also above average. In the early 1960s, Pakistan was seen as a model of economic development around the world, and there was much praise for the way its economy was progressing. Later, economic mismanagement in general, and fiscally imprudent economic policies in particular, caused a large increase in the country's public debt and led to slower growth in the 1990s.

Historically, Pakistan's overall economic output (GDP) has grown every year since a 1951 recession. Despite this record of sustained growth, Pakistan's economy had, until a few years ago, been characterized as unstable and highly vulnerable to external and internal shocks. However, the economy proved to be unexpectedly resilient in the face of multiple adverse events concentrated into a four-year period

— the Asian financial crisis;

— economic sanctions — according to Colin Powell, Pakistan was "sanctioned to the eyeballs";

— global recession;

— severe rioting in the port city of Karachi;

— a severe drought — the worst in Pakistan's history, lasting four years;

— heightened perceptions of risk as a result of military tensions with India — with as many as a million troops on the border, and predictions of impending (potentially nuclear) war; and

— the post-9/11 military action in neighboring Afghanistan, with a massive influx of refugees from that country.

Despite these adverse events, Pakistan's economy kept growing, and economic growth accelerated towards the end of this period. This resilience has led to a change in perceptions of the economy, with leading international institutions such as the IMF, World Bank, and the ADB praising Pakistan's performance in the face of adversity.

## Modern Trends

Pakistan's economic outlook has brightened in recent years in conjunction with rapid economic growth and a dramatic improvement in its foreign exchange position as a result of its current account surplus and a consequent rapid growth in hard currency reserves. Pakistan's nuclear tests in May 1998 triggered the imposition of economic sanctions by the G-7. International default was narrowly averted by the partial waiver of sanctions and the subsequent reinstatement of Pakistan's IMF ESAF/EFF in early 1999, followed by Paris Club and London Club rescheduling. The Sharif government had difficulty meeting the conditionality of the IMF program, which was suspended in July 1999, and resumed later during Musharraf's administration. Having improved its finances, the government stated in 2004 that it would no longer require IMF assistance, and the assistance program ended in that year.

The administration of President Pervez Musharraf has sought and received debt relief from international lenders, reducing its external debt from $32 billion to a discounted present value less than half of that. The government is using Pakistan's surplus to prepay expensive debt and replace it with commercial debt, which it has been able to obtain at low interest rates as a result of its improved credit rating.

Musharraf's economic agenda includes measures to widen the tax net, privatize public sector assets, and improve its balance of trade. Pakistan has made governance reforms, privatization, and deregulation the cornerstones of its economic revival.

Although it has received a positive endorsement from supranational financial institutions such as the World Bank, the International Monetary Fund and the Asian Development Bank, as well as improved credit ratings from Standard & Poor's and Moody's, Pakistan is still experiencing a costly dearth of foreign direct investment.

Pakistan's Finance Minister, Shaukat Aziz, who has been credited with Pakistan's economic turnaround, was elected to the office of Prime Minister on 28 August 2004.

Pakistan's current account surplus put upward pressure on the Pakistani rupee, which rose from 64 rupees per dollar to 57 rupees per dollar. The State Bank of Pakistan (the central bank) stabilized the rise by lowering interest rates and buying dollars.

After short-term Pakistani T-bond rates fell below 2%, with government borrowing having declined, banks greatly expanded their lending to businesses and consumers. Construction activity, sales of durable goods such as trucks and automobiles, and housing purchases have all jumped to record levels. Private sector credit expanded by 28.5% in 2003.

Despite rapid growth in domestic automobile manufacturing, imports have also risen to meet the increased demand. Major automakers, such as BMW, Toyota, and Honda have invested in manufacturing facilities in the country.

### Macroeconomic Reform

According to many sources, the Pakistani government has made substantial economic reforms since 2000, and medium-term prospects for job creation and poverty reduction are the best in nearly a decade.

Government revenues have greatly improved in recent years, as a result of economic growth, tax reforms - with a broadening of the tax base, and more efficient tax collection as a result of self-assessment schemes and corruption controls in the Central Board of Revenue - and the privatization of public utilities and telecommunications. Pakistan is aggressively cutting tariffs and assisting exports by improving ports, roads, electricity supplies and irrigation projects. Islamabad has raised development spending from about 2% of GDP in the 1990s to 4% in 2003, a necessary step towards reversing the broad underdevelopment of its social sector.

Liberalization in the international textile trade has already yielded benefits for Pakistan's exports, and the country also expects to profit from freer trade in agriculture. As a large country, Pakistan hopes to take advantage of significant economies of scale, and to replace China as the largest textile manufacturer as the latter China moves up the value-added chain. These industries play to Pakistan's relative strengths in low labor costs.

A perception of stability in the nation's monetary policies has contributed to a reduction in money-market interest rates, and a great expansion in the quantity of credit, changing consumption and investment patterns in the nation. Pakistan's domestic natural gas production, and its significant use of CNG in automobiles, has cushioned the effect of the oil-price shock of 2004-2005. Pakistan is also moving away from the doctrine of import substitution which some developing countries dogmatically pursued in the twentieth century. The Pakistani government is now pursuing an export-driven model of economic growth successfully implemented by South East Asia and now highly successful in China. abcdefg In 2005, the World Bank reported that

> "Pakistan was the top reformer in the region and the number 10 reformer globally — making it easier to start a business,

> reducing the cost to register property, increasing penalties for violating corporate governance rules, and replacing a requirement to license every shipment with two-year duration licenses for traders."

In addition, reduced tensions with India and the ongoing peace process raise new hopes for a prosperous and stable South Asia, with more intra-regional trade. Shahid Javed Burki, former vice president of World Bank and who was in charge of the bank's Latin American division when Mexico was hit by the crisis in 1994, said Pakistan is facing symptoms that preceded the Mexican financial crisis more than 10 years ago. He points to the nation's current account deficit, 'excessive' speculative business activity and weak banking system.

## Economy Today

In the first four years of the twenty-first century, Pakistan's KSE 100 Index was the best-performing stock market index in the world. Pakistan's manufacturing sector has experienced double-digit growth in recent years, with large-scale manufacturing growing by 18% in 2003. A reduction in the fiscal deficit has resulted in less government borrowing in the domestic money market, lower interest rates, and an expansion in private sector lending to businesses and consumers. Foreign exchange reserves continued to reach new levels in 2003, supported by robust export growth and steady worker remittances.

Measured by purchasing power, Pakistan has a 30 million strong middle class enjoying per capita incomes of $8000-$10,000, according to Dr. Ishrat Husain, Governor of the State Bank of Pakistan. In addition, Pakistan has a growing upper class with relatively high per capita incomes. However, Pakistan has no individual with as much as a billion US dollars, according to Forbes magazine and has the distinction of being (by population) the largest nation to have no billionaires. On measures of income inequality, the country ranks slightly better than the median.

Pakistan government spent over 1 trillion Rupees on poverty alleviation programs during the past four years, cutting poverty from 32.1 percent in 2000-01 to 25.4 percent in 2004-05. The rural poverty has declined from 39 percent to 31.8 percent and urban poverty from 22.7 percent to 17.1 percent.

## Factors Affecting Economy

### *Demographics*

With a per capita GDP of about $2080 the World Bank considers Pakistan a low-income country. Pakistan has a large informal economy, which the government is trying to document and assess. Approximately 50% of adults are literate, and life expectancy is about 64 years or less. The population, about 155 million in 2004, is growing at about 1.96%.

Relatively few resources have been devoted to socio-economic development or infrastructure projects. Inadequate provision of social services and very high birth rates in the past have contributed to a persistence of poverty. An influential recent study concluded that the fertility rate peaked in the 1980s, and has since fallen sharply. Pakistan has a family-income Gini index of 41, close to the world average of 39.

### *Employment*

The high population growth in the past few decades has ensured that a very large number of young people are now entering the labor market. Among the seven most populous Asian nations, Pakistan has a lower population density than Bangladesh, Japan, India, and the Philippines. In the past, excessive red tape made firing, and consequently hiring, difficult. Significant progress in taxation and business reforms has ensured that many firms now are not compelled to operate in the underground economy. The nations of Iran, Germany, France and previously Pakistan had one thing in common; high costs of entry into the market for firms and excessive restriction on labor. The result: high unemployment. In recent years, employment rates in Pakistan have been unexceptional compared to other countries.

## Currency System

The basic unit of currency is the Rupee, which is divided into 100 paisas. Since the turn of the century, a strengthening economy and large current-account surplus has caused the rupee's exchange rate to rise in value. In response, Pakistan's central bank has prevented the rupee from rising too much, by lowering interest rates and buying dollars, in order to preserve the country's export competitiveness. As of 2005, one US dollar is approximately equal to 60 rupees.

The Pakistani rupee depreciated against the US dollar until the turn of the century, when Pakistan's large current-account surplus pushed the value of the rupee up versus the dollar. Pakistan's central bank then stabilized by lowering interest rates and buying dollars, in order to preserve the country's export competitiveness.

## Structure of Economy

In 1947, when Pakistan became independent, agriculture accounted for about 53% of its GDP. While per-capita agricultural output has grown since then, it has been outpaced by the growth of the non-agricultural sectors, and the share of agriculture has dropped to roughly one-fifth of Pakistan's economy. In recent years, the country has seen rapid growth in industries (such as apparel, textiles, and cement) and services (such as telecommunications, transportation, advertising, and finance).

## Economic Sectors

Pakistan's service sector accounts for about 51% of GDP. Transport, storage, communications, finance, and insurance account for 24% of this sector, and wholesale and retail trade about 30%. Pakistan is trying to promote the information industry and other modern service industries through incentives such as long-term tax holidays.

### *Financial Services*

A reduction in the fiscal deficit has resulted in less government borrowing in the domestic money market, lower interest rates, and an expansion in private sector lending to businesses and consumers. Foreign exchange reserves continued to reach new levels in 2003, supported by robust export growth and steady worker remittances.

### *Tax Incentives & IT Industry*

The Government of Pakistan has, over the last few years, granted numerous incentives to technology companies wishing to do business in Pakistan. A combination of decade-plus tax holidays, zero duties on computer imports, government incentives for venture capital and a variety of programs for subsidizing technical education, are intended to give impetus to the nascent Information Technology industry. This in recent years has resulted in impressive growth in that sector. Pakistan saw an increase in IT exports of 50% from 2003-4 to 2004-5, with total exports standing at $48.5 million. This year the government has set an export goal of $72 million. Exports account for 11% of the total revenues of the IT sector in Pakistan. Compared to India, Pakistan's IT sector is still in the infantile stage, but recent trends have led economists to be optimistic about the IT industries future prospects in Pakistan.

Paging and mobile (cellular) telephone were adopted early and freely. Cellular phones and the Internet were adopted through a rather laissez-faire policy with a proliferation of private service providers that led to fast adoption. Both have taken off and in the last few years of the 1990s and first few years of the 2000s. With a rapid increase in the number of internet users and ISPs, and a large English-speaking population, Pakistani society has seen major changes.

— Pakistan has more than 20 million internet users as of 2005. The country is said to have a potential to absorb up to 50 million mobile phone Internet users in the next 5 years thus a potential of nearly 1 million connections per month.

— Almost all of the main government departments, organizations and institutions have their own websites.

— The use of search engines and instant messaging services is also booming. Pakistanis are some of the most ardent chatters on the Internet, communicating with users all over the world. Recent years have seen a huge increase in the use of online marriage services, for example, leading to a major re-alignment of the tradition of arranged marriages.

— As of 2005 there were 6 cell phone companies operating in the country with nearly 28 million mobile phone users in the country.

— Wireless local loop and the landline telephony sector has also been liberalized and private sector has entered thus increasing the teledensity rate from less than 3% to more than 10% in span of two years.

### *Agriculture*

Pakistan's principal natural resources are arable land and water. About 25% of Pakistan's total land area is under cultivation and is watered by one of the largest irrigation systems in the world. Agriculture accounts for about 23% of GDP and employs about 44% of the labor force. The most important crops are wheat, sugarcane, cotton, and rice, which together account for more than 75% of the value of total crop output.

Pakistan's largest food crop is wheat. In 2005, Pakistan produced 21,591,400 metric tons of wheat, more than all of Africa (20,304,585 metric tons) and nearly as much as all of South America (24,557,784 metric tons), according to the FAO. Pakistan is a net food exporter, except in occasional years when its harvest is adversely affected by droughts. Pakistan exports rice, cotton, fish, fruits, and vegetables and imports vegetable oil, wheat, cotton, pulses and consumer foods.

The economic importance of agriculture has declined since independence, when its share of GDP was around 53%. Following the poor harvest of 1993, the government introduced agriculture assistance policies, including increased support prices for many agricultural commodities and expanded availability of agricultural credit. From 1993 to 1997, real growth in the agricultural sector averaged 5.7% but has since declined to about 4%. Agricultural reforms, including increased wheat and oilseed production, play a central role in the government's economic reform package.

### *Energy*

Pakistan has extensive energy resources, including fairly sizable natural gas reserves, some proven oil reserves, coal (Pakistan has the fourth-largest coal reserves in the world), and a large hydropower potential. However, the exploitation of energy resources has been slow due to a shortage of capital and domestic political constraints. Domestic petroleum production totals only about half the country's oil needs, and the need to import oil has contributed to Pakistan's trade deficits and past shortages of foreign exchange. The current government has announced that privatization in the oil and gas sector is a priority, as is the substitution of indigenous gas for imported oil, especially in the production of power. Pakistan is a world leader in the use of compressed natural gas (CNG) for personal automobiles.

### *Minerals*

Important minerals found in Pakistan are gypsum, limestone, chromites, iron ore, rock salt, silver, gold, precious stones, gems, marble, copper, coal, graphite, sulphur, fire clay, silica. The salt range in Punjab Province has large deposits of pure salt. Balochistan province is a mineral rich area having substantial mineral, oil and gas reserves which have not been exploited to their full capacity. The province has significant quantities of copper, chromite and iron, and pockets of antimony and zinc in the south and gold in the far west. Natural gas was discovered near Sui in 1952, and the province has been gradually developing its oil and gas projects over the past fifty years.

### *Industry*

Pakistan's industrial sector accounts for about 24% of GDP. Cotton textile production and apparel manufacturing are Pakistan's largest industries, accounting for about 64% of total exports. Other major industries include cement, fertilizer, edible oil, sugar, steel, tobacco, chemicals, machinery, and food processing. The government is privatizing large-scale parastatal units, and the public sector accounts for a shrinking proportion of industrial output, while growth in overall industrial output (including the private sector) has accelerated. Government policies aim to diversify the country's industrial base and bolster export industries.

### *Manufacturing*

In FY 2002-03, real growth in manufacturing was 7.7%. In the twelve months ending 30 June 2004, large-scale manufacturing grew by more than 18% compared to the previous twelve-month period.

### *Construction*

After the devastating 2005 Kashmir earthquake Pakistan has instituted stricter building codes. The cost of construction in Pakistan will increase 30 to 50% due to implementation of a new building code which requires strengthening of structures to withstand earthquake of 8 to 8.5 magnitude. The demand for cement has increased due to reconstruction after the earthquake. The prices of cement has increased by 50% and Pakistan government banned export of cement to lower the prices and the reconstruction costs.

Dubai Ports World, annouced on June 1st, 2006 that it will spend $10 billion to develop transport infrastructure and real estate in Pakistan.Dubai Ports World is also discussing the possibility of the company taking over operational management of Gwadar port in Balochistan. Emaar Properties, announced on May 31, 2006 three real estate developments in the cities of Islamabad and Karachi in Pakistan. The projects, with a total investment of AED 8.8 billion (US$2.4 billion), will include a series of master planned communities that will set new benchmarks in commercial, residential and retail property within Pakistan.

## Economic Aid

Pakistan receives economic aid from several sources as loans and grants. The International Monetary Fund (IMF), World Bank (WB), Asian Development Bank (ADB), etc provides long term loans to Pakistan. Pakistan also receives bilateral aid from developed and oil-rich countries.

The Asian Development Bank will provide close to $4 billion development assistance to Pakistan during 2006-08. The World Bank unveiled a lending program of up to $6.5 billion for Pakistan under a new four-year, 2006-2009, aid strategy showing a significant increase in funding aimed largely at beefing up the country's infrastructure. Japan will provide $500 million annual economic aid to Pakistan.

## Remittance

The remittance of Pakistanis living abroad has played important role in Pakistan's economy and foreign exchange reserves. The Pakistanis settled in Western Europe and North America are important sources of remittance to Pakistan. Since 1973 the Pakistani workers in the oil rich Arab states have been sources of billions dollars of remittance. Pakistan received nearly $4 billion dollars in remittance in 2005. An IMF research paper has revealed that workers' remittances contribute 4% to the GDP of Pakistan and are equivalent to about 22 percent of annual exports of goods and services.

## Investment

The Foreign direct investment (FDI) in Pakistan soared by 180.6 per cent year-on-year to US$2.22 billion and portfolio investment by 276 per cent to $407.4 million during the first nine months of fiscal year 2006, the State Bank of Pakistan (SBP) reported on April 24. During July-March 2005-06, FDI year-on-year increased to $2.224 billion from only $792.6 million and portfolio investment to $407.4 million, whereas it was $108.1 million in the corresponding period last year, according to the latest statistics released by the State Bank.

## Foreign Trade

Pakistan is a member of the World Trade Organization, and has bilateral and multilateral trade agreements with many nations and international organizations. Fluctuating world demand for its exports, domestic political uncertainty, and the impact of occasional droughts on its agricultural production have all contributed to variability in Pakistan's trade deficit. In the six months to December 2003, Pakistan recorded a current account surplus of $1.761 billion, roughly 5% of GDP. Pakistan's exports continue to be dominated by cotton textiles and apparel, despite government diversification efforts. Exports grew by 19.1% in FY 2002-03. Major imports include petroleum and petroleum products, edible oil, chemicals, fertilizer, capital goods, industrial raw materials, and consumer products.

Past external imbalances left Pakistan with a large foreign debt burden. Principal and interest payments in FY 1998-99 totaled $2.6 billion, more than double the amount paid in FY 1989-90. Annual debt service peaked at over 34% of export earnings before declining. With a current account surplus in recent years, Pakistan's hard currency reserves have grown rapidly. Improved fiscal management, greater transparency and other governance reforms have led to upgrades in Pakistan's credit rating. Together with lower global interest rates, these factors have enabled Pakistan to prepay, refinance and reschedule its debts to its advantage. Despite the country's current account surplus and increased exports in recent years, Pakistan still has a large merchandise-trade deficit. The budget deficit in fiscal year 1996-97 was 6.4% of GDP. The budget deficit in fiscal year 2003-04 is expected to be around 4% of GDP.

In the late 1990s, Pakistan received about $2.5 billion per year in loan/grant assistance from international financial institutions (e.g., the IMF, the World Bank, and the Asian Development Bank) and bilateral donors. Increasingly, the composition of assistance to Pakistan shifted away from grants toward loans repayable in foreign exchange. All new U.S. economic assistance to Pakistan was suspended after October 1990, and additional sanctions were imposed after Pakistan's May 1998 nuclear weapons tests. The sanctions were lifted by president George W. Bush after Pakistani president Musharraf allied Pakistan with the U.S in its war on terror. Having improved its finances, the government refused further IMF assistance, and consequently the IMF program was ended.The government is also reducing tariff barriers with bilateral and multilateral agreements.

While the country has a current account surplus and both imports and exports have grown rapidly in recent years, it still has a large merchandise-trade deficit. The budget deficit in fiscal year 2004-2005 was 3.4% of GDP. The budget deficit in fiscal year 2005-06 is expected to be over 7% of GDP. Economists believe that the soaring trade deficit would have an adverse impact on Pakistani rupee by depreciating its value against dollar and other currencies.

One of the main reasons that contributed to the increase in trade deficit is the increased imports of earthquake relief related items, especially tents, tarpaulin and plastic sheets to provide temporary shelter to the survivors of earthquake of October 8th, 2005 in Azad Jammu and Kashmir and parts of the NWFP, an official said. The rise in the trade gap was also fuelled by high oil import prices, food items, machinery and automobiles.

Pakistan has suffered the highest ever $9.427 billion trade deficit during the first 10 months (July 2005 to April 2006) of the current fiscal year against the trade deficit of $4.868 billion during the same period last year, showing an increase of 93.65 percent. The Petroleum Ministry says that this year the bill of oil imports was expected to reach $6.5 billion against $4.6 billion in the last fiscal year, which is the main reason behind the all-time high trade deficit. Pakistan's total imports in first ten month of current fiscal year stood at $22.95 billion, up 40.38 percent, and exports at $13.52 billion, with 17.80 percent increase over the corresponding period of the last fiscal year.

**Exports**

The exports in the first ten months of 2006 financial year (July 2005 to June 2006) were $13.52 billion showing an increase of 17.80% compared to $11.48 billion corresponding period last fiscal year. Pakistan exports rice, furniture, cotton fiber, cement, tiles, marble, textiles, clothing, leather goods, sports goods (renowned for footballs/soccer balls), surgical instruments, electrical appliances, software, carpets, and rugs, ice cream, livestock meat, chicken, powdered milk, wheat, seafood (especially shrimp/prawns), vegetables, processed food items, Pakistani assembled Suzukis (to Afghanistan and other countries), defense equipment (submarines, tanks, radars), salt, marble, onyx, engineering goods, and many other items. Exports are projected to be $17 billion in current financial year.

**Imports**

The imports in the first ten months of 2006 financial year (July 2005 to June 2006) amounted to $22.95 billion showing an increase of 40.38% compared to $16.35 billion in corresponding period last fiscal year. Imports are projected to be over $27 billion in current financial year. Pakistan's single largest import category is petroleum and petroleum products. Other imports include: industrial machinery, construction machinery, trucks, automobiles, computers, computer parts, medicines, pharmaceutical products, food items, civilian aircraft, defense equipment, iron, steel, toys, electronics, and other consumer items.

**Deficit**

Pakistan's trade deficit is $9.427 billion, almost 8.6 percent of Gross Domestic Product (GDP), due to its high import bill and the rise in prices during the first ten months of the current fiscal year. Economists believe that the soaring trade deficit would depreciate the Pakistani rupee against dollar and other currencies. The demand by local importers for dollars in the coming months would increase to finance their surplus imports. Independent economic experts say that the trade deficit would cross $13 billion current fiscal year. The rise in the trade gap has been attributed to high oil import bill, and rise in the prices of food items, machinery and automobiles.

**Bonds**

Pakistan is expected to sell a dual-tranche sovereign bond worth $750 million on March 23, 2006 that analysts said should ensure a favorable reception in the bond market. The 10-year tranche would be $500 million and the 30-year portion $250 million. Pricing is expected during New York trading hours on March 23, 2006. The sources said that the 10-year tranche was expected to be priced at around 7.125 percent, while the longer-dated tranche was expected to be sold at around 7.875 percent, the top end of the indicative yield range of 7.75 to 7.875 percent. The bonds, comprising 10-year and 30-year tranches, had generated $1.5 billion in orders and a total size of as much as $1.25 billion had been anticipated for what is Pakistan's third foray into the international debt market since 2004.

# 10

# GOVERNMENT AND POLITICS

Nation building remains a difficult process in Pakistan. But although the country has undergone a succession of traumatic sociopolitical experiences since achieving independence in 1947, it continues to demonstrate its resilience and its capacity to survive and adapt to changing circumstances. Joining the community of nations as a bifurcated state, with its two wings separated by 1,600 kilometers of foreign soil, Pakistan was faced with the immediate task of absorbing large numbers of refugees from India in the months immediately following partition. The new nation struggled with severe economic disadvantages made acutely painful by a shortage of both administrative personnel and the material assets necessary to establish and sustain its fledgling government. With the death of Mohammad Ali Jinnah—the revered Quaid-i-Azam (Great Leader)—only thirteen months after independence, the nation was dealt another severe blow.

Created to provide a homeland for the Muslims of the Indian subcontinent, Pakistan was heir to a government structure and a political tradition that were essentially Western and secular. From its inception, Pakistan has worked to synthesize Islamic principles with the needs of a modern state. The young nation was immediately challenged by a host of other factors affecting national development, including ethnic and provincial tensions, political rivalries, and security considerations. The country subsequently survived civil war and the resultant loss of its East Wing, or East Pakistan, which became the independent nation of Bangladesh in December 1971, and has accommodated an influx of refugees resulting from the Soviet occupation of Afghanistan (December 1979-February 1989), which over the course of the conflict exceeded 3.2 million people.

Pakistan has had difficulty in establishing stable, effective political institutions. The country has experimented with a variety of political systems, has endured periods of martial law, and has had five constitutions, one inherited from the British and four indigenous creations since independence. Its political parties have suffered from regionalism, factionalism, and lack of vision.

Power has shifted between the politicians and the civilmilitary establishment, and regional and ethnic forces have threatened national unity. However, the impulse toward cohesion has been stronger than the impetus toward division, and the process of nation building has continued. The return to democracy in 1988, and the peaceful, constitutional transfer of power to new governments in 1990 and 1993 testify to Pakistan's progress in the quest for political stability.

Pakistan, in its comparatively short history, has tried various forms of parliamentary, military, and presidential governments in its efforts to achieve political stability. At independence Pakistan was governed by the Government of India Act of 1935 as amended by the authority of the India Independence Act of 1947. The amended act provided at the center for a governor general (as successor to the British viceroy) as head of state and for a Constituent Assembly with two separate functions—to prepare a constitution and to be a federal legislature until the constitution came into effect.

At the outset, however, this structure of governor general and parliamentary legislature took on singular characteristics tailored to the personality, prestige, and unique position occupied by Jinnah, Pakistan's first governor general. At independence, he was the supreme authority, the founder of the state, and the chief political leader.

As head of the All-India Muslim League, in 1940 he mobilized the political effort that in just seven years won Pakistan's independence. His ultimate authority came not from military power, not from the support of the bureaucracy, and not from constitutional prerogatives but from the political support of the people. In these circumstances, Jinnah chose to unite in himself the functions of head of state and the power of chief executive and party boss. In addition to his position as governor general, he was elected president of the Constituent Assembly.

For the office of governor general to be held by an active party politician who continued as political leader was an innovation. Initially, the arrangement may have seemed necessary to preserve national unity after independence and to facilitate the work of the new government. When Jinnah died, the prime minister, Liaquat Ali Khan, and the cabinet assumed increased power, in more traditional roles, and Khwaja Nazimuddin, as the new governor general, became a more traditional, nonpolitical head of state.

Liaquat, however, found it difficult to establish his political authority. Whether the transfer of effective power to Liaquat while Jinnah was still alive might have created a precedent for future political stability in Pakistan is a moot point. Liaquat's assassination, three years later in October 1951, was the catalyst for a series of constitutional and political crises that over the years seemed almost endemic.

Pakistan has provided a unique setting for experiments in synthesizing Islamic principles with the needs of a modern state. Although Pakistan's independence movement was articulated in Western terminology and centered on the right of national selfdetermination , it was also rooted in the Islamic concept of society and of what constitutes legitimate political authority for a Muslim.

The basis of the ideal Muslim polity is the sharia, the sacred law of Islam as embodied in the Quran. Efforts to apply Quranic law in a modern political context have had a direct impact on Pakistan's political history and have also complicated the nation's constitutional evolution.

## Politics of Pakistan

Politics of Pakistan takes place in a framework of a federal presidential republic, whereby the President of Pakistan is both head of state and head of government, and of a pluriform multi-party system. Executive power is exercised by the government. Legislative power is vested in both the government and parliament.

Pakistan has been ruled by both democratic and military governments. The first decade was marred with political unrest and instability resulting in frequent collapses of civilian democratic governments. From 1947 to 1958 as many as seven Prime Ministers of Pakistan either resigned or were ousted. This political instability paved the way for Pakistan's first military take over.

On October 7th 1958 Pakistan's civilian and first President Iskander Mirza in collaboration with General Mohammad Ayub Khan abrogated Pakistan's constitution and declared Martial Law.

General Ayub Khan was the president from 1958 to 1969, and General Yahya Khan from 1969 to 1971. Civilian rule continued from 1972 to 1977 under Zulfikar Ali Bhutto, but he was deposed by General Zia-Ul-Haq. General Zia was killed in a plane crash in 1988, after which Benazir Bhutto, daughter of Zulfikar Ali Bhutto, was elected as the

Prime Minister of Pakistan. She was the youngest woman ever to be elected the Head of Government and the first woman to be elected as the Head of Government of a Muslim country. Her government was followed by that of Nawaz Sharif, and the two leaders alternated until the military coup by General Pervez Musharraf in 1999. Since the resignation of President Rafiq Tarar in 2001, Musharraf has been the President of Pakistan.

Nation-wide parliamentary elections were held in October 2002, with the PML-Q winning a plurality of seats in the National Assembly of Pakistan, and Zafarullah Khan Jamali of that party emerging as Prime Minister. Jamali resigned on June 26, 2004. PML-Q leader Chaudhry Shujaat Hussain became interim PM, and was succeeded by Finance Minister and former Citibank Vice President Shaukat Aziz, who was elected Prime Minister on August 27, 2004 by a National Assembly vote of 191 to 151.

The Pakistan's federal cabinet on April 12, 2006 decided that general elections would be held after the completion of the assemblies constitutional term by the end of 2007 or beginning of 2008.

## Constitution of Pakistan

Pakistan's Constitution may be amended by a vote of two-third of both houses of the Parliament of Pakistan.

Pakistan's many constitutional changes are reflected by the following key constitutional amendments:

— Eighth Amendment to the Constitution of Pakistan which gave the president executive powers

— Thirteenth Amendment to the Constitution of Pakistan which removed the president's reserve powers to dissolve the National Assembly and call elections before the end of its term.

— Fourteenth Amendment to the Constitution of Pakistan which institutionalized party discipline, diminishing the ability of the legislature to dismiss a Prime Minister by Confidence Voting, especially if the Prime Minister is also the leader of a party that has a majority rather than just a plurality.

— Seventeenth Amendment to the Constitution of Pakistan which restored the president's reserve powers, but made them subject to the approval of the Supreme Court of Pakistan.

## Form of Government

Pakistan's independence was won through a democratic and constitutional struggle. Although the country's record with parliamentary democracy has been mixed, Pakistan, after lapses, has returned to this form of government. The constitution of the Islamic Republic of Pakistan adopted in 1985 provides for a federal parliamentary system with a president as head of state and a popularly elected prime minister as head of government.

## Executive Branch

### *President*

The president, in keeping with the constitutional provision that the state religion is Islam, must be a Muslim. Elected for a five-year term by an Electoral College consisting of members of the Senate and National Assembly and members of the provincial assemblies, the president is eligible for reelection. But no individual may hold the office for more than two consecutive terms.

The president may resign or be impeached and may be removed from office for incapacity or gross misconduct by a two-thirds vote of the members of the parliament. The president generally acts on the advice of the prime minister but has important residual powers. One of the most important—a legacy of Zia—is contained in the Eighth Amendment which gives the president the power to dissolve the National Assembly "in his discretion where, in his opinion . . . a situation has arisen in which the Government of the Federation cannot be carried on in accordance with the provisions of the Constitution and an appeal to the electorate is necessary."

The Thirteenth Amendment which was passed in 1997, revoked this power. In December 2003, the President's power was partially restored by the Seventeenth Amendment. In April 2004, the Presidency's influence was augmented by an Act of Parliament that established the National Security Council, a body chaired by the President.

### *Prime Minister*

The prime minister is appointed by the members of the National Assembly through a vote. The prime minister is assisted by the Federal Cabinet, a council of ministers whose members are appointed by the president on the advice of the prime minister. The Federal Cabinet comprises the ministers, ministers of state, and advisers.

As of early 1994, there were thirty-three ministerial portfolios: commerce; communications; culture; defense; defense production; education; environment; finance and economic affairs; food and agriculture; foreign affairs; health; housing; information and broadcasting; interior; Kashmiri affairs and Northern Areas; law and justice; local government; minority affairs; narcotics control; parliamentary affairs; petroleum and natural resources production; planning and development; railroads; religious affairs; science and technology; social welfare; special education; sports; state and frontier regions; tourism; water and power; women's development; and youth affairs.

### *Parliament: The Legislative Branch*

The bicameral federal legislature consists of the Senate (upper house) and National Assembly (lower house). According to Article 50 of the Constitution, the National Assembly, the Senate and the President together make up a body known as the Majlis-i-Shoora (Council of Advisers).

Pakistan's democracy has no recall method. However, past governments have been dismissed for corruption by the President's invocation of Article 58 of the Constitution. The President's power to dismiss the Prime Minister and dissolve the National Assembly was removed by the Thirteenth Amendment and partially restored by the Seventeenth Amendment.

### *Senate*

The Senate is a permanent legislative body with equal representation from each of the four provinces, elected by the members of their respective provincial assemblies. There are representatives from the Federally Administered Tribal Areas and from Islamabad Capital Territory. The chairman of the Senate, under the constitution, is next in line to act as president should the office become vacant and until such time as a new president can be formally elected. Both the Senate and the National Assembly can initiate and pass legislation except for finance bills. Only the National Assembly can approve the federal budget and all finance bills. In the case of other bills, the president may prevent passage unless the legislature in joint sitting overrules the president by a majority of members of both houses present and voting. Unlike the National Assembly, the Senate cannot be dissolved by the President.

### *National Assembly*

Members of the National Assembly are elected by universal adult suffrage (over eighteen years of age in Pakistan). Seats are allocated to each of the four provinces, the Federally Administered Tribal Areas, and Islamabad Capital Territory on the basis of population. National Assembly members serve for the parliamentary term, which is five years, unless they die or resign sooner, or unless the National Assembly is dissolved.

Although the vast majority of the members are Muslim, about 5 percent of the seats are reserved for minorities, including Christians, Hindus, and Sikhs. Elections for minority seats are held on the basis of separate electorates at the same time as the polls for Muslim seats during the general elections.

*Federal Offices*

Other offices and bodies having important roles in the federal structure include the attorney general, the auditor general, the Federal Land Commission, the Federal Public Service Commission, the Central Election Commission, and the Wafaqi Mohtasib (Ombudsman).

### *Provincial Governments*

Pakistan subdivides into 4 provinces 1 territory, and 1 capital territory.

1. Balochistan
2. Federally Administered Tribal Areas
3. Islamabad Capital Territory
4. North-West Frontier Province
5. Punjab
6. Sindh

Each province has a Provincial Assembly, a directly-elected legislature. Members are elected for five-year terms. Each

Assembly elects a Chief Minister, who then selects the ministers of his or her cabinet.

Pakistan's four provinces enjoy considerable autonomy. Each province has a governor, a Council of Ministers headed by a chief minister appointed by the governor, and a provincial assembly. Members of the provincial assemblies are elected by universal adult suffrage. Provincial assemblies also have reserved seats for minorities.

Although there is a well-defined division of responsibilities between federal and provincial governments, there are some functions on which both can make laws and establish departments for their execution. Most of the services in areas such as health, education, agriculture, and roads, for example, are provided by the provincial governments. Although the federal government can also legislate in these areas, it only makes national policy and handles international aspects of those services.

### *Local Governments*

Pakistan's provinces are divided into zillas. A zilla is further subdivided into tehsils (roughly equivalent to a borough in an integrated multi-tier (federated) systemic context, such as the one to be found in Montreal and Birmingham or known as arondissements in French context. Tehsils may contain villages or municipalities. Pakistan's system is the one that applies an integrated federated systemic framework most comprehensively, so far.

This methodology is not new to the region,as it is similar to what is referred to as the Panchayat Raj system in India that was introduced by Britain during colonial era. In India it was implemented in some regions and not others; and then allowed to lie fallow. It got new life after the very successful West Bengal revival in the 1970s, which eventually inspired the 1990s Constitutional Amendment making it national policy.

There are over five thousand local governments in Pakistan. Since 2001, the vast majority of these have been led by democratically elected local councils, each headed by a Nazim. Council elections are held every four years.

## Judicial Branch

The judiciary includes the Supreme Court, provincial high courts, and other lesser courts exercising civil and criminal jurisdiction.

### *Supreme Court*

The Supreme Court has original, appellate, and advisory jurisdiction. The Chief Justice of the Supreme Court is appointed by the president; the other Supreme Court judges are appointed by the president after consultation with the chief justice. The chief justice and judges of the Supreme Court may remain in office until age sixty-five.

### *Provincial & High Courts*

Judges of the provincial high courts are appointed by the president after consultation with the chief justice of the Supreme Court, as well as the governor of the province and the chief justice of the high court to which the appointment is being made. High courts have original and appellate jurisdiction.

There is also a Federal Shariat Court consisting of eight Muslim judges, including a chief justice appointed by the president. Three of the judges are ulama, that is, Islamic Scholars, and are well versed in Islamic law. The Federal Shariat Court has original and appellate jurisdiction. This court decides whether any law is repugnant to the injunctions of Islam. When a law is deemed repugnant to Islam, the president, in the case of a federal law, or the governor, in the case of a provincial law, is charged with taking steps to bring the law into conformity with the injunctions of Islam. The court also hears appeals from decisions of criminal courts under laws relating to the enforcement of hudud laws that is, laws pertaining to such offenses as intoxication, theft, and unlawful sexual intercourse.

In addition, there are special courts and tribunals to deal with specific kinds of cases, such as drug courts, commercial courts, labor courts, traffic courts, an insurance appellate tribunal, an income tax appellate tribunal, and special courts for bank offenses. There are also special courts to try terrorists. Appeals from special courts go to high courts except for labor and traffic courts, which have their own forums for appeal. Appeals from the tribunals go to the Supreme Court.

### *Mohtasib*

A further feature of the judicial system is the office of Mohtasib (Ombudsman), which is provided for in the constitution. The office of Mohtasib was established in many early Muslim states to ensure that no wrongs were done to citizens. Appointed by the president, the Mohtasib holds office for four years; the term cannot be extended or renewed.

The Mohtasib's purpose is to institutionalize a system for enforcing administrative accountability, through investigating and rectifying any injustice done to a person through maladministration by a federal agency or a federal government official. The Mohtasib is empowered to award compensation to those who have suffered loss or damage as a result of maladministration.

Excluded from jurisdiction, however, are personal grievances or service matters of a public servant as well as matters relating to foreign affairs, national defense, and the armed services. This institution is designed to bridge the gap between administrator and citizen, to improve administrative processes and procedures, and to help curb misuse of discretionary powers.

## Political Parties

Pakistan has a multi-party system, with numerous parties in which no one party often has a chance of gaining power alone, and parties must work with each other to form coalition governments.

Major parties and coalitions ranked by seats in Parliament are given below:

1. Pakistan Muslim League (Q) (PML Quaid-e-Azam; the party supporting Pervez Musharraf)
2. Pakistan People's Party (PPP) with its parliamentary wing Pakistan People's Party Parliamentarian (PPPP) headed by Benazir Bhutto)
3. Muttahhida Majlis-e-Amal Pakistan (MMA), a coalition of religious parties consisting of the Jamaat-e-Islami (JI), Jamiat Ulema-e-Islam (Assembly of Islamic Clergy), Jamiat Ulema-e-Pakistan (assembly of Pakistani Clergy), and Tehrik-e-Islami
4. Pakistan Muslim League (N) (PML "Nawaz group")
5. Muttahida Qaumi Movement (formerly known as the Muhajir Qaumi Movement, a name is still maintained by one or more splinter groups)

## Factors Affecting Government and politics

Government and politics bear the imprint of Pakistan's diversity. Despite the loss of the country's East Wing in 1971, the body politic remains a varied and volatile mix of ethnic, linguistic, and regional groups, and provincialism and ethnic rivalries continue to impede the progress of national integration. Although Islam is a unifying force, and the majority of Pakistanis are Sunni Muslims, there is considerable cultural diversity within and among the country's four provinces, and coreligionists' identification as Sindhis, Punjabis, Baloch, or Pakhtuns is strong.

### *Regional and Ethnic Factors*

Added to the indigenous human mosaic are the more than 7 million muhajirs (refugees or immigrants from India and their descendants) from various parts of India. Economic and political rivalries persist between the muhajirs and the indigenous populations of the provinces of Pakistan. These contests often turn violent and have contributed significantly to national unrest and instability. Ethnic riots have cost hundreds of lives and destroyed millions of dollars worth of property. A further challenge to national stability results from the approximately 1.4 million Afghan refugees who in early 1994 still had not returned to their country. Linguistic diversity is also a divisive force. Some twenty languages are spoken, and although Urdu is the official language, it is not the native tongue of the majority of the population. Islam provides a tenuous unity in relation to such diversity. Efforts to build national consensus *in the face of these obstacles remains central to effective government in Pakistan.*

### *The Civil Service*

The bureaucracy, particularly the higher civil service, has been a continuing source of stability and leadership and a counterweight to political upheaval and government instability. This cadre originated in the prepartition Indian Civil Service, whose members were well educated, well trained, and dedicated to a tradition of efficiency and responsibility. In time, the British recruited indigenous people, who were among India's best and brightest, into the Indian Civil Service ranks.

At partition, out of more than 1,100 Indian Civil Service officers, scarcely 100 were Muslims, and eighty-three of them opted to go to Pakistan. Because none of them held a senior rank equivalent to that of a secretary (and administrators were urgently needed to staff senior posts in the new state), this initial group was augmented by quick promotions in the Civil Service of Pakistan (CSP) through ad hoc appointments from other services and through retention, for a time, of some British officers. The CSP prided itself on being the backbone of the nation, the "steel frame" as it was sometimes called, and played a key role in Pakistan's survival in the difficult years following independence.

Although Jinnah commended its contribution, he also warned CSP cadres to stay out of politics and to discharge their duties as public servants. After Jinnah's death, however, in the subsequent absence of strong political leadership, members of the CSP assumed an extraordinary role in the country's policy-making process. When the CSP was disbanded in 1973 and the various services were amalgamated into one administrative system, the expertise of its former members was much valued, and they continued to hold critical positions in the country's administrative apparatus through subsequent transitions in government. It is not surprising, then, that a later president of Pakistan, Ghulam Ishaq Khan (1988-93) was once a member of the CSP.

### *The Military*

Another significant aspect of Pakistan's political legacy is its military forces and, in particular, the role of the largest of these forces, the army. The military remains one of the country's most cohesive national institutions. Since independence it has oscillated between indirect and direct political control, remaining a major power.

The military's sense of mission in defending and preserving the Islamic state of Pakistan has always been strong. For Muslim members of the British Indian Army, the transfer of loyalties from the colonial to the ideological state was not difficult. Successors to the historical legacy of the Muslim armies of the once powerful Mughal Empire, Muslim soldiers could relate to a new role of protecting the faith and the state embodied in Pakistan. The military also provided alternative political leadership in times of crisis. Military regimes in Pakistan have legitimated their actions by the doctrine of necessity, stepping in temporarily when political crises have reached a deadlock and threatened the state.

# Part III. Bangladesh

# 11

# HISTORY

Bangladesh became one of the youngest major nation states following a pair of twentieth century secessions from India (1947) and Pakistan (1971). The region's history combines Indo-Aryan, Assamese, Munda, Dravidian, Mughal, Persian, Turkic and British influences. Bangladesh's territory became part of the state of Bengal as part of the Mughal Empire for two centuries and also during the succeeding two centuries of British rule. During the twentieth century, its resilient inhabitants seem to have suffered one trauma after another. Sheikh Mujibur Rahman (Mujib) led the nation to independence in 1971, but he and his successor Ziaur Rahman (Zia) were both assassinated only in a span of six years. Their legacies (and families) define Bangladesh's faltering democracy to this day.

## Ancient Period

Remnants of civilization in the greater Bengal region date back three millennia. From the sixth century BCE, much of Bengal was a part of the powerful kingdom of Magadha, which was an ancient Indo-Aryan kingdom of ancient India, mentioned in both the Ramayana and the Mahabharata. It was also one of the four main kingdoms of India at the time of Buddha, having risen to power during the reigns of Bimbisara (c. 544-491 BCE) and his son Ajatashatru

(c. 491-460 BCE). Magadha spanned to include most of Bihar and much of Bengal.

Magadha formed one of the sixteen Maha Janapadas (Sanskrit, "great country"). The Magadha Empire included republican communities such as Rajakumara. Villages had their own assemblies under their local chiefs called Gramakas. Their administrations were divided into executive, judicial, and military functions. Bimbisara was friendly to both Jainism and Buddhism and suspended tolls at the river ferries for all ascetics after the Buddha was once stopped at the Ganges River for lack of money.

In 326 BCE, the army of Alexander the Great approached the boundaries of the Magadha Empire. The army, exhausted and frightened by the prospect of facing another giant Indian army at the Ganges River, mutinied at the Hyphasis (modern Beas) and refused to march further East. Alexander, after the meeting with his officer, Coenus, was convinced that it was better to return.

Magadha was the seat of the Maurya Empire, founded by Chandragupta Maurya, which extended over nearly all of South Asia and parts of Persia and Afghanistan under Ashoka the Great; and, later, of the powerful Gupta Empire, which extended over the northern Indian subcontinent and parts of Persia and Afghanistan. Mauryan artifacts from Bogra date back to the third and second centuries BCE.

Greek and Roman writings refer to the Bengal as Gangaridai (Land of the Ganges) between the third century BCE and first century CE.

### Early Medieval Period

The name Bengal may have been derived from the Vanga, one of several early tribes in the region. By the sixth century, the Gupta Empire ruling over the northern Indian subcontinent was largely broken up. Eastern Bengal became the Vanga kingdom while the Gauda king Shashanka rose in the west, and vied for regional power with northern India. But this burst of Bengali power did not last beyond his death, as Bengal descended afterwards into a period marked by disunity and foreign invasion.

The first independent Buddhist king of Bengal, Gopala I came to power in 750 in Gaur by democratic election. Gopala founded the Buddhist Pala dynasty which lasted for four centuries (750-1120 AD), ushering in a period of relative stability and prosperity. At its peak, under Dharmapala the empire extended into much of Bihar and once more wrestled for control of the subcontinent. The Pala empire did not extend into southeastern Bengal which saw several independent dynasties and kingdoms during this time including the Khadgas, Devas, Harikela and Varmans. The east and west would come under one ruler only during the twelfth century Sena dynasty. The Sena dynasty brought a revival of Hinduism and cultivated Sanskrit literature.

## Arrival of Islam

Islam made its first appearance in Bengal during the twelfth century AD when Sufi missionaries arrived. Later occasional Muslim invaders reinforced the process of conversion by building mosques, madrassas and Sufi Khanqahs. Beginning in 1202 a military commander from the Delhi Sultanate, Ikhtiar Uddin Muhammad bin Bakhtiar Khilji, overran Bihar and Bengal as far east as Rangpur, Bogra and the Brahmaputra River.

The defeated Laksmanasena and his two sons moved to a place then called Vikramapura (south of Dhaka), where their diminished dominion lasted until the late thirteenth century. The period after Bakhtiar Khilji's death in 1206 devolved into infighting among the Khiljis - representative of a pattern of succession struggles and intra-empire intrigues during later Turkish regimes. Ghiyasuddin Iwaz Khalji prevailed and extended the Sultan's domain south to

Jessore and made the eastern Bang province a tributary. The capital was made at Lakhnauti on the Ganges near the older Bengal capital of Gaur. Two Turkish attempts to push east of the broad Jamuna and Brahmaputra rivers were repulsed, but a third led by Mughisuddin Tughral conquered the Sonargaon area south of Dhaka to Faridpur, bringing the Sena Kingdom officially to an end by 1277.

Bengal was sufficiently remote from Delhi that its governors would declare independence on occasion, styling themselves as Sultans of Bengal. It was Iliyas Shah who would make that title last, founding an independent dynasty that lasted from 1342-1487 which successfully repulsed attempts by Delhi to reign them in. They continued to reel in the territory of modern-day Bengal, reaching to Khulna in the south and Sylhet in the east.

The sultans advanced civic institutions and became more responsive and "native" in their outlook, having cut loose from Delhi. Considerable architectural projects were completed in Gaur including the massive Adina Mosque and the 1479 Darasbari Mosque which still stands in Bangladesh near the border. The Sultans of Bangalah were patrons of Bengali literature and began a process in which a common Bengali culture and identity would coalesce.

The Iliyas Shahi dynasty gave way to a similar Husain Shahi dynasty that ruled from 1494-1538. Its domain extended all the way to the port of Chittagong, which witnessed the arrival of the first Portuguese merchants. The Sultan of Bengal, which continued to rule from Gaur, had to contend with rising Afghan activity on his northwestern border. Eventually the Afghans broke through and sacked the capital in 1538 where they remained for several decades until the arrival of the Mughals. Their most impressive achievement was Sher Shah's construction of the Grand Trunk Road connecting Sonargaon, Delhi and Peshawar.

## Mughal Period

Bengal came once more under the suzerainty of Delhi as the Mughals conquered it in 1576. Not far from Sonargaon, Dhaka rose from the mists of obscurity as a Mughal provincial capital. But it remained remote and thus a difficult to govern region—especially the section east of the Brahmaputra River—outside the mainstream of Mughal politics. The Bengali ethnic and linguistic identity further cystallized during this period, since the whole of Bengal was united under an able and long-lasting administration. Furthermore its inhabitants were given sufficient autonomy to cultivate their own customs and literature.

The Mughal onslaught against the Afghan Sultan began with the battle of Rajmahal in 1576, led by Khan Jahan. In 1612, during Emperor Jahangir's reign, the defeat of Sylhet completed the Mughal conquest of Bengal, except for Chittagong. At this time the capital was established at Dhaka. Chittagong was later annexed in order to stifle Arakanese raids from the east. During the great Aurangzeb's reign, the local Nawab made the haunting mistake of selling three villages, including one then known as Kalikata, to the British. A well-known Dhaka landmark, Lalbagh Fort was built during Aurangzeb's sovereignty as well.

History repeated itself as the frontier Bengal province broke off from a Delhi-based empire around the time Aurangzeb's death in 1707. Murshid Quli Khan ended Dhaka's century of grandeur as he shifted the capital to Murshidabad ushering in a series of independent Bengal Nawabs.

## British Rule

Portuguese traders and missionaries were the first Europeans to reach Bengal in the latter part of the fifteenth century. They were followed by representatives of the

Dutch, the French, and the British East India Company. Calcutta was in fact Britain's initial foothold on the Indian subcontinent and remained a focal point of their activity. The British gradually extended their commercial contacts and administrative control beyond Calcutta to the rest of Bengal.

The British East India Company gained official control of Bengal following the Battle of Plassey in 1757. This was the first conquest, in a series of engagements that ultimately lead to the expulsion of other European competitors, the defeat of the Mughals and the consolidation of the subcontinent under the rule of a corporation — a doubly unique event. Calcutta (nowadays Kolkata) on the Hooghly became a major trading port for the Muslin and Jute produced in Dhaka and the rest of Bengal.

Scandals and the bloody rebellion known as the Sepoy Mutiny prompted the British government to intervene in the affairs of the East India Company. In 1858, authority in India was transferred from the Company to the crown and the rebellion was brutally surpressed. Rule of India was organized under a Viceroy and continued a pattern of economic exploitation.

Famine racked the subcontinent many times, including at least two major famines in Bengal. The British Raj was politically organized into seventeen Provinces—of which Bengal was one of the most significant—most headed by a Governor. For a brief period in the early twentieth century, an abortive attempt was made to divide Bengal into two zones, West Bengal and East Bengal & Assam.

### Creation of Pakistan

As the independence movement throughout British-controlled India began in the late nineteenth century gained momentum during the twentieth century, Bengali politicians played an active role in Gandhi's Congress Party and Jinnah's Muslim League, exposing the opposing forces of ethnic and religious nationalism. By exploiting the latter, the British probably intended to distract the independence movement, for example by partitioning Bengal in 1905 along religious lines (the split only lasted for seven years). At first the Muslim League sought only to ensure minority rights in the future nation. But after faring poorly in the 1936 elections, in 1940 Jinnah shifted decisively towards the idea of a separate Islamic Pakistan.

Non-negotiable was the inclusion of the Muslim parts of Punjab and Bengal in this new state. The stakes grew as a new Viceroy Mountbatten was appointed expressly for the purpose of effecting a graceful British exit. Communal violence in Noakhali and Calcutta sparked a surge in support for the Muslim League, which won a majority of Bengal's Muslim seats in 1946. Accusations have been made that Hindu and Muslim nationalist instigators were involved in the latter incident.

British India was partitioned and the independent states of India and Pakistan were created in 1947; the region of Bengal was divided along religious lines. The predominantly Muslim eastern half of Bengal became the East Bengal (later renamed East Pakistan) state of Pakistan and the predominantly Hindu western part became the Indian state of West Bengal.

Pakistan's history from 1947 to 1971 was marked by political instability and economic difficulties. In 1956 a constitution was at last adopted, making the country an "Islamic republic within the Commonwealth". The nascent democratic institutions foundered in the face of military intervention in 1958, and the government imposed martial law between 1958 and 1962, and again between 1969 and 1971.

Almost from the advent of independent Pakistan in 1947, frictions developed between East and West Pakistan, which were separated by more than 1,000 miles of Indian territory. East Pakistanis felt exploited by the West Pakistan-dominated central government. Linguistic, cultural, and ethnic differences also contributed to the estrangement of East from West Pakistan.

When Mohammad Ali Jinnah died in September 1948, Khwaja Nazimuddin became the Governor General of Pakistan while Nurul Amin was appointed the Chief Minister of East Bengal. Nurul Amin continued as the Chief Minister of East Bengal until 2 April 1954. The abolition of the Zamindari system in East Bengal (1950) and the Language Movement were two most important events during his tenure.

## The Language Movement

The Language Movement began in 1948 and reached its climax in the killings of 21 February 1952, and ended in the adoption of Bangla as one of the state languages of Pakistan. The question as to what would be the state language of Pakistan was raised immediately after its creation.

The central leaders and the Urdu-speaking intellectuals of Pakistan declared that Urdu would be the state language of Pakistan, just as Hindi was the state language of India. Bengalis strongly resisted attempts to impose Urdu as the sole official language of Pakistan. The students and intellectuals of East Pakistan, however, demanded that Bangla be made one of the state languages, which was the native language of the majority (54% native speakers as opposed to 7% native Urdu speakers) in the whole of Pakistan anyway.

After a lot of controversy over the language issue, the final demand from East Pakistan was that Bangla must be the official language and the medium of instruction in East Pakistan and for the central government it would be one of the state languages along with Urdu. The first movement on this issue was mobilised by Tamaddun Majlish headed by Professor Abul Kashem. Gradually many other non-communal and progressive organisations joined the movement, which finally turned into a mass movement.

**Political Situation: 1954 - 1970**

The first election for East Bengal Provincial Assembly was held between 8 March and 12 March 1954. The Awami Muslim League, krishak sramik party and nezam-e-Islam formed the United Front, on the basis of 21-points agenda.

Notable pledges contained in the 21-points were:

making Bangla one of the state languages

— autonomy for the province

— reforms in education

— independence of the judiciary

— making the legislative assembly effective, etc.

The United Front won 215 out of 237 Muslim seats in the election. The ruling Muslim League got only nine seats. Khilafat-E-Rabbani Party got one, while the independents got twelve seats. Later, seven independent members joined the United Front while one joined the Muslim League.

There were numerous reasons for the debacle of the Muslim League. Above all, the Muslim League regime angered all sections of the people of Bengal by opposing the demand for recognition of Bangla as one of the state languages and by ordering the massacre of 1952.

The United Front got the opportunity to form the provincial government after winning absolute majority in the 1954 election. Of the 222 United Front seats, the Awami Muslim League had won 142, Krishak-Sramik Party forty eight, Nezam-i-Islam nineteen and Ganatantri Dal thirteen.

The major leaders of the United Front were Huseyn Shaheed Suhrawardy and Maulana Abdul Hamid Khan

Bhasani of Awami Muslim League and AK Fazlul Huq of Krishak-Sramik Party. Suhrawardy and Bhasani did not take part in the election and Fazlul Huq was invited to form the government. But a rift surfaced at the very outset on the question of formation of the cabinet. The unity and solidarity among the component parties of the United Front soon evaporated. Finally, on 15 May, Fazlul Huq arrived at an understanding with the Awami Muslim League and formed a 14-member cabinet with five members from that party.

But this cabinet lasted for only fourteen days. The Muslim League could not concede defeat in the elections in good grace. So, they resorted to conspiracies to dismiss the United Front government. In the third week of May, there were bloody riots between Bengali and non-Bengali workers in different mills and factories of East Bengal. The United Front government was blamed for failing to control the law and order situation in the province.

Fazlul Huq was then quoted in an interview taken by the New York Times correspondent John P Callaghan and published in a distorted form that he wanted the independence of East Bengal. Finally, on 29 May 1954, the United Front government was dismissed by the central government and Governor's rule was imposed in the province, which lasted till 2 June 1955.

Curiously enough within two months of his sacking, Fazlul Huq was appointed the central Home Minister. As Home Minister, Fazlul Huq utilised his influence to bring his party to power in East Bengal. Naturally, the United Front broke up. The Muslim members of the United Front split into two groups. In 1955 the Awami Muslim League adopted the path of secularism and non-communalism, erased the word 'Muslim' from its nomenclature and adopted the name of Awami League.

Great differences began developing between the two wings of Pakistan. While the west had a minority share of

Pakistan's total population, it had the maximum share of revenue allocation, industrial development, agricultural reforms and civil development projects. Pakistan's military and civil services were dominated by the fair-skinned, Persian-cultured Punjabis and Afghans. Only one regiment in the Pakistani Army was Bengali. And many Bengali Pakistanis could not share the natural enthusiasm for the Kashmir issue, which they felt was leaving East Pakistan more vulnerable and threatened as a result.

## Bangladesh Liberation War

After the Awami League won all the East Pakistan seats of the Pakistan's National Assembly in the 1970-71 elections, West Pakistan opened talks with the East on constitutional questions about the division of power between the central government and the provinces, as well as the formation of a national government headed by the Awami League.

The talks proved unsuccessful, however, and on March 1, 1971, Pakistani President Yahya Khan indefinitely postponed the pending national assembly session, precipitating massive civil disobedience in East Pakistan.

After the military crackdown by the Pakistan army since the night of March 25, 1971 Sheikh Mujibur Rahman was arrested and the political leaders dispersed, mostly fleeing to neighbouring India where they organized a provisional government afterwards. The people were at a loss. At this crucial moment with a sudden forced political vacuum, the Eighth East Bengal Regiment under the leadership of Major Ziaur Rahman revolted against the Pakistan Army and took up the Bangladesh flag as its mainstay on the night of March 26 - March 27, 1971. Major Zia declared the independence of Bangladesh.

As fighting grew between the army and the Bengali Mukti Bahini ("freedom fighters"), an estimated ten million Bengalis, mainly Hindus, sought refuge in the Indian states of Assam, Tripura and West Bengal.

The crisis in East Pakistan produced new strains in Pakistan's troubled relations with India. The two nations had fought a war in 1965, mainly in the west, but the refugee pressure in India in the fall of 1971 produced new tensions in the east. Indian sympathies lay with East Pakistan, and on December 3, 1971, India intervened on the side of the Bangladeshis. On December 16, 1971, Pakistani forces surrendered, and Bangladesh ("Country of Bangla") was finally established the following day. The new country changed its name to Bangladesh on January 11, 1972 and became a parliamentary democracy under a constitution. Shortly thereafter on March 19 Bangladesh signed a friendship treaty with India.

## Post-Independence Period

In January 1975 economic and political difficulties led to Sheikh Mujib's assumption of the presidencey with greatly increased powers. On August 15, 1975, he was killed in a military coup.

Following two further coups (November 3 and November 6), Major General Ziaur Rahman emerged as de facto ruler, assuming the presidency in April 1977. In May 1981, Zia in turn fell victim to a failed coup attempt; ten months later, on March 24, 1982, Lt. General Hossain Mohammad Ershad took power, holding office until his resignation (December 6, 1990) amid corruption allegations.

Democracy was restored in 1991. The Bangladesh Nationalist Party (BNP) of Khaleda Zia, General Zia's widow, won power in the elections held in February 1991. The next election in June 1996 was won by the rival Awami League under Mujib's daughter Sheikh Hasina. In 2001, a four-party alliance including Khaleda Zia's BNP and Jamaat-e-Islami, returned to power after a landslide victory in the polls.

# 12

# GEOGRAPHY

Bangladesh is a low-lying, riverine country located in South Asia with a largely marshy jungle coastline of 710 kilometers (440 mi) on the northern littoral of the Bay of Bengal. Formed by a deltaic plain at the confluence of the Ganges (Padma), Brahmaputra (Jamuna), and Meghna Rivers and their tributaries, Bangladesh's alluvial soil is highly fertile, but vulnerable to flood and drought. Hills rise above the plain only in the Chittagong Hill Tracts in the far southeast and the Sylhet division in the northeast.

Straddling the Tropic of Cancer, Bangladesh has a tropical monsoonal climate characterized by heavy seasonal rainfall, high temperatures, and high humidity. Natural calamities, such as floods, tropical cyclones, tornadoes, and tidal bores affect the country almost every year. Bangladesh also is affected by major cyclones—on average 16 times a decade. One cyclone struck the southeastern coast in May 1991, killing 136,000 people.

## Physiography

The physiography of Bangladesh is characterized by two distinctive features: a broad deltaic plain subject to frequent flooding, and a small hilly region crossed by swiftly flowing rivers. The country has an area of 144,000 square kilometers and extends 820 kilometers north to south and 600 kilometers east to west. Bangladesh is bordered on the west, north, and east by a 2,400-kilometer land frontier with India and, in the southeast, by a short land and water frontier (193 km) with Burma (Myanmar). On the south is a highly irregular deltaic coastline of about 600 kilometers, fissured by many rivers and streams flowing into the Bay of Bengal. The territorial waters of Bangladesh extend 12 nautical miles, and the exclusive economic zone of the country is 200 nautical miles (370 km).

Roughly 80 % of the landmass is made up of fertile alluvial lowland called the Bangladesh Plain. The plain is part of the larger Plain of Bengal, which is sometimes called the Lower Gangetic Plain. Although altitudes up to 105 meters above sea level occur in the northern part of the plain, most elevations are less than 10 meters above sea level; elevations decrease in the coastal south, where the terrain is generally at sea level. With such low elevations and numerous rivers, water—and concomitant flooding—is a predominant physical feature. About 10,000 square kilometers of the total area of Bangladesh is covered with water, and larger areas are routinely flooded during the monsoon season.

The only exceptions to Bangladesh's low elevations are the Chittagong Hills in the southeast, the Low Hills of Sylhet in the northeast, and highlands in the north and northwest. The Chittagong Hills constitute the only significant hill system in the country and, in effect, are the western fringe of the northsouth mountain ranges of Burma and eastern India. The Chittagong Hills rise steeply to narrow ridge lines, generally no wider than 36 meters, with altitudes from 600 to 900 meters above sea level. At 1,046 meters altitude, the highest elevation in Bangladesh is found at Keokradong, in the southeastern part of the hills. Fertile valleys lie between the hill lines, which generally run north-south. West of the Chittagong Hills is a broad plain, cut by rivers draining into the Bay of Bengal, that rises to a final chain of low coastal hills, mostly below 200 meters, that attain a maximum elevation of 350 meters. West of these hills is a narrow, wet coastal plain located between the cities of Chittagong in the north and Cox's Bazar in the south.

About 67 % of Bangladesh's nonurban land is arable. Permanent crops cover only 2 %, meadows and pastures cover 4 %, and forests and woodland cover about 16 %. The country produces large quantities of quality timber, bamboo; and sugarcane. Bamboo grows in almost all areas, but high-quality timber grows mostly in the highland valleys. Rubber planting in the hilly regions of the country was undertaken in the 1980s, and rubber extraction had started by the end of the decade. A variety of wild animals are found in the forest areas, such as in the Sundarbans on the southwest coast, which is the home of the worldfamous Royal Bengal Tiger. The alluvial soils in the Bangladesh Plain are generally fertile and are enriched with heavy silt deposits carried downstream during the rainy season.

## Climate

Bangladesh has a tropical monsoon climate characterized by wide seasonal variations in rainfall, high temperatures, and high humidity. Regional climatic differences in this flat country are minor. Three seasons are generally recognized: a hot, muggy summer from March to June; a hot, humid and rainy monsoon season from June to November; and a warm-hot, dry winter from December to February. In general, maximum summer temperatures range between 38 and 41 °C. April is the hottest month in most parts of the country. January is the coolest (but still hot) month, when the average temperature for most of the country is 26-30 °C during the day and around 20°C at night.

Winds are mostly from the north and northwest in the winter, blowing gently at one to three kilometers per hour in northern and central areas and three to six kilometers per hour near the coast. From March to May, violent thunderstorms, called northwesters by local English speakers, produce winds of up to 60 kilometers per hour. During the intense storms of the early summer and late monsoon season, southerly winds of more than 160 kilometers per hour cause waves to crest as high as 6 meters in the Bay of Bengal, which brings disastrous flooding to coastal areas.

Heavy rainfall is characteristic of Bangladesh. With the exception of the relatively dry western region of Rajshahi, where the annual rainfall is about 1600 mm, most parts of the country receive at least 2300 mm of rainfall per year. Because of its location just south of the foothills of the Himalayas, where monsoon winds turn west and northwest, the region of Sylhet in northeastern Bangladesh receives the greatest average precipitation. From 1977 to 1986, annual rainfall in that region ranged between 3280 and 4780 mm per year. Average daily humidity ranged from March lows of between 55 and 81 % to July highs of between 94 and 100 %, based on readings taken at selected stations nationwide in 1986.

About 80 % of Bangladesh's rain falls during the monsoon season. The monsoons result from the contrasts between low and high air pressure areas that result from differential heating of land and water. During the hot months of April and May hot air rises over the Indian subcontinent, creating low-pressure areas into which rush cooler, moisture-bearing winds from the Indian Ocean. This is the southwest monsoon, commencing in June and usually lasting through September.

Dividing against the Indian landmass, the monsoon flows in two branches, one of which strikes western India. The other travels up the Bay of Bengal and over eastern India and Bangladesh, crossing the plain to the north and northeast before being turned to the west and northwest by the foothills of the Himalayas.

Natural calamities, such as floods, tropical cyclones, tornadoes, and tidal bores—destructive waves or floods caused by flood tides rushing up estuaries—ravage the country, particularly the coastal belt, almost every year. Between 1947 and 1988, 13 severe cyclones hit Bangladesh, causing enormous loss of life and property.

In May 1985, for example, a severe cyclonic storm packing 154 kilometer-per-hour winds and waves 4 meters high swept into southeastern and southern Bangladesh, killing more than 11,000 persons, damaging more than 94,000 houses, killing some 135,000 head of livestock, and damaging nearly 400 kilometers of critically needed embankments.

Annual monsoon flooding results in the loss of human life, damage to property and communication systems, and a shortage of drinking water, which leads to the spread of disease. For example, in 1988 two thirds of Bangladesh's 64 districts experienced extensive flood damage in the wake of unusually heavy rains that flooded the river systems. Millions were left homeless and without potable water.

Half of Dhaka, including the runways at the Zia International Airport—an important transit point for disaster relief supplies—was flooded. About 2 million tons of crops were reported destroyed, and relief work was rendered even more challenging than usual because the flood made transportation of any kind exceedingly difficult. A tornado in April 1989 killed more than 600 people.

There are no precautions against cyclones and tidal bores except giving advance warning and providing safe public buildings where people may take shelter. Adequate infrastructure and air transport facilities that would ease the sufferings of the affected people had not been established by the late 1980s. Efforts by the government under the Third Five-Year Plan (1985-90) were directed toward accurate and timely forecast capability through agrometeorology, marine meteorology, oceanography, hydrometeorology, and seismology. Necessary expert services, equipment, and training facilities were expected to be developed under the United Nations Development Programme.

## River Systems

The rivers of Bangladesh mark both the physiography of the nation and the life of the people. About 700 in number, these rivers generally flow south. The larger rivers serve as the main source of water for cultivation and as the principal arteries of commercial transportation. Rivers also provide fish, an important source of protein.

Flooding of the rivers during the monsoon season causes enormous hardship and hinders development, but fresh deposits of rich silt replenish the fertile but overworked soil. The rivers also drain excess monsoon rainfall into the Bay of Bengal. Thus, the great river system is at the same time the country's principal resource and its greatest hazard.

The profusion of rivers can be divided into five major networks. The Jamuna-Brahmaputra is 292 kilometers long and extends from northern Bangladesh to its confluence with the Padma. Originating as the Yarlung Zangbo Jiang in China's Xizang Autonomous Region (Tibet) and flowing through India's state of Arunachal Pradesh, where it becomes known as the Brahmaputra (Son of Brahma), it receives waters from five major tributaries that total some 740 kilometers in length. At the point where the Brahmaputra meets the Tista River in Bangladesh, it becomes known as the Jamuna. The Jamuna is notorious for its shifting subchannels and for the formation of fertile silt islands (chars). No permanent settlements can exist along its banks.

The second system is the Padma-Ganges, which is divided into two sections: a 258-kilometer segment, the

Ganges, which extends from the western border with India to its confluence with the Jamuna some 72 kilometers west of Dhaka, and a 126-kilometer segment, the Padma, which runs from the Ganges-Jamuna confluence to where it joins the Meghna River at Chandpur. The Padma-Ganges is the central part of a deltaic river system with hundreds of rivers and streams—some 2,100 kilometers in length—flowing generally east or west into the Padma.

The third network is the Surma-Meghna system, which courses from the northeastern border with India to Chandpur, where it joins the Padma. The Surma-Meghna, at 669 kilometers by itself the longest river in Bangladesh, is formed by the union of six lesser rivers. Below the city of Kalipur it is known as the Meghna. When the Padma and Meghna join together, they form the fourth river system—the Padma-Meghna—which flows 145 kilometers to the Bay of Bengal.

This mighty network of four river systems flowing through the Bangladesh Plain drains an area of some 1.5 million square kilometers. The numerous channels of the Padma-Meghna, its distributaries, and smaller parallel rivers that flow into the Bay of Bengal are referred to as the Mouths of the Ganges. Like the Jamuna, the Padma-Meghna and other estuaries on the Bay of Bengal are also known for their many chars.

A fifth river system, unconnected to the other four, is the Karnaphuli. Flowing through the region of Chittagong and the Chittagong Hills, it cuts across the hills and runs rapidly downhill to the west and southwest and then to the sea. The Feni, Karnaphuli, Sangu, and Matamuhari—an aggregate of some 420 kilometers—are the main rivers in the region. The port of Chittagong is situated on the banks of the Karnaphuli. The Karnaphuli Reservoir and Karnaphuli Dam are located in this area. The dam impounds the Karnaphuli River's waters in the reservoir for the generation of hydroelectric power.

During the annual monsoon period, the rivers of Bangladesh flow at about 140,000 cubic meters per second, but during the dry period they diminish to 7,000 cubic meters per second. Because water is so vital to agriculture, more than 60 % of the net arable land, some 91,000 km², is cultivated in the rainy season despite the possibility of severe flooding, and nearly 40 % of the land is cultivated during the dry winter months.

Water resources development has responded to this "dual water regime" by providing flood protection, drainage to prevent overflooding and waterlogging, and irrigation facilities for the expansion of winter cultivation. Major water control projects have been developed by the national government to provide irrigation, flood control, drainage facilities, aids to river navigation and road construction, and hydroelectric power. In addition, thousands of tube wells and electric pumps are used for local irrigation. Despite severe resource constraints, the government of Bangladesh has made it a policy to try to bring additional areas under irrigation without salinity intrusion.

Water resources management, including gravity flow irrigation, flood control, and drainage, were largely the responsibility of the Bangladesh Water Development Board. Other public sector institutions, such as the Bangladesh Krishi Bank, the Bangladesh Rural Development Board, the Bangladesh Bank, and the Bangladesh Agricultural Development Corporation were also responsible for promotion and development of minor irrigation works in the private sector through government credit mechanisms.

# 13

# SOCIETY AND CULTURE

The culture of Bangladesh has a unique history, dating back more than 2500 years ago. The land, the rivers and the lives of the common people formed a rich heritage with marked differences from neighboring regions. It has evolved over the centuries, and encompasses the cultural diversity of several social groups of Bangladesh.

The culture of Bangladesh is composite, and over centuries has assimilated influences of Hinduism, Jainism, Buddhism, and Islam. It is manifested in various forms, including music, dance and drama; art and craft; folklores and folktales; languages and literature, philosophy and religion, festivals and celebrations, as also in a distinct cuisine and culinary tradition.

## Religion in Bangladesh

Bangladesh is ethnically homogeneous, with Bengalis comprising 98% of the population. Most Bangladeshis (about 83%) are Muslims, but Hindus constitute a sizable (16%) minority. There are also a small number of Buddhists, Christians, and Animists.

Muslims constitute 88 percent of the population of Bangladesh, most of them Sunnis. The remainder of the population follow Hinduism (11%), Buddhism and

Christianity. There are also small populations of Sikhs, Bahá'ís, animists and Ahmadis. Religion has always been a strong part of identity, but this has varied at different times. A survey in late 2003 confirmed that religion is the first choice by a citizen for self-identification; atheism is extremely rare.

### *Islam*

The large scale conversion to Islam of the population of what was to become Bangladesh began in the thirteenth century and continued for hundreds of years. Conversion was generally collective rather than individual, although individual Hindus who became outcastes or who were ostracized for any reason often became Muslims. Islamic egalitarianism, especially the ideals of equality, brotherhood, and social justice, attracted numerous Buddhists and lower caste Hindus. Muslim missionaries were responsible for most conversions.

Most Muslims in Bangladesh are Sunnis, but there is a small Shi'a community. Most of those who are Shi'a reside in urban areas. Although these Shi'as are few in number, Shi'a observance commemorating the martyrdom of Ali's sons, Hasan and Husayn, is widely observed by the nation's Sunnis.

### *Hinduism*

Hinduism is the second largest religious affiliation in Bangladesh, covering about 10.5% of the population as of 1991 census. Bangladeshi Hinduism closely resembles the forms and customs of Hinduism practised in neighbouring West Bengal, with which Bangladesh was united until the partition of India in 1947.

### *Buddhism*

About 0.5% of Bangladesh population adheres to the

Theravada school of Buddhism. Most of the practitioners are from the south-eastern district of Chittagong and Chittagong Hill Tracts.

Most of the followers of Buddhism in Bangladesh live in the south-eastern region, especially in the Chittagong district. Also, there are people of Arakanese descent living in the sub-tropical Chittagong Hill Tracts. Most of these people belong to the Chakma, Chak, Marma, Tenchungya and the Khyang, who since time immemorial have practiced Buddhism. Other tribals, notably those who practice Animism, have come under some Buddhist influence, and this is true in the case of the Khumi and the Mru, and to a lesser extent on the other tribals.

Bangladesh has a unique place in the history of Buddhism, mainly for two reasons. Firstly, Bengal was the last stronghold of Indian Buddhism where it could survive as a socio-cultural force until the 12th century, despite its disappearance from other parts of the Indian subcontinent. Secondly, it is generally claimed that Bengal was the home of a form of Buddhism, namely, the Tantric Buddhism. Tantric Buddhism is a later development in Bengal and therefore it remains to be seen what specific factors are responsible for turning the pure form of Buddhism into tantricism and whether the mystic and esoteric practices in the Buddhism of Bangladesh are of distinctively Bengali origin.

## Langauge

Bangla or Bengali is an Indo-Aryan language of East South Asia, evolved from Sanskrit and Prakrit. The traditional English rendering is "Bengali", but recently the rendering "Bangla" has been gaining currency in English. With nearly 200 million native speakers, Bangla is one of the most widely spoken languages of the world. Bangla is the second most commonly spoken language in India. Along with

Assamese, it is geographically the most eastern of the Indo-European languages.

Owing to the Bengal renaissance in the 19th and 20th centuries, Bangla literature emerged among the richest in South Asia, and includes luminaries such as Rabindranath Tagore, the first Asian to be awarded a Nobel Prize.

## Literature

The first evidence of Bangla literature is Charyapada or Charyageeti, buddhist hymns or dohas from the 8th century. Iswarchandra Bandyopadhyaya (popularly known as "Vidyasagar" which means 'ocean of knowledge') was mainly known as a social reformer. But his contribution to the Bengali literature also plays a significant role. He laid the foundation of modern Bengali language.

Vidysagar realized the need of educating women in the society. With his tireless effort to uplift the status of women in the society, he was able to establish some Girl's schools in different places of Bengal. But there was no good Bengali text book for basic Bengali education. He wrote Bengali books with basic language construct and fundamentals, like, "Barnaparichay", "Bodhoday", "Kathamala" etc. and then easy grammar books like "Upakramonika" and "Byakaron Kaumudi". He also introduced some basic books for Mathematical logic. Rabindranath Tagore called him as the father of modern Bengali language. Vidyasagar translated some masterpieces of Sanskrit and English literature into Bengali

Possibly the most prolific writer in Bangla is Nobel laureate Rabindranath Tagore. Tagore dominated both the Bengali and Indian philosophical and literary scene for decades. His 2,000 Rabindrasangeets play a pivotal part in defining Bengali culture, both in West Bengal and Bangladesh. He is the author of the national anthems of both India and Bangladesh, both composed in Bangla. Other notable Bangla works of his are Gitanjali, a book of poems for which he was awarded the Nobel Prize for Literature in 1913, and many short stories and a few novels.

In a similar category is Kazi Nazrul Islam, a Muslim who was invited to post-partition Bangladesh as the National Poet and whose work transcends sectarian boundaries. Adored by Bengalis both in Bangladesh and West Bengal, his work includes 3,000 songs, known as both as nazrul geeti and "nazrul sangeet". He is frequently called the rebel poet mainly because of his most famous and electrifying poem "Bidrohi" or "The Rebel", and also because of his strong sympathy and support for revolutionary activities leading to India's independence from British Rule. His songs and poems were frequently used during the Bangladesh Liberation War as well.

Michael Madhusudan Dutt, a Christian by conversion, is best known for his Ramayana-based masterpiece, "The Slaying of Meghnadh,", which essentially follows in the poetic tradition of Milton's Paradise Lost. Those who have read it consider this work a world-class epic poem of the modern era. Michael Madhusudan Dutta is also credited with the introduction of sonnets to Bangla literature.

Parichand Mitra, a 19th century author, is widely considered to be the first Bengali novelist for his novel "Alaler Ghore Dulal". Bankim Chandra Chattopadhyay , another 19th century author, was also one of the earliest and leading Bengali novelists and is popularly known as the author of India's first national song, "Bande Matarom". Sarat Chandra Chattopadhyay was one of the most popular novelists of early 20th century whose speciality was exploring complex human psychology and drama. Tarashankar Bandopadhay was another famous novelist whose works feature a realistic picture of the many-colored fabric of life in rural Bengal in a pioneering modernish style of prose in fiction.

Jibanananda Das was a famous poet who, along with Buddhadev Basu, marks the beginning of the move to transcend the Tagore legacy. The new genere of Bengali poets departed considerably from Tagore's ideological style and adoped realism in their writing more pronouncedly. Titled polli-kobi (Poet of the Village) for works relating to the villages and countryside of Bengal, Jasimuddin is particularly famous for his poems that have become major highlights for pedagogical purposes in both West Bengal and Bangladesh.

Seminal Hindu religious works in Bangla include the many songs of Ramprasad Sen. His works (still sung today) from the 17th century cover an astonishing range of emotional responses to the goddess Kali, detailing complex philosophical statements based on Vedanta teachings and more visceral prouncements of his love of the goddess. There are also the laudatory accounts of the lives and teachings of the Vaishnava saint Chaitanya Mahaprabhu (the Choitanyo Choritamrit) and Devi Advaitist Shri Ramakrishna (the Ramakrishna Kathamrita, translated roughly as Gospel of Ramakrishna). There is also a large body of Islamic literature, that can be traced back atleast to Noornama by Abdul Hakim. Bishad Sindhu depicting the death of Hussain in Karbala is very popular novel written by Mir Mosharraf Hossain. Later works influenced by Islam include devotional songs written by Nazrul, and popularized by Abbas Uddin, among others.

The mystic Bauls of the Bengal countryside who preached the boundless spiritual truth of Sôhoj Pôth (the Simple, Natural Path) and Moner Manush (The Man of The Heart) drew on Vedantic philosophy to propound transcendental truths in song format, traveling from village to village proclaiming that there was no such thing as Hindu, Muslim or Christian, only moner manush.

The literature discussed so far can be more or less regarded as the common heritage of both Bangladesh and

West Bengal. Since the partition of Bengal in 1947, the east and west parts of Bengal have also developed their own distinctive literatures. For example, the Naxalite movement has influenced much of West Bengal's literature, whereas the Liberation War has had a similarly profound impact on Bangladeshi literature.

Major literary figures in Bangladesh include Shamsur Rahman, Sufia Kamal, Hasan Azizul Huq, Akhtaruzzaman Ilias and Humayun Azad , to name a few. Some notable writers from West Bengal are Sunil Gangopadhyay, Shankha Ghosh, Shakti Chattopadhyay, Mahasweta Devi and Joy Goswami.

## Music

Bangladesh is traditionally very rich in its musical heritage. From the ancient times, music documented the lives of the people. Also, music was widely patronized by the rulers.

Bangla music in ancient times was mostly linked to prayer. Due to the immense influence of Hindu mythology, most folk songs are related to some sort of praise of the gods and their creation. Songs were associated with particular groups of people, such as fishermen, cart-drivers, hermits and so on. Most songs were based on classical themes.

Modernisation of Bangla music occurred at different times and most of these modernisation processes happened independently of western influence. Most notable of these changes were:

— Popularity of folk music of Sufi genres: introduction of non-Hindu notions and philosophy in music

— Works of Rabindranath Tagore: introduction of variations of classical music to music

— Works of Kazi Nazrul Islam: introduction of complicated musical composition and use of music as a revolutionary tool

— Modernisation of folk music: bringing folk music into mainstream

— Fusion work: fusion of traditional music with electronic instruments and Western work to revitalise and re-popularise Bangla music in a society increasingly overwhelmed by the West

Rabindranath Tagore, a Nobel Laureate poet, wrote thousands of songs that are cherished even today. A famous writer of Bengal whose music was very popular in Bangladesh is Kazi Nazrul Islam. Lalon Fokir is a popular Bangladeshi mystic poet, famous for his spiritual tunes.

The music of Bangladesh can be broadly categorized among the following genres:

### *Classical Music*

Bangla classical, like classical music in the rest of the Sub-continent, is based on modes, called ragas (rag, in Bangla). All traditional Bangla music was based on classical music or on its variation. Some of the most talented classical musicians of the subcontinent come from Bangladesh including Ustad Allauddin Khan.

### *Rabindra Sangeet*

Rabindra sangeet is the best-known genre of Bangla music outside Bengal. The main origin of Rabindra sangeet is the works of Nobel laureate poet, novelist and play writer, Rabindranath Tagore. (Rabindra sangeet literally means music of Rabindra).

Rabindra sangeet itself is broadly classified into few sub-genres:

— puja porjai (prayer songs)

— prem porjai (love songs) [some argue prem porjai is actually a part of puja porjai]

— bichitra porjai

— swadesh porjai (patriotic songs)

— (seasonal songs)

All categories are tied by a common theme of philosophy and love. Tagore also composed most of the songs himself. Hence, a common compositional similarity is visible. All songs are based on minor variations of Sub-continental musical modes or ragas.

Rabindra sangeet forms an integral part of almost any Bengali cultural festival and is seen as one of the most important parts of Bengali cultural heritage. These songs have also been used in several movies, both in Bengali and non-Bengali cinema. The national anthems of both Bangladesh and India are Rabindra sangeets; these are "Amar Shonar Bangla" (Oh My Precious Bengal, the melody is based on a folk tune by Gogon Harkara) and "Jana Gana Mana" (Ruler of the Minds of All People, written in an older form of Bangla, closer to Sanskrit, that can be readily re-interpreted in almost all Indian languages) respectively.

In Bangladesh, until recently, Rabindra sangeet has practically been synonymous with two names: Rezwana Choudhury Bonya and Sadi Mohammad.

### *Nazrul Geeti*

Nazrul geeti, literally meaning "music of Nazrul", are the works of Kazi Nazrul Islam, national poet of Bangladesh and active revolutionary during Indian independence movement.

Unlike Rabindra sangeets mentioned above, Nazrul geetis incorporate revolutionary notions as well as more spiritual and philosophical themes. Islam used his music as a major way of disseminating his revolutionary notions, mainly by the use of strong words and powerful, but catchy, tunes. Among the revolutionary songs, Karar Oi

Louho Kopat (Prison-doors of Steel) is best known and has been used several movies - especially those made during the pre-independence period of Bangladesh.

Islam also incorporated influences from Western India. He played an active role in carrying out a fusion between Western Indian ghazals and traditional Bengali classical music. (Ghazals are poems in Urdu presented with a semi-classical tune, popular in Western India.) Nazrul geetis that do not incorporate themes of protest essentially form what is now called Bangla ghazal. The music involves variation on ragas (modes) along with complicated timing based almost entirely on vocal work and complex structure.

Due to Islam's revolutionary nature and lifestyle, Nazrul geeti was not mainstream for a very long time (and possibly still is not as commercially promoted as Rabindra sangeet). Bangladeshi singer and composer, Firoza Begum, played a very big role in popularising Nazrul geeti in both Bangladesh and West Bengal. Sohorab Hossain also played a crucial role in making Nazrul geeti mainstream.

### *Folk Songs*

Bangla folk music has a long history. Several people contributed to what has become one of the most important musical influences in lives of Bengalis on both sides of the (West Bengal-Bangladesh) border. Among these are Lalon Fokir, Hason Raja and Ramesh Shill. Abbas Uddin was a key player in popularising folk music later on.

Folk music can clearly be distinguished and classified into several sub-genres:

— *Baul*: mainly inspired by Lalon Fokir and his Sufi way of living and almost exclusively performed by hermits who have adopted such (Sufi) life style

— *Bhandari*: devotional music from the South (mainly Chittagong)

— *Bhatiali*: music of fishermen and boatman, almost always tied by a common raga (mode), sung solo

— *Bhawaiya*: song of bullock-cart drivers of the North (Rangpur)

— *Gajir geet*: tradition song from the North (Rangpur)

— *Gombhira:* song (originating in Chapai Nawabganj, in the North) performed with a particular distinctive rhythm and dance with two performers, always personifying a man and his grand father, discussing a topic to raise social awareness

— *Hason Raja*: devotional songs written by music composer Hason Raja (from Sylhet near Assam) that was recently repopularised as popular dance music

— *Jaari*: song that involves musical battle between two groups

— *Jatra Pala*: songs associated exclusively with plays (performed on-stage) that usually always involve historical themes presented in a very colourful way

— *Kirtan*: devotional song depicting love of Hindu god Krishno and his (best-known) wife, Radha

— *Pala*: songs from the haor (lake) area in Sylhet, Kishoregonj, and Netrokona usually performed on stage live by folk singers

— *Kobi gaan*: poems sung with simple music usually presented on stage as a musical battle between poets

— *Lalon*: best known of all folk songs and the most import sub-genre of Baul songs, almost entirely attribute to spiritual writer and composer, Lalon Fokir of Kustia (Western Bangladesh, near the border with West Bengal)

— *Mursiya*: Islamic songs of devotion of the Shi'ah groups based mainly on Western influences

— *Shaari:* song of boatmen sung in group to match the beat of the oar movement

— *Upojatiyo*: songs of the minor ethnic groups - worth oting, this is not really a classification since songs of these ethnic groups (of which there are at least 13 different groups) vary widely and have very distinct and intriguing characteristics

— *Letto's song:* songs from Mymensingh (North of Dhaka) that also allegedly influenced Nazrul geeti

— *Wedding songs*: sung all over Bangladesh but always tied by similar tunes and by, obviously, a common theme, marriage

Of these several groups, Baul song is best known and was further enriched by works of Lalon. All folk songs are characterised by simple musical structure and words. Before advent of radio, stage performances of folk singers used to be possibly the only entertainment for the vast rural population of Bengal. After arrival of new communication and digital media, many of the folk songs were modernised and incorporated into modern songs.

***Baul geeti***

Baul geeti has been such a huge influence in Bangladeshi music that it deserves being called a genre on its own. However, although Baul geeti can be characterised by particular nature of music and presentation, in general, the genre is actually also defined by a definite cult. In order to understand Baul geeti, it is necessary to understand its creators.

Baul geeti is almost exclusively performed by Bauls (hermits) who are followers of Sufism in Bangladesh. (Note that traditionally bauls were Hindus; Sufism was started following the lifestyle of Lalon Shah.) In Bangladesh, in the early days of Bauls who claimed to be Muslims, with greater focus on love of the society and harmony with nature, baul geeti had to go through a major struggle of survival as did the Bauls themselves. Bauls were subjected to harsh teasing and isolation. However, with time, Islamists were forced by the general population to accept the Bauls and their spiritual music as part of the society.

Current day Bauls in Bangladesh are Sufis and have given up claims to be Muslims. Most live simple lives on an absolute minimum, earned mainly from performing their music. Baul songs always incorporate simple words expressing songs with deeper meanings involving Creation, society, lifestyle and human emotions. The songs are performed with very little musical support to the main carrier, the vocal. Bauls, bohemian by nature and belief, leave on grand expeditions, writing and performing music on their entire trip to earn living and disseminate notion of love and spirituality.

Ektara (literally, the one-string), Dotara (literally, the two-strings), ba(n)shi (flute made from bamboo shoot)) and cymbals are used in the presentation of Baul geeti. Although, in recent days, Baul geeti has lost popularity mainly due to disruption of the lifestyle of the bauls by urbanisation and westernisation, the songs have permanently altered Bangla music, especially in the form of Lalon geeti.

Baul songs were hugely promoted by Fokir Alamgeer and Feroz Shahi in Bangladesh.

### *Lalon Geeti*

Lalon geeti is the work of composer and philosopher, Lalon Shah (also known as Lalon Fokir). Most of his songs are extensions of Baul geeti. However, his songs are always more philosophical in nature, involving greater thought about abstract themes.

Lalon geeti originated in Kushtia and has been popularised throughout the two Bengals (West Bengal and Bangladesh) by various artists. Among the proponents of Lalon geeti, Farida Parveen is particularly worth mentioning for her extensive work in modernising tunes.

### *Adhunik Gaan*

Adhunik songeet literally means "modern songs". Although, to outsiders, this may seem an extremely ambiguous way of nomenclature, it has particular motivations. Bangla music traditionally has been classified mainly by the region of origin and the creators of the musical genre, such as Nazrul geeti (written and composed by Kazi Nazrul Islam), ghombhira (unique to a specific area in Bangladesh), etc. However, this prevented the ability to classify any music that failed to fit into any of the classes.

In the period just before Indian independence (Bengal, under British rule, was a part of one massive India that does not exactly correspond to the India of current day), several new minor musical groups emerged, mainly as playback songs for movies. These songs failed to fit into any particular genre, but seemed to be tied together by common theme of "music for the masses". Most of the music tended to be aimed at the mainstream audience - popular catchy tunes with simple words that were far moved from the classical ragas (modes). Hence, a miscellaneous category, Adhunik songeet, was created, since, at that time, this music was "modern".

Although over time these so-called "modern" songs have become fairly old, they continue to be called by the same name. Interestingly, this group of song has grown faster than any other, since it is a miscellaneous category that can accommodate anything that fails to fit elsewhere. The common theme continues to exist. So, although the nomenclature itself might not be as insightful, the genre itself is still well-defined. Among the main contributors to

Adhunik songeet were several singers from both West Bengal and Bangladesh. The list can never be completed, but some of the more prolific ones from Bangladesh are:

### *Modern music*

In the post-independence period, Adhunik songeet continued to attract large proportiones of music enthusiasts. However, with time, newer generations demanded more upbeat music. Starting late 80's, music involving political theme have started to gain popularity once again, in a similar fashion to growht of Nazrul geeti had gained popularity during the revolution against the British Monarch and the War of Independence of Bangladesh.

Pop music initially started with the so-called band music. And as the name suggests, the music was heavily influenced by Western Music. It is worth noting that pop music of Bangladesh had an assorted history. Artists of the "Adhunik Gaan" and folk (especially new wave) genre also contributed to the pop music from time to time. This further popularized pop music with the masses.

Bangla rock was started by Azam Khan, Miles and LRB. Hassan (associated with Ark) and James (associated with Feelings and, later, Nagar Baul) contributed in popularizing rock music. However, hard-rock did not begin until arrival of bands like Rockstrata, and later Warfaze among many others in the early 90s.

Current day rock and metal bands have progressed a long way from the initiators of the genre in Bangladesh. Deeply influenced by the progressive rock music of the West, and with the latest technology and equipments at their disposal, many of the new rock musicians are trying to follow westren bands instead of trying to develop their own identity and style.

Recently, the death metal scene of Bangladesh has generated considerable buzz among the young audience with the arrival of bands like Severe Dementia, Barzak, Voodoo Economix, Annex, Necropolis, Ashes and Dripping Gore. Though the quality of words is very poor and the music seriously lacks originality.

## Media

One of the most effective means for the ruling political party to control the nation was through manipulation of the news media. In the 1980s, the government's National Broadcasting Authority monopolized telecommunications within the country. Thus the party that controlled the government effectively decided the content of the country's broadcasts. Until the early 1980s, the government also ran a number of daily and weekly newspapers. Such newspapers printed the ruling party's version of the news.

As part of Ershad's policy of divesting government-owned properties, however, these official sources of propaganda were removed from government control, thus ending a legacy left over from the Mujib period. Each major political party in the late 1980s had one or more newspapers that supported it, and each used its own newspapers to publish its official views.

Bengali society has the longest tradition of freedom of the press in South Asia, and its dozens of weekly and daily newspapers, press associations, and publishers guarantee that almost any opinion finds expression. Ruling regimes have countered this independence by exercising press censorship. Repression of the media has varied from banning certain publications for extended periods of time to officially pressuring publishers to regulate the content of news articles. For example, the English-language Bangladesh Observer was banned for three months in 1987, and the weekly Banglar Bani (Bengal's Message) was banned through much of 1987 and 1988. The weekly Joyjatra (Victory March) was banned in February 1988 for publishing "objectionable comments" referring to the possibility of Ershad's resignation.

In 1988 the government closed the Dainik Khabor (Daily News) for ten weeks under the Special Powers Act of 1974 because the newspaper had released an article with a map making Bangladesh look like part of India, thus inflicting "injury to the independence and sovereignty of the country." In addition, the operations of the British Broadcasting Corporation were banned under the Special Powers Act from December 14, 1987, to May 2, 1988, and one of its correspondents was jailed for allegedly having manufactured "continuing hostile and tendentious propaganda."

Bangladeshi journalists are unionized, and they sometimes strike back at government censorship. During the 1988 parliamentary elections, journalists staged a walkout to protest attempts by the government's Press Information Department to restrict news and photographic coverage of election violence and opposition demonstrations. The continuing struggle between the press and the government regularly kept at least six newspapers on the list of banned publications in the late 1980s.

With a 29-percent literacy rate, newspapers and journals are not widely read in Bangladesh. For example, despite the publication of 62 daily newspapers, only 22 percent of all urban households in 1982 reported regularly reading them; a dismal 2.5 percent was reported for rural areas.

Both Radio Bangladesh and Bangladesh Television were established in 1971, and both came under state control in 1972. In 1984 they merged to form the National Broadcasting Authority. In 1988 the twelve home service stations and twelve FM stations of Radio Bangladesh offered a total of eighty-five hours of daily programming. Radio Bangladesh also transmitted to Southeast Asia, the Middle East, Africa, and Western Europe via its shortwave station at Dhaka. Seven and one-half hours of daily programming were broadcast in six languages: Bangla, English, Arabic, Hindi, Urdu, and Nepali. The television service operated two channels, with eight and one-half hours of daily programming, relayed by twelve stations for reception throughout the country.

However, outside Dhaka the number of television sets was very small, and television was not yet a significant medium when compared with radio, press, and word-of-mouth communications. Statistics from the early 1980s indicated that about 29 percent of the country's urban households had radios, and only 6.7 percent had television sets. In the countryside, broadcast communications were even less available: 13 percent of all rural households had radios, and only 0.2 percent had televisions.

**Sports and Games**

Sports and games form an integral part of Bangladeshi's life. In the villages one might see a passel of kids kicking a football, or in some dusty alley one might see kids playing cricket. Though Bangladesh is not a major sporting power in any sense, Bangladeshi athletes and sportspersons have brought her many laurels.

Cricket is a game which has a massive and passionate following in Bangladesh. There is a strong domestic league which on many occasions also saw Test players from many countries (Sri Lanka, India, Pakistan, England) gracing the cricket fields of Bangladesh.

Bangladesh has now joined the elite group of countries eligible to play Test cricket. The Bangladesh national cricket team goes by the nick-name of the Tigers - after the Royal Bengal Tiger which too calls Bangladesh its home.

Sports organisation in Bangladesh has undergone many changes in different periods before and after its independence. The Bangladesh Sports Control Board was established in 1972. There are 29 registered federations under this board. These include federations for popular games such as football, cricket, hockey, tennis, badminton, volleyball, handball, chess, and carom as well as for wrestling, weightlifting, squash, billiard, and snooker, which are less popular in Bangladesh. Other recognised sports organisations in the country are the district and divisional sports organisations, university sports organisations, and the sports bodies of the armed forces, police and ansar, as well as of public sector corporations, boards and departments such as Bangladesh Biman, BJMC, BTMC, PWD, and Bangladesh Railway.

Sport clubs have a significant contribution to the development of sports in the country. Prominent among the clubs of Bangladesh are Abahani Krirachakra, Arambag, Ajax, Azad Sporting, Brothers Union, Dhaka Mohammedan Sporting, Dhaka Wanderers, Dilkusha Sporting, GMCC, Kalabagan, Muktijoddha Sangsad, Rahmatganj, Suryatarun, Victoria Sporting, and Wari. Some of these clubs are reputed for their glorious past while others earned a name by excellent performance at national level at present.

## Bengali Cuisine

Bengali cuisine is a style of food preparation that originated in Bengal, a region in the northeast of South Asia which is now divided between the independent country of Bangladesh and the Indian state of West Bengal. Bengali meal is well known for the vast domination of rice and various preperation from sweet water fishes etc. Bengali cuisine is rich and varied with the use of many specialized spices and flavours. It is known to be one of the best among the Indian cuisines.

Bangladesh is famous for its distinctive culinary tradition, and delicious food, snacks and savories. Boiled rice constitutes the staple food, and is served with a variety of vegetables, fried as well as curries, thick lentil soups, and fish and meat preparations of beef, mutton and chicken.

Sweetmeats of Bangladesh are mostly milk based, and consist of several delights including Roshgulla, Sandesh, Rosmalai, Gulab Jamun, Kalo Jamun, Chom Chom. Several other sweet preparations are also available.

Bengali food has inherited a large number of influences, both foreign and Indian, from both a turbulent history and strong trade links with many parts of the world. Bengal is fairly ancient; it was originally a Dravidian and tribal society that was extensively settled upon by the Aryans during the Gupta era, it fell under the sway of various Muslim rulers from the early thirteenth century onwards, and was then ruled by the British for two centuries (1757-1947).

Every layer of historical influence endures to the present day; the tribals have traditionally abided as hunter-gatherers in the dense forests of the Sunderbans while the rest of Bengal turned heavily agrarian, farming the extremely fertile Ganges delta for rice, vegetables and cash crops such as jute. There was also significant pisciculture in ponds and lakes, along with fishing in the many rivers.

## Festivals and Celebrations

Festivals and celebrations are integral part of the culture of Bangladesh. Prominent and widely celebrated festivals are Pohela Baishakh, Independence day, National Mourning Day, Id-ud-fitra, Id-ud-zoha, Muharram, Durga puja, and Language Martyrs' Day.

## Traditional Ceremonies

### *Weddings*

A traditional wedding is arranged by Ghotok's (matchmakers), who are typically friends or relatives of the couple. The matchmakers facilitate the introduction, and also help agree the amount of any settlement.

In older times, the settlement was a dowry to be paid by the bride's family to the groom. However, in the last 30 to 40 years, dowry has been declared illegal, and it is discouraged. Even then, it persists, especially in rural areas. These days, the settlement is likely to take the form of a Mahr which is paid by the groom to the bride.

The amount of the settlement is set so as to avoid too many zeroes in the amount, such as 10001 rather than 10000; the final zeroes being said by some to signify bad luck.

Weddings are traditionally in four parts: the bride's Gaye Holud, the groom's Gaye Holud, the Nika and the Bou Bhaat. These often take place on separate days. The first event in a wedding is an informal one: the groom presents the bride with a ring marking the "engagement".

### *Gaye Holud*

The Gaye Holud is in preparation for the Nika. For the bride's Gaye Holud, the groom's family - minus the groom himself - go in procession to the bride's home. They carry with them the bride's wedding outfit, wedding decoration including turmeric paste and henna, sweetmeats and gifts. They also take a large fish cooked and decorated. The procession traditionally centers on the (younger) female relative and friends of bride, and they are traditionally all in matching clothes, mostly yellow, orange or red in colour.

The bride is seated on a dias, and the henna is used to decorate the bride's hands and feet with elaborate abstract designs. The turmeric paste is applied by the bride's friends to her body. This is said to soften the skin, but also colours her with the distinctive yellow hue that gives its name to this ceremony. The sweets are then fed to the bride by all involved, piece by piece. There is, of course, a feast for the guests. The groom's Gay Holud comes next, and has the same form as the bridal ceremony.

### Nika

The actual wedding ceremony or Nika follows the Gaye Holud ceremonies. The wedding ceremony is arranged by the bride's family. On the day, the younger members of the bride's family barricade the entrance to the venue, and demand gifts of the groom in return for allowing him to enter. There is typically much good-natured pushing and shoving involved. Another custom is for the bride's younger siblings or cousins to steal the groom's shoes for ransom; to get them back the groom must usually pay off the children. The bride and groom are seated separately, and a priest, accompanied by the parents and a Wakil (witness) from each side formally asks the groom for his consent to the union, and then the bride for hers.

At this time, the amount of the dowry is verified, and if all is well, the formal papers are signed, and the couple are seated side by side on a dias. The brides dupatta (headcovering) is draped over both, and a mirror placed in front. The groom is then supposed to say something romantic on what is notionally the first time he has laid eyes on his bride. Everybody celebrates the union with a feast. While seated on the dias, the bride's entourage will make attempts to steal the groom's shoes, which they will return for a ransom. Once the return of the shoes is negotiated, the bride takes tearful leave of her family. Finally, the happy couple make their way from the venue to the groom's home, where a bridal room has been prepared.

### Bou Bhaat

The reception, also known as Bou-Bhaat ("bride rice"), is a party given by the groom's family in return for the wedding party. It is typically a much more relaxed affair, with only the second-best wedding outfit being worn.

# 14

# ECONOMY

In the late 1980s, Bangladesh continued to be called the "largest poorest" country and to be singled out as "the test case for development." A great deal that had happened in the economy since independence in 1971 supported the hope that the country would eventually overcome its dependence on foreign aid and would approach relative self-sufficiency. In the meantime, success was measured in more limited and immediate accomplishments: greater production of food grains year by year, greater vigor shown by the private sector in generating investment capital and using it productively, and measurable growth and diversification of exports. The government continued to depend on the donor community to provide the bulk of the resources needed to promote human development in the form of nutrition, health, and education programs. The most active donors continued to give Bangladesh good marks for its economic performance.

In 1971, the year Bangladesh achieved independence from Pakistan, the new nation was referred to in foreign circles as an "international basket case," a wounded combatant almost beyond hope of recovery. Bangladeshis themselves, recalling the "international basket case" characterization, often choose the metaphor "bottomless basket," implying that no matter how much assistance is given to the economy, there will always be a need for more. It is a tribute to the Bangladeshi people, to the constructiveness and generosity of other nations, and to the strength of the human spirit that the gloomiest fears have not materialized. The firsttime observer of Bangladesh may still perceive the country as poverty stricken, overpopulated, and with little prospect for a sunnier future. In its first seventeen years of independence, Bangladesh did not prosper, nor was it able to improve substantially the quality of life for its huge population, but it did not lose ground either. If the prospects for rapid economic development were not noticeably better in 1988 than they were in 1972, it was encouraging that Bangladesh was active in economic fields that were not foreseen even a few years earlier—e.g., as a major producer and exporter of ready-made garments and frozen seafood. And if the economy still seemed dangerously poised on the brink of disaster—a drought, a typhoon, or excessive flooding threatens every year—the government, the people, and the international community had combined to limit the scope of disasters, and the economy of Bangladesh had continued to struggle upward.

## Historical Perspective

East Bengal—the region that was to become East Pakistan and later Bangladesh — was a prosperous region of South Asia until modern times. It had the advantages of a mild, almost tropical climate, fertile soil, ample water, and an abundance of fish, wildlife, and fruit. The standard of living compared favorably with other parts of South Asia. As early as the thirteenth century, the region was developing as an agrarian economy. It was not entirely without commercial centers, and Dhaka in particular grew into an important entrepôt during the Mughal Empire. The British, however, on their arrival in the early seventeenth century, chose to develop Calcutta as their commercial and administrative center in South Asia. The development of East Bengal was thereafter limited to agriculture. The colonial infrastructure of the eighteenth and nineteenth centuries reinforced East Bengal's function as the primary producer—chiefly of rice and jute—for processors and traders in Calcutta and beyond.

Some of the same factors that had made East Bengal a prosperous region became disadvantages during the nineteenth and twentieth centuries. As life expectancy increased, the limitations of land and the annual floods increasingly became constraints on economic growth. Traditional agricultural methods became obstacles to the modernization of agriculture. Geography severely limited the development and maintenance of a modern transportation and communications system.

The partition of British India and the emergence of India and Pakistan in 1947 severely disrupted the former colonial economic system that had preserved East Bengal (now East Pakistan) as a producer of jute and rice for the urban industrial economy around Calcutta. East Pakistan had to build a new industrial base and modernize agriculture in the midst of a population explosion. The united government of Pakistan expanded the cultivated area and some irrigation facilities, but the rural population generally became poorer between 1947 and 1971 because improvements did not keep pace with rural population increase.

Pakistan's five-year plans opted for a development strategy based on industrialization, but the major share of the development budget went to West Pakistan, that is, contemporary Pakistan. The lack of natural resources meant that East Pakistan was heavily dependent on imports, creating a balance of payments problem. Without a substantial industrialization program or adequate agrarian expansion, the economy of East Pakistan steadily declined. Blame was placed by various observers, but especially those in East Pakistan, on the West Pakistani leaders who not only dominated the government but also most of the fledgling industries in East Pakistan.

## Economic Reconstruction

The economic situation facing Bangladesh as it emerged from the war of independence in 1971 included the highest rural population density in the entire world, an annual population growth rate between 2.5 and 3 percent, chronic malnutrition for perhaps the majority of the people, and the dislocation of between 8 and 10 million people who had fled to India and returned to independent Bangladesh by 1972. The new nation had few experienced entrepreneurs, managers, administrators, engineers, or technicians.

There were critical shortages of essential food grains and other staples because of wartime disruptions. External markets for jute had been lost because of the instability of supply and the increasing popularity of synthetic substitutes. Foreign exchange resources were minuscule, and the banking and monetary system was unreliable. Although Bangladesh had a large work force, the vast reserves of undertrained and underpaid workers were largely illiterate, unskilled, and underemployed.

Commercially exploitable industrial resources, except for natural gas, were lacking. Inflation, especially for essential consumer goods, ran between 300 and 400 percent. The war of independence had crippled the transportation system. Hundreds of road and railroad bridges had been destroyed or damaged, and rolling stock was inadequate and in poor repair. The new country was still recovering from a severe cyclone that hit the area in 1970 and cause 250,000 deaths. India, by no means a wealthy country and without a tradition of giving aid to other nations, came forward immediately with massive economic assistance in the first months after the fighting ended. Between December 1971 and January 1972, India committed US$232 million in aid to Bangladesh, almost all of it for immediate disbursement. The largest single element in Indian aid was 900,000 tons of food grains. The United States and the World Bank thereafter became leading foreign aid donors, and the World Bank organized a consortium known as the Bangladesh Aid Group, comprising twenty-six international financial institutions and foreign governments interested in assisting Bangladesh's development.

## Economic Policy and Planning

After West Pakistani owners of industrial enterprises fled in 1971, the government of Bangladesh seized their plants as abandoned properties. The government suddenly found itself managing and operating more than 300 medium- and large-scale industrial plants, which represented nearly 90 percent of the value of all such enterprises in the new nation. It organized public corporations to oversee the major industries: jute, textiles, sugar, steel, paper and paperboard, fertilizer, chemicals, pharmaceuticals, engineering and shipbuilding, minerals, oil and gas, food and allied products, and forest products. With government control over major industries and massive inputs of foreign aid, the economy gradually returned to the levels of the late 1960s, but it was still among the world's poorest and least developed countries.

The main government institution responsible for coordinating national rehabilitation and development was the Planning Commission. Sheikh Mujibur Rahman (Mujib), the first president of Bangladesh, led the formation of the national-level Planning Commission, which prepared plans that directed economic priorities for five-year periods. The First Five-Year Plan covered the period July 1973 to June 1978. It was succeeded by a two-year plan, covering the period July 1978 to June 1980, which was followed by a year-long hiatus. The Second Five-Year Plan (1981-85) and the Third Five-Year Plan (1985-90) put the planning process back on track. The broad objectives of the Third Five-Year Plan were to reduce poverty, bring down the rate of population growth to 1.8 percent annually, increase exports by 5.9 percent and domestic savings by 10 percent, attain self-sufficiency in food production, and realize an annual growth of the gross domestic product of 5.4 percent. These ambitious goals went well beyond the previous actual performance of the economy.

Five-year plans are financed through the development, or capital budget, which was separate from the government's revenue, or administrative, budget. The Third Five-Year Plan envisaged a total outlay of more than US$12 billion, approximately 65 percent of which was destined for public sector projects. About 55 percent of the needed funds were to come from foreign sources, including private investment, the aid programs of international financial institutions, and bilateral donor nations. Foreign commitments in the early and mid-1980s were around US$1.7 billion per year (exclusive of external private investment, which in any case was not significant). The portion of the development budget to come from domestic sources (45 percent) represented a substantial increase from the 15 to 20 percent of earlier development budgets.

The Planning Commission translates the multiyear development plan into public investment through the Annual Development Programme. The commission also ensures that public programs and policies are in conformity with its long-term strategy through its project approval process and through its advisory position on the country's highest economic decision-making bodies, the National Economic Council and its Executive Committee. The National Economic Council in the late 1980s was chaired by the president of Bangladesh and included all government ministers plus the governor of the Bangladesh Bank and the deputy chairman and members of the Planning Commission.

The Executive Committee of the National Economic Council made most of the decisions on major development projects and development issues in general. The committee included the ministers of key economic sectors (finance, planning, industries, commerce, and public works) and, according to the agenda, any other sectors concerned. A third organization involved in the planning mechanism is the Project Evaluation Committee, which monitors the progress of five-year-plan programs.

## Joint Ventures and Foreign Investment

Despite its early concentration on developing a socialist economy, the government became increasingly open to private investment. The 1974 New Investment Policy restored certain rights to private and foreign investors. In December 1975, President Ziaur Rahman promulgated the Revised Investment Policy, which allowed greater private sector activity and authorized joint ventures with public sector corporations in a number of previously reserved areas, provided that the government retained 51 percent ownership.

The Dhaka Stock Exchange was reactivated in 1976, and the Bangladesh Investment Corporation was established the same year to provide financing for bridge construction and underwriting facilities to the private sector. Investment ceilings for private industry were abolished in 1978. Then, in 1980, the government delineated a more liberal attitude toward foreign direct investment in the Foreign Private Investment (Promotion and Protection) Act. Growth of investment nonetheless remained slow, and industry was still dominated by relatively inefficient public enterprises and governed by an elaborate system of administrative controls.

In June 1982, the new government of Hussain Muhammad Ershad introduced its own New Industrial Policy, calling for a significant increase in private sector activity and denationalization of selected public sector enterprises. The government transferred 650 industrial enterprises to private hands, leaving only 160 under public ownership. In 1986 the government announced a comprehensive revision of its industrial policy, setting out objectives and strategies to accelerate the pace of industrialization. The policy also emphasized private and foreign investment in high technology, export-oriented, and labor-intensive industries. The revised policy increased the number of sectors open to private investment, liberalized the tariff structure, reduced quantitative import restrictions, and furthered privatization of state-managed enterprises.

The role of the public sector in the late 1980s was limited to seven fields: arms, ammunition, and sensitive defense equipment; electrical power generation, transmission, and distribution; management and exploitation of reserved forests; telecommunications; air, water, and railroad transportation; atomic energy; and currency note printing and coin minting. In addition, public sector involvement was still possible, alone or jointly with private participants, in projects where investment was not forthcoming from the private sector. The only consistent moneymakers among public sector industrial corporations were the Bangladesh Petroleum Corporation, the Bangladesh Chemical Industries Corporation (Tk18.7 crore), and the Bangladesh Forest Industries Development Corporation (Tk5.8 crore).

In 1987 an amendment to the Bangladesh Industrial Enterprises (Nationalisation) Ordinance was adopted, providing the legal basis for plans to sell up to 49 percent of government shares in remaining nationalized enterprises. The fact that the government would retain the majority was understood by some as a political gesture to workers and entrenched management opposed to privatization.

An export processing zone was established officially at the port city of Chittagong in 1980. But because of political controversy and indecision surrounding the project from the moment it was proposed, the Bangladesh Export Processing Zones Authority did not actually begin functioning until March 1983, when a program of inducements was offered to investors opening up enterprises. Zone enterprises enjoyed a tax holiday of 5 years (10 years for pioneer industries), subsequent rebate of 50 percent of income tax on export sales, freedom from duties on both imports and exports, and guaranteed full repatriation of profits and capital. Additional export processing zones were contemplated for Khulna and Dhaka.

In addition to the broad policies encouraging foreign investment, the government of Bangladesh has entered into bilateral investment treaties with eight countries: Belgium, Britain, Federal Republic of Germany (West Germany), France, the Republic of Korea (South Korea), Romania, Turkey and the United States. As of early 1988, similar treaties were at various stages of negotiation with ten other countries. These treaties included such assurances as unrestricted currency transfers, compensation for expropriation, dispute settlement procedures, and taxation treatment. In addition, Bangladesh has signed agreements for the avoidance of double taxation with Britain, Canada, Sweden, Singapore, and South Korea.

Even with a reasonably attractive framework in place, the flow of private capital to Bangladesh has been slow. Estimates from the Organization for Economic Cooperation and Development indicated that for the 1980-84 period foreign direct investment in Bangladesh averaged only US$3.4 million per year.

The Bangladesh Ministry of Industries listed just sixty-eight existing and forty-one "sanctioned" joint venture and multinational companies in Bangladesh in 1987. The largest amounts of foreign private investment were from other Asian countries—Japan foremost, with smaller amounts from South Korea, Singapore, Taiwan, and Hong Kong—and from Britain and other countries in Western Europe.

American investment of about US$20 million in 1987 was concentrated in the physical assets of a life insurance company, the manufacturing operations of three pharmaceutical firms, and a vegetable oil processing and storage plant.

## Currency Fluctuation

At independence the value of the taka, Bangladesh's unit of currency, was set between 7.5 and 8.0 to US$1. With the exception of FY 1978, the taka's value relative to the dollar declined every year from 1971 through the end of 1987. To help offset this phenomenon, Bangladesh first used the compensatory financing facility of the International Monetary Fund in FY 1974.

Despite the increasing need for assistance, the Mujib government was initially unwilling to meet the IMF's conditions on monetary and fiscal policy. By FY1975, however, the government revised its stance, declaring a devaluation of the taka by 56 percent and agreeing to the establishment by the World Bank of the Bangladesh Aid Group.

Between 1980 and 1983, the taka sustained a decline of some 50 percent because of a deterioration in Bangladesh's balance of payments. Between 1985 and 1987, the taka was adjusted in frequent incremental steps, stabilizing again around 12 percent lower in real terms against the United States dollar, but at the same time narrowing the difference between the official rate and the preferential secondary rate from 15 percent to 7.5 percent.

Accompanying this structural adjustment was an expansion in the amount of trade conducted at the secondary rate, to 53 percent of total exports and 28 percent of total imports. In mid-1987, the official rate was relatively stable, approaching Tk31 to US$1.

**Toward a Market Economy**

Following the violent events of 1971 during the fight for independence, Bangladesh—with the help of large infusions of donor relief and development aid—slowly began to turn its attention to developing new industrial capacity and rehabilitating its economy. The statist economic model adopted by its early leadership, however—including the nationalization of much of the industrial sector—resulted in inefficiency and economic stagnation. Beginning in 1975, the government gradually gave greater scope to private sector participation in the economy, a pattern that has continued.

A few state owned enterprises have been privatized, but many, including major portions of the banking and jute sectors, remain .under government control. Population growth, inefficiency in the public sector, and limited natural resources and capital have continued to restrict economic growth. In the mid-1980s, there were encouraging, if halting, signs of progress.

Economic policies aimed at encouraging private enterprise and investment, denationalizing public industries, reinstating budgetary discipline, and liberalizing the import regime were accelerated. From 1990-1993. In 1985 1989-1993, the government successfully followed an enhanced structural adjustment facility (ESAF) with the International Monetary Fund.

Although the Khaleda Zia Government (1991-1996) initially took significant strides toward pro-market reform, including tax reform and allowing increased foreign direct investment in the gas and power sectors, preoccupation with its domestic political troubles stalled progress on this critical front in the last year of its tenure.

The government of Prime Minister Sheikh Hasina, elected in June 1996, indicated that it would continue along the path toward privatization and open-market reform, but progress has been slow, especially in privatization. While the Awami League government has managed to maintain economic growth levels around 4%-5%, and single-digit inflation—except for a period of months after the 1998 floods—per capita income levels still remain distressingly low, at less than $1 per day.

Efforts to achieve Bangladesh's macroeconomic goals have been problematic. The privatization of public sector industries has proceeded at a slow pace, due in part to worker unrest in affected industries. The government also has proven unable to resist demands for wage hikes in government-owned industries. Economic growth has been further slowed by a largely dysfunctional banking system which has impeded access to capital-state-owned banks, which control about three-fourths of deposits and loans, and carry classified loan burdens of about 50%. Some efforts are being made to alleviate this problem through microcredit programs such as Grameen Bank.

## Agriculture

Most Bangladeshis earn their living from agriculture. Although rice and jute are the primary crops, wheat is assuming greater importance. Tea is grown in the northeast. Because of Bangladesh's fertile soil and normally ample water supply, rice can be grown and harvested three times a year in many areas.

Due to a number of factors, Bangladesh's labor-intensive agriculture has achieved steady increases in food grain production despite the often unfavorable weather conditions. These include better flood control and irrigation, a generally more efficient use of fertilizers, and the establishment of better distribution and rural credit networks. With 20.2 million metric tons produced in 1999, rice is Bangladesh's principal crop. By comparison, wheat output in 1999 was 1.9 million metric tons. Population pressure continues to place a severe burden on productive capacity, creating a food deficit, especially of wheat. Foreign assistance and commercial imports fill the gap. Underemployment remains a serious problem, and a growing concern for Bangladesh's agricultural sector will be its ability to absorb additional manpower. Finding alternative sources of employment will continue to be a daunting problem for future governments, particularly with the increasing numbers of landless peasants who already account for about half the rural labor force.

## Industry and Investment

Fortunately for Bangladesh, many new jobs—1.5 million, mostly for women—have been created by the country's dynamic private ready-made garment industry, which grew at double-digit rates through most of the 1990s. Despite the country's politically motivated general strikes, poor infrastructure, and weak financial system, Bangladeshi entrepreneurs have shown themselves adept at competing in the global garments marketplace. Bangladesh's exports to the U.S. surpassed $1.9 billion in 1999.

Bangladesh also exports significant amounts of garments and knitwear to the EU market. The country has done less well, however, in expanding its export base—garments account for more than three-fourths of all exports, dwarfing the country's historic cash crop, jute, along with leather, shrimp, pharmaceuticals and ceramics. Bangladesh has been a world leader in its efforts to end the use of child labor in garment factories.

On July 4, 1995, the Bangladesh Garment Manufacturers Export Association, International Labour Organization, and UNICEF signed a memorandum of understanding on the elimination of child labor in the garment sector. Implementation of this pioneering agreement began in fall 1995, and by the end of 1999, child labor in the garment trade virtually had been eliminated.

The labor-intensive process of shipbreaking for scrap has developed to the point where it now meets most of Bangladesh's domestic steel needs. Other industries include sugar, tea, leather goods, newsprint, pharmaceutical, and fertilizer production.

The Bangladesh government continues to court foreign investment, something it has done fairly successfully in private power generation and gas exploration and production, as well as in other sectors such as cellular telephony, textiles, and pharmaceuticals. In 1989, the same year it signed a bilateral investment treaty with the United States, it established a Board of Investment to simplify approval and start-up procedures for foreign investors, although in practice the board has done little to increase investment.

Bangladesh also has established successful export processing zones in Chittagong and Dhaka, and has given the private sector permission to build and operate competing EPZs-initial construction on a Korean EPZ started in 1999. In June 1999, the AFL-CIO petitioned the U.S. Government to deny Bangladesh access to U.S. markets under the Generalized System of Preferences (GSP), citing the country's failure to meet promises made in 1992 to allow freedom of association in EPZs.

Bangladesh has made significant strides in economic sector since independence in 1971. Although the economy has improved vastly in the 1990s, Bangladesh still suffers in the area of foreign trade in South Asian region. Despite major impediments to growth like the inefficiency of state-owned enterprises, a rapidly growing labor force that cannot be absorbed by agriculture, inadequate power supplies, and slow implementation of economic reforms, Prime Minister Begum Khaleda Zia's government has made some headway improving the climate for foreign investors and liberalizing the capital markets; for example, it has negotiated with foreign firms for oil and gas exploration, better countrywide distribution of cooking gas, and the construction of natural gas pipelines and power stations. Progress on other economic reforms has been halting because of opposition from the bureaucracy, public sector unions, and other vested interest groups. The especially severe floods of 1998 increased the country's reliance on large-scale international aid. So far the East Asian financial crisis has not had major impact on the economy.

# 15

# GOVERNMENT AND POLITICS

The quest for representative government has been an important feature of the history of Bangladesh. The independence struggle of the eastern Bengali peoples against the British, partition from India in 1947, and secession from Pakistan in 1971 set the stage for the people of Bangladesh to create a democratic political system. The Constitution, as it was initially promulgated in 1972, embodied the democratic yearnings of the long struggle for independence and guaranteed human rights and political freedoms within a system of checks and balances similar to those existing in the British and United States governments. But later events ended these hopes.

Sheikh Mujibur Rahman (Mujib), hero of the 1971 war of independence, amended the Constitution and assumed dictatorial powers. His successors, most of whom were military men who seized power during various times of trouble, also ruled through autocratic means. As a result, successive regimes established single-party systems representing military interests, with the leader wielding almost absolute power.

Yet the struggle for democracy was still alive in Bangladesh as of the late 1980s. The single-party system of the 1970s and 1980s was unable to satisfy the varied political movements and interest groups of the nation.

Opposition parties—although they represented conflicting views and were as unwilling as the ruling regime to share power—remained a vital force that commanded the loyalties of a large proportion of the population.

Socialist and communist parties, centrist parties representing the policies of defunct regimes, and conservative Islamic parties— each with a completely different vision of the path that Bangladesh should follow but united in their opposition to the rule of President Hussain Muhammad Ershad—all vied for power in the late 1980s. Their refusal to participate in parliamentary politics under Ershad, who had seized power in 1982, relegated the opposition to illegal activities and demonstrations on campuses and in the streets that periodically brought economic life to a standstill in urban areas. The ineffectiveness and confrontational position of the opposition only strengthened the regime's hold over Parliament and the civil service and allowed the military to continue its strong autocratic rule.

Remarkably, the policies of Bangladesh's autocratic military rulers have been characterized by a commitment to democratic ideals and an adherence to the Constitution. Ershad seized power in the name of the Constitution, and he sought to legitimize his position by claiming that he brought stability to the country in order to guarantee democratic freedom.

One of Ershad's most significant moves toward democracy was the establishment of a system of local elections that allowed voters to choose members of local representative councils. In the short term, this democratic reform allowed local elites to control government patronage, and it also made them docile supporters of the regime. Nevertheless, by the late 1980s the local councils had become training grounds for new political leaders and forums for democratic competition throughout the nation.

Bangladesh has pursued a neutralist policy in international relations in a continuing effort to secure economic aid from every possible foreign source. Bangladesh in 1988 was one of the few countries in the world on good terms with both the United States and the Soviet Union and their allies and with China, the Islamic world, and most Third World nations. Bangladesh has played an active role in the United Nations (UN), the Nonaligned Movement, and other international groupings, and it was the driving force behind the establishment of the South Asian Association for Regional Cooperation, which offered promise for economic cooperation.

Bangladesh was neutral, but it was forceful on a number of international issues. The Cambodian, Palestinian, and South African issues have elicited strong stands from Dhaka, and complicated bilateral problems with India have invoked intense displays of hostility and national pride among Bangladeshis in the years since independence.

## Structure of the Government

### *Constitution*

The Constitution of Bangladesh has formed the basis for the nation's political organization since it was adopted on November 4, 1972. Many abrupt political changes have caused suspension of the Constitution and have led to amendments in almost every section, including the total revision of some major provisions. It is notable, however, that every regime that came to power since 1972 has couched major administrative changes in terms of the Constitution and has attempted to legitimize changes by legally amending this basic document.

According to the Constitution, the state has a positive role to play in reorganizing society in order to create a free and equal citizenry and provide for the welfare of all. The government is required to ensure food, shelter, clothing, medical care, education, work, and social security for the people. The government must also build socialism by implementing programs to "remove social and economic inequality" and "ensure the equitable distribution of wealth among citizens." These far-reaching goals represented the viewpoints of many members of the 1972 Constituent Assembly and the early Awami League (People's League) government, who were deeply influenced by socialist ideology.

Another sector of public opinion, however, has always viewed private property and private enterprise as the heart of social and economic development. This viewpoint is also part of the constitutional principles of state policy, which equally recognize state, cooperative, and private forms of ownership.

The Constitution thus mandates a high degree of state involvement in the establishment of socialism, although it explicitly preserves a private property system. In practice, the Constitution has supported a wide range of government policies, ranging from those of the nationalized, interventionist state of Mujib's time to the increasing deregulation and reliance on market forces under presidents Ziaur Rahman (Zia) and Ershad.

The framers of the Constitution, after emerging from a period of intense repression under Pakistan, took great pains to outline the fundamental rights of citizens even before describing the government's structure. According to the section on fundamental rights, all men and women are equal before the law, without discrimination based on religion, race, caste, sex, or place of birth.

The Constitution also guarantees the right to assemble, hold public meetings, and form unions. Freedom of speech and of the press are ensured. Persons who have been arrested must be informed of the charges made against them, and they must be brought before a magistrate within twenty-four hours.

The Constitution, however, adds that these guarantees are subject to "any reasonable restrictions imposed by law," leaving open the possibility of an administrative decision to revoke fundamental rights. Furthermore, there is a provision for "preventive detention" of up to six months. Those being held under preventive detention do not have the right to know the charges made against them, nor to appear before a magistrate, and a legal advisory board may extend this form of detention after seeing the detainee.

The Constitution does not define the circumstances or the level of authority necessary for the revocation of constitutional guarantees or for the enforcement of preventive detention. During the many occasions of civil disorder or public protest that have marked Bangladeshi political life, the incumbent administration has often found it useful to suspend rights or jail opponents without trial in accordance with the Constitution.

The Islamic religion was the driving force behind the creation of Pakistan, and it has remained an important component of Bangladeshi ideology. The Constitution as originally framed in 1972 explicitly described the government of Bangladesh as "secular," but in 1977 an executive proclamation made three changes in wording that did away with this legacy. The proclamation deleted "secular" and inserted a phrase stating that a fundamental state principle is "absolute trust and faith in the Almighty Allah." The phrase bismillah ar rahman ar rahim (in the name of Allah, the beneficent, the merciful) was inserted before the preamble of the Constitution.

Another clause states that the government should "preserve and strengthen fraternal relations among Muslim countries based on Islamic solidarity." These changes in terminology reflected an overt state policy aimed at strengthening Islamic culture and religious institutions as central symbols of nationalism and at reinforcing international ties with other Islamic nations, including wealthy Arab oil-producing countries. Domestically, state support for Islam, including recognition of Islam as the state religion in the Eighth Amendment to the Constitution in June 1988, has not led to official persecution of other religions. Despite agitation by Jamaat e Islami (Congregation of Islam) and other conservative parties, there was no official implementation of sharia (Islamic law) as of mid-1988.

The Constitution is patterned closely on the British and United States models inasmuch as it includes provisions for independent legislative, executive, and judicial branches of government. When it first came into effect, the Constitution established a Britishstyle executive, with a prime minister appointed from a parliamentary majority as the effective authority under a titular president.

In 1975 the Fourth Amendment implemented "Mujibism" (named for Mujib), mandating a single national party and giving the president effective authority, subject to the advice of a prime minister. The later governments of Zia and Ershad preserved the powers of the presidency and strengthened the office of the chief executive through amendments and their personal control of the highest office in the land. Because of this concentration of power in individual leaders, the Bangladeshi Constitution gives much greater authority to the executive branch than does the United States Constitution.

In fact, the legislature and the courts have few constitutional avenues for checking presidential power, while the executive has many tools for dominating the other branches of the government.

## Legislature

The legislative branch of the government is a unicameral Parliament, or Jatiyo Sangsad (House of the People), which makes the laws for the nation.

Members of Parliament, who must be at least twenty-five years old, are directly elected from territorial constituencies. Parliament sits for a maximum of five years, must meet at least twice a year, and must meet less than thirty days after election results are declared. The president calls Parliament into session. The assembly elects a speaker and a deputy speaker, who chair parliamentary activities. Parliament also appoints a standing committee, a special committee, a secretariat, and an ombudsman.

Parliament debates and votes on legislative bills. Decisions are decided by a majority vote of the 300 members, with the presiding officer abstaining from voting except to break a tie. A quorum is sixty members. If Parliament passes a nonmoney bill, it goes to the president; if he disapproves of the bill, he may return it to Parliament within fifteen days for renewed debate. If Parliament again passes the bill, it becomes law. If the president does not return a bill to Parliament within fifteen days, it automatically becomes law. All money bills require a presidential recommendation before they can be introduced for debate in Parliament.

Parliament has the ability to reject the national budget or to delay implementation. It is therefore in the best interests of the executive as well as the entire nation that budgets submitted to Parliament should be designed to please the majority of its members. The legislature is thus a potentially powerful force for enacting laws over the objections of the president or for blocking presidential financial initiatives. In practice, however, because most members of Parliament have been affiliated with the president's party, the legislature has typically served the interests of the president.

The Bangladeshi and British parliaments have accommodated political parties in a similar manner. After elections, a single political party or a coalition of parties must form a government— that is, they must form a block of votes within Parliament that guarantees the passage of bills they may introduce. Once a parliamentary majority is formed, the president chooses the majority leader as prime minister and appoints other members of the majority as cabinet ministers.

Parliament can function for a full five-year term if a single party or coalition can continue to guarantee a majority. If, however, opposition members attract enough votes to block a bill, the president can dissolve Parliament and call for new elections. In order to prevent widespread bribing of members, or the constant defection of members from one party to another, the Constitution declares that party members who abstain, vote against their party, or absent themselves lose their seats immediately. In practice, whenever Parliament has been in session, a single party affiliated with the president has been able to command a solid majority.

## Executive

### *Presidency*

The president, who must be at least thirty-five years old, is directly elected by all voters for a five year term, and according to the provisions of the Sixth Amendment (1981) he may be reelected. He is commander in chief of the armed forces, oversees the conduct of all foreign affairs, appoints the vice president for a five-year term, and has the power to convene and dissolve Parliament.

The president also chooses cabinet ministers, who run the government bureaucracy; heads a secretariat that devises money bills for introduction into Parliament; and appoints the members of the Elections Commission, who supervise all aspects of elections. In addition, the president appoints, without the need for parliamentary approval, Supreme Court justices and lower court judges. Parliament, in turn, can only impeach the president with a two-thirds vote and can only remove the president from office because of malfeasance or illness with a vote of three-fourths of its members.

The president has a number of extraordinary constitutional means of wielding power and influence. In the case of a constitutionally defined "grave emergency" threatening "the security or economic life of Bangladesh," the president may issue a proclamation of emergency, which eliminates all restrictions on state power and the protection of fundamental rights. A state of emergency may last 120 days, or longer with Parliament's approval. If the president determines that "immediate action" is necessary, he may promulgate any ordinance he wants, as long as it is laid before Parliament for approval at its next session—that is, if it has not already been repealed.

Added to the considerable power of being able to place persons in preventive detention, these are a potent array of powers controlled directly, and without means for external control, by the president. The Fifth Amendment (1979) allows the president to amend the Constitution, without action by Parliament, by conducting a general referendum allowing a majority of citizens to approve an amendment. Constitutional amendments approved by Parliament must be passed by a two-thirds majority.

The increase in executive power has been the most important trend in the development of the Bangladeshi Constitution. This increase has developed because, in practice, even the very large scope of presidential authority has proved insufficient to protect civilian governments from military coups or to provide military leaders with sufficient legitimacy to preserve their power. Thus Mujib established a constitutional dictatorship, and both Zia and Ershad ruled for extended periods as chief martial law administrators in order to consolidate their hold over the country and to safeguard their influence by increasing their executive powers. Through the extended periods when Parliament was suspended, proclamations of the president or the chief martial law administrator amended the Constitution, not only to strengthen the office of the president but also to legitimize presidential acts.

### *Council of Ministers*

The president administers the country through the Council of Ministers—the cabinet—which is headed by the prime minister, a presidential appointee. Up to one-fifth of the members of the cabinet may be persons from outside Parliament, allowing experts to participate in the administration of the country, and the president may attract influential politicians to his party by offering them prestigious ministerial posts. The number of ministers in the cabinet has therefore varied over time, according to presidential political strategies.

There were nineteen ministers in the 1982 cabinet of President Abdul Fazal Muhammad Ahsanuddin Chowdhury, but by mid-1988 Ershad had increased the number to twenty-eight. Variations in the number of ministries do not signify the creation or cancelation of government programs but simply the reclassification of government services. For example, in 1982 finance and planning programs were administered by a single ministry with two divisions, but in 1988 a separate ministry was created for each.

In addition to changes in the status of various governmental divisions, discontinuities have occurred when the president has periodically dismissed ministers or moved them to different ministries. In the midst of this flux, administrative continuity is provided by the secretariats of the various ministries and regions, staffed by senior members of the Bangladesh Civil Service. Ministerial secretaries have often wielded a great deal of power because they are experienced and have numerous personal contacts in their fields, whereas ministers are typically professional politicians who hold office only for a short time.

## Judiciary

The government operates courts in the regions, districts, and subdistricts that make up the local administrative system. The judges in these courts are appointed by the president through the Ministry of Law and Justice or the Ministry of Home Affairs. Most cases heard by the court system originate at the district level, although the newer subdistrict courts experienced an increased caseload in the late 1980s. Upon appeal, cases may go up to the Supreme Court, but litigation may be very slow; in 1987 there were 29 Supreme Court judges dealing with 21,600 pending cases.

The Supreme Court, as of June 1988, had permanent benches—called the High Court Division— in Dhaka, Comilla, Rangpur, Barisal, Sylhet, Chittagong, and Jessore. It hears appeals from district courts and may also judge original cases. The Appellate Division of the Supreme Court in Dhaka reviews appeals of judgment by the High Court Division. The judges of both divisions are appointed by the president.

At the grass-roots level, the judicial system begins with village courts. An aggreived party may make an official petition, which requires a fee, to the chairman of the union council (the administrative division above the village), who may call a session of the village court with himself as chairman and two other judges nominated by each of the parties to the dispute. The parties may question the impartiality of the chairman and have him replaced. The majority of cases end at the village court level, which is inexpensive and which hands down judgments that reflect local opinion and power alignments.

There are occasions, however, when the union council chairman may reject an official petition to constitute a village court or when one party desires a higher opinion. In these cases, the dispute goes to a government court at the subdistrict level. Cases may wind their way up from district courts to permanent benches of the High Court Division.

Once cases leave the village courts, they become expensive affairs that may last for years, and few citizens have the financial resources to fund a lengthy court battle.

Rapid political changes in independent Bangladesh have compromised the court system. The Constitution originally stated that the president could remove members of the Supreme Court only if two-thirds of Parliament approved, but the Proclamation (Amendment) Order of 1977 included a clause that eliminated the need for parliamentary involvement. The clause set up the Supreme Judicial Council, consisting of the chief justice and the next two senior judges.

The council may determine that a judge is not "capable of properly performing the functions of his office" or is "guilty of gross misconduct." On their advice, the president may remove any judge. In addition, executive action has completely eliminated judicial authority for long periods. For example, under martial law regulations enacted in 1982, the Supreme Court lost jurisdiction over the protection of fundamental rights, and all courts operated under provisions of law promulgated by the chief martial law administrator; special and summary martial law courts handed down judgments that were not subject to review by the Supreme Court or any other court.

Furthermore, the Fifth Amendment and the Seventh Amendment placed martial law proclamations and judgments outside the review of the court system. In these ways, the courts have been forced to serve the interests of the ruling regime, rather than standing as an independent branch of government.

## Civil Service

The implementation of government policies and projects is the duty of the Bangladesh Civil Service, a corps of trained administrators who form the nation's most influential group of civilians. The importance of the bureaucracy dates back to the colonial period, when the Indian Civil Service provided an elite, educated, and dedicated body of professional administrators.

After the partition of India in 1947, when almost all administrative organs had to be created afresh, both East Pakistan and West Pakistan heavily relied on the managerial expertise of professional managers from the old Indian Civil Service. When Bangladesh became independent in 1971, the members of the civil service who joined the new nation brought with them the heritage of the colonial system. This heritage included administrative competence, which proved invaluable in running a young Bangladesh, and an expectation by the elite of benefits and power.

In mid-1988 the civil service was composed of twenty-eight separate services. There were twenty grades, with promotion to higher grades based on merit and seniority, dependent on annual confidential reports filed by the individuals' supervisors. Recruitment to the civil service occurred through open competition within a quota system. Forty percent of all new positions were allotted on the basis of merit; 30 percent were reserved for former freedom fighters (Mukti Bahini), and 20 percent were allotted to women. The quotas were distributed among districts on the basis of population. Eligibility depended on an entrance examination, which included English, Bangla, and mathematics sections, plus a personal interview.

The Public Services Commission, as mandated by the Constitution, conducted the examinations for the civil service. The recruitment system attempted to eliminate the entrenched power of the old elites and to decrease the bias that favored candidates from wealthy, urban families. Although in the late 1980s it appeared that the new rules for recruitment and promotion might widen the backgrounds of civil service personnel and their supervisors, the older, senior members of the service continued to dominate the administration.

Since independence, membership in the civil service has been one of the most desirable careers in the country. For senior civil servants, benefits included government housing at a standard rate of 7.5 percent of base salary, transportation, medical care, and a pension. Equally important were the prestige and influence that accompanied an administrative career. For example, there was great power in directing a division of a ministerial secretariat in Dhaka, or one of its attached departments, subordinate offices, or autonomous bodies.

Positions in the countryside were less popular, but the long tradition of bureaucratic elitism and subservience to government officials made the local administrator of the civil service an influential person in the community. In the late 1980s, the centralization of power and influence within the civil service remained one of the prime targets of administrative changes designed to decentralize politics and economic development throughout Bangladesh.

## Local Administration

During the early British period, when modified versions of Mughal (1526-1858) and earlier administrations were adopted, the closest the government came to the rural society was the zamindar, an administrator with concurrent judicial functions, who ensured revenue flows from the localities to the central government and handled a wide variety of official business. Government from the top down was the general rule for the Indian Civil Service and later the Pakistani and early Bangladeshi civil services. After 1971 the government of Bangladesh saw the benefits of involving more people in democratic decision-making and development programs, but the progress of reform was slow.

In 1959 General Mohammad Ayub Khan's government inaugurated a "basic democracies" program designed to involve villagers in development programs, with direct elections to union councils and indirect elections to bodies serving larger administrative units. Mujib's government held elections for union councils, but the coup of 1975 prevented their effective functioning.

In 1980 Zia's government announced the Self-Sufficient Village Government Plan, but this project ended when Zia was assassinated in 1981. In 1982 Ershad appointed the Committee for Administrative Reorganization/Reforms, which led to the establishment of the National Implementation Committee for Administrative Reorganization. These bodies built a comprehensive plan for administrative decentralization based on the subdistrict.

Bangladesh is divided into four main territorial divisions. In the late 1980s, the four divisions were divided into twenty-one regions, and the regions were subdivided into sixty-four districts. Below the district level, there were further urban and rural subdivisions. Urban areas include four municipal corporations (Dhaka, Chittagong, Rajshahi, and Khulna, each of which included several municipalities), eightyseven municipalities (pourashavas) and thirty townships (thanas). The four divisions had the same name as the four municipal corporations.

The countryside had 460 subdistricts (upazilas), which were further divided into 4,401 unions (the rough equivalent of an urban ward); these, in turn, contained 60,315 mouzas (groups of two or more villages—about 20 percent of the total) and single villages (about 80 percent of the total). A further subdivision, equivalent to the rural mouza, was the mahalla, which was found in urban areas. Each mouza or mahalla, the size of which was determined by census data-gathering techniques, contained about 250 households. An average village in the late 1980s contained 1,300 to 1,400 people. An average union contained about 15 villages and a population of about 20,000, and an average subdistrict had 8 to 10 unions with about 200,000 people.

Throughout its history, one of the main challenges to the Bangladeshi government has been finding ways to involve people in democratic politics at every administrative level.

According to the decentralization plan in effect in mid-1988, each rural mouza had its own council (parishad) of elected representatives chosen by local voters (persons aged eighteen and over). At the next administrative level, the chairmen of the union councils were directly elected by voters within their jurisdictions. The remaining members of the union council were chosen by the mouza councils, with each member of the union council representing three or four villages. The chairmen of the union councils formed the voting membership of the council at the subdistrict level, along with three appointed women and another appointed member, usually a former freedom fighter.

The chairman of the subdistrict council was directly elected by subdistrict voters. Thus the people had a direct electoral role at the village level, and they had a voice in choosing influential chairmen at the union and subdistrict levels. In the late 1980s, plans called for the expansion of representation at the district level, and the controversial District Council (Zila Parishad) Bill of 1987 was the first step in this direction. By mid-1988, however, these plans had not been implemented; the region and division levels remained administrative units of the civil service and had no political significance.

Local participatory politics met the civil service in the subdistrict council. In the late 1980s, the chief government official in charge of local projects and development efforts was the subdistrict project management (upazila nirbahi) officer, who directed a staff of about 250 technical and administrative officers. Nirbahi officers were part of the staff appointed by central authorities in Dhaka, and they received their pay, benefits, and promotion from the civil service. Their direct supervisors, however, were the subdistrict council chairmen. The subdistrict councils, through their chairmen, were expected to make plans for public works and development projects within their own territories, spend allocated government funds, and direct the development activities of nirbahi officers and their staff. Nirbahi officers and other subdistrict technical personnel were allowed to participate in subdistrict council meetings, but only as nonvoting members.

Civil service members, heirs of a long tradition of elite government, took orders from subdistrict council chairmen because the latter wrote the annual evaluations of nirbahi officers which served as the basis for promotion within the civil service. In this way, elected representatives of the people at the local level exercised direct control over civil servants and government projects in their own area.

In the late 1980s, the administrative apparatus at the urban level was comprised of a governing council with an elected chairman, elected commissioners (no more than 10 percent of whom were women), and several ex officio members. A mayor and deputy mayors were elected from among the council members.

The decentralization scheme implemented under Ershad's government was the most ambitious attempt in the history of Bangladesh to bring responsible government to the local level. The system officially began with elections in 1983 for four-year terms to union councils and with elections in 1984 for three-year terms to subdistrict councils. However, there were major problems with this scheme of decentralized administration.

First, the electoral system tended to represent only the wealthiest and most influential members of society. These persons made decisions that strengthened their own patronage networks and influence at the local level; the poorest strata in society had little direct voice in elected committees.

Second, the subdistrict councils were designed to create and implement development activities in their areas, but they were typically slow to draft five-year plans or carry through broad-based development efforts. Most of their projects emphasized construction or public works, (e.g., school buildings or irrigation canals, and they sometimes neglected the personnel and training components necessary for social involvement.

Third, civil service members have long lacked respect for local politicians, looking to their own advancement from their supervisors in Dhaka. They have often been slow to cooperate with elected members of local committees. For example, although the subdistrict council chairman was responsible for writing the nirbahi officer's annual evaluation, the officer was expected to submit the evaluation form to the subdistrict council chairman, and in many cases these forms did not appear, thus preventing the chairmen from exercising control.

Finally, the entire system of decentralized politics was viewed by opposition politicians as a patronage network designed to attract local elites to the party of the regime in power. Observers tended to conclude that instead of furthering decentralized democracy, the system only strengthened the national party controlled from Dhaka.

## Party Politics

The government estimated in 1988 that there were 102 different political parties in Bangladesh. The majority of these parties were based solely in urban areas and had tiny constituencies. Many of them were formed by small cliques of like-minded intellectuals or by political leaders who, with their small followings, had broken away from larger political groups. There was a steady turnover in the composition of the smaller fringe groups, which nevertheless continued to organize periodic demonstrations and issue press releases. Amid the welter of conflicting groups, there were five main political forces in the country that had long histories or some claim to support from wide constituencies. At the center in 1988 was the pro-government Jatiyo Party. Opposing it were two centrist parties, the Awami League, led by Mujib's daughter, Hasina, and the Bangladesh Nationalist Party, led by Khaleda Zia. To the left were the pro-Soviet Bangladesh Communist Party, factions of the Jatiyo Samajtantrik Dal, and other socialist groups advocating revolutionary change. To the right was a group of parties, including Jamaat e Islami and the Muslim League, that called for an increased role for Islam in public life. All of the minor political parties in Bangladesh clustered around the policies and the activities of these five main political forces.